FIGHTING FOR FAIRNESS

FIGHTING FOR FAIRNESS

THE LIFE STORY OF HALL OF FAME SPORTSWRITER

SAM LACY

by SAM LACY with MOSES J. NEWSON

TIDEWATER PUBLISHERS
CENTREVILLE, MARYLAND

Library of Congress Cataloging-in-Publication Data

Lacy, Sam, 1903–
    Fighting for fairness : the life story of Hall of Fame
sportswriter Sam Lacy / by Sam Lacy with Moses J. Newson.
        p.   cm.
    Includes index.
    ISBN 0-87033-512-X (hardcover)
    1. Lacy, Sam, 1903–   . 2. Sportswriters—United States—
Biography.   3. Afro-American sportswriters—Biography.
4. Discrimination in sports—United States—History.   I. Newson,
Moses J., 1927–   . II. Title.
GV742.42.L33A3   1998
070.4'49796'092—dc21
[b]   98-45957
                                                                    CIP

Manufactured in the United States of America
First edition

To my son Tim Lacy and my daughter Michaelyn Harris
—S.L.

To my loving wife Lucille and our four daughters,
Claudette, Kathaleen, Patricia, and Shawn
—M.J.N.

CONTENTS

Foreword, viii

Acknowledgments, x

CHAPTER 1   High Times, Low Times, 3

CHAPTER 2   Growing Up in D.C., 14

CHAPTER 3   The 1930s, 30

CHAPTER 4   Blacks and Sports, 49

CHAPTER 5   Branch Rickey, Jackie Robinson, 55

CHAPTER 6   Separate Housing, Other Issues, 87

CHAPTER 7   'Skins, Colts, Birds, 110

CHAPTER 8   Leadership Barriers, 118

CHAPTER 9   The Fairways, Airways, 135

CHAPTER 10   Sports Jeopardy, 149

CHAPTER 11   Women, Olympics, South Africa, 167

CHAPTER 12   1990s Stats Show Progress Made, Needed, 186

A Collection of Lacy Columns, 210

Biography, 244

Index, 247

FOREWORD

Sam Lacy's coverage of sports competition and sports personalities is must reading for sports historians, sports journalists, coaches, athletes, spectators, and certainly the general reader.

His book, *Fighting for Fairness: The Life Story of Hall of Fame Sportswriter Sam Lacy*, provides insider information about Jackie Robinson's performances on and off the field as a great all-around athlete, and it describes his unparalleled impact on major league baseball. There are interesting stories about other great athletes whose performances in tennis, track, football, and basketball are legendary.

Lacy is one of the country's super sports journalists. His unique presentation of sports stories is great reading entertainment.

The writer's presentation not only provides compelling insights into his work as a journalist but also serves as a revelation of the impact of sports on society.

—Dr. LeRoy T. Walker
Former President, United States Olympic Committee

For more than sixty years, Sam Lacy has been part of the national and international sports scene. He has played for and managed semipro baseball and basketball teams; he has covered six Olympiads; he has been a sports commentator in Baltimore on both radio and television; he's been a sports editor on two major black newspapers and currently is sports editor of the *Afro-American* newspapers in Baltimore, Maryland, where his sports column, "A to Z," is one of the most informative, evenly balanced (and opinionated) sports commentaries in America.

Sam Lacy was fighting for equal rights for all Americans thirty years before civil rights became a rallying point for many minorities. He has been the recipient of many honors and awards, including an Honorary Doctorate of Laws Degree from Morgan State University, a Doctor of Humane Letters from Loyola College of Baltimore, and induction into the Society of Professional Journalists Hall of Fame.

Fighting for Fairness is not just a book about the life of a Baseball Hall of Fame sportswriter; it is also an insightful tome covering the history of sports and the impact blacks have had on sports and society in America.

Sam Lacy writes about the great black jockeys; tennis great Arthur Ashe; the superstars of baseball's Negro Leagues; and Jackie Robinson's breaking the color line in baseball, especially interesting because Lacy had been fighting for the integration of baseball long before Jackie Robinson was selected to be the first black major league baseball player.

Sam Lacy takes the reader behind the scenes of these and many other events. You will find Lacy's impressions of Casey Stengel and others. Some stadium press boxes were still segregated after Jackie Robinson and other early black players were accepted on the field. Lacy recalls those days and the reader will find out which writers attempted to keep those doors closed to the black press and which writers helped give all accredited sportswriters access and credentials.

Fighting for Fairness is not just another sports book. It is an important informational and historical reference guide, an excellent book, from "A to Z."

—Bill White
Former President, National Baseball League

ACKNOWLEDGMENTS

The authors thank everyone who helped and supported us in this effort, especially John J. Oliver Jr., Chairman and CEO of the *Afro-American* newspapers, Tim Lacy, Paul Evans, Barry Beckham, Robert E. Greene, Sandra Eubanks Brown, and staffers at the Library of Congress, Howard University, Morgan State University, and Enoch Pratt Library.

FIGHTING FOR FAIRNESS

CHAPTER 1

HIGH TIMES, LOW TIMES

When you're two sunrises short of your ninety-fourth birthday, in a way, every day becomes special. But by late afternoon of October 21, 1997, my living room telephone started bringing me such unforgettably thrilling news that I'm sure there must have been an expression of sheer happiness on my face.

Larry Whiteside of the *Boston Globe* was calling from Cleveland, where members of the Baseball Writers Association of America would select someone for 1998 enshrinement in the writers wing of the National Baseball Hall of Fame and Museum in Cooperstown, New York. He wanted to clarify some information about me.

Whiteside and Dave Anderson of the *New York Times* (who I later learned were my primary sponsors), believed they had the votes to make me the forty-ninth sportswriter, and the second African-American, to have my picture placed in the Scribes and Mikemen exhibit as the 1997 winner of the J.G. Taylor Spink Award.

3

Though I didn't think I'd ever be inducted into the Hall of Fame, I still found myself anxiously waiting for the outcome of the vote, which turned out to be 23-21 in my favor.

Jeff Idelson, executive director for communications and education for the Baseball Hall of Fame, called to confirm my selection. He told me he'd be happy to see me back at Cooperstown again, and he hoped I'd bring along my son Tim, as I had on a previous visit, to participate in a program there. Later, I received a congratulatory call from Ricky Clemons, director of public relations for the National Baseball League and administrative assistant to National League president Leonard Coleman.

By now, I suppose, I was floating on air, reflecting on the many ways I'd been blessed over the years, only to have the entire assortment of career recognitions topped off by this one. My mind floated some, also. This made-my-day vote came in Cleveland, where I first had expected to address baseball team owners about integration in 1943, before community leaders shunted me aside. Whiteside writes for a daily in Boston—the city where the Red Sox team was the last in the major leagues to hire a black player. And Anderson writes in the city that fielded a team with the only manager with whom I could never strike up a good relationship during the early years of baseball integration—Casey Stengel.

I never worked with Whiteside, although we were together on a program in New York a few years back. He said he had admired my work since he was a youngster. Now Dave Anderson is one of the great sports guys I've known forever. We were together for the Long Island University 1997 series on "Race, Sports and the American Dream."

While surprised at being selected for the Hall, I had known for some weeks that my name had been put forward. The last time his hometown team was in Baltimore, Patrick Reusse of the *Minneapolis Star-Tribune* invited me to breakfast, and before we parted, he asked if I knew I was one of the Hall finalists. I certainly did not know until that day.

When he told me another finalist was Hal Leibovitz of the *Cleveland Plain Dealer*, I did know that I would be elated no matter the outcome. I'd known Hal for many years and would have been pleased to see him make the Hall. I told that to Reusse there at the hotel.

Many deserving writers don't make it to the Hall that ensconces the likes of Grantland Rice, Damon Runyon, Heywood C. Broun, Red Smith,

Dick Young, Milton Richman, Ken Smith, and Wendell Smith, who in 1993 became the first African-American selected for the Spink Award for meritorious contributions to baseball writing. Smith wrote for the *Pittsburgh Courier* and the daily *Chicago American*. He was inducted posthumously in 1994, having died in 1972 at the age of fifty-eight.

I'd considered at least two reasons why I might not make the Hall of Fame. For one, I never wrote sports for a daily newspaper; for another, my work covered many sports areas. When I became the first of my race admitted to membership in the Baseball Writers Association in 1948, my sponsors, Kenny Smith of the *New York Mirror* and Joe King of the *New York World Telegram*, argued that the thirteen issues a week the *Baltimore Afro-American* published at the time should qualify me.

I remained a member from 1948 to 1982. After my membership was transferred to the association's Baltimore chapter, that chapter dropped me because the *Afro-American* is not a daily.

Uniquely, the 1998 ceremony was the first time the Hall of Fame inducted three black persons at the same time. I went into the writers wing. Larry Doby, of Paterson, New Jersey, who became the first of his race to play in the American League in July 1947 with Bill Veeck's Cleveland Indians, was chosen for the major leagues veterans section. And Joe "Bullet" Rogan, a hard-throwing pitcher who also played infield and outfield for the Kansas City Monarchs from 1920 to 1938, was picked for the African-American section. He died in 1940. Doby, seventy-three and a longtime friend, was plucked from the Newark Eagles by Veeck and spent most of his thirteen years in the majors with the Indians and White Sox. Doby had 253 homers, 970 RBIs, and a .283 batting average. He served as manager of the White Sox during the last half of the 1978 season, making him the second of his race to manage a major league team. In 1998, he was still working as a special assistant to Gene Budig, American League president.

None of my other many awards approached the magnitude of Cooperstown, but it's easy to reel off a few that encouraged me to look back with pride at the years I've toiled as a sportswriter—even though my dream as a young man was to star as a professional player rather than write about others.

My 1994 induction into the Hall of Fame of the Society of Professional Journalists, Washington, D.C., chapter, was a thriller. Maybe part of that one was the setting. It was a long way from the tiny ghetto printing shop where I worked as a kid to the rostrum of the prestigious National Press Club in the nation's capital, where a crowd in the auditorium was applauding an elitist group of journalists including nationally syndicated exposé-columnist Jack Anderson, *New York Times* financial editor Hobart Rowan, and Cable News Network boss Edith Lewin.

And me.

For me, who as a youth in Washington, D.C., had shined shoes and kowtowed for nickel tips from white men who patiently allowed me to "pretty up" their shoes while having their hair cut at a downtown barbershop, and who at age twelve had shouldered two golf bags heavier than my own weight over eighteen holes of a hilly country club on a weekend when most kids were being spiffed up for Sunday fun, this was big—super big!

Of course, there'd been other times when unexpected honors had come my way, including having been placed in the Miller Brewing Company's "Gallery of Journalistic Greats" along with such personalities as pioneer African-American publisher John Russwurm, nationally syndicated artist-cartoonist E. Simms Campbell, United Nations assignee Mal Goode, White House correspondent Ethel Payne, and *Washington Post* columnist William Raspberry. That, too, was special.

Maybe I was so touched on these and other occasions because of an inner feeling that my crusade against racism in sports, waged over a sixty-four year career on behalf of all of my people and often taking on members of the mainstream media, had been deemed worthy of these distinguished tributes.

That kind of acceptance was not always a hallmark of life in America for its black citizens. Indeed, every day of the early decades on my beat brought the real possibility of being smacked in the face by another unpleasant reminder of the great divide that separated the races.

Sportswriter or not, that was a fact of life for millions of black Americans. Once I was in the writing business, fighting against racial discrimination through my sports pages and columns came naturally. There wouldn't be any of that nonsense about keeping politics out of sports.

These days, I've been tagged the dean of black sportswriters, probably because at age ninety-four I'm still at it. I've always maintained that, for me, being called "dean" means only that I have lived longer than the rest.

Almost all the interviews and stories about me focus on the role I played in the fight to bring down the barriers against black baseball players in the major leagues. However, starting with my first writing job with the *Washington Tribune*, at that time a black weekly newspaper, and through well more than half a century as writer and editor for the *Afro-American* newspapers in Baltimore, Maryland (widely known as the AFRO), my challenge and commitment has been to cover as much of the sports scene as possible—no matter the obstacles that confronted me.

Wherever minority male and female athletes competed, reporting their wins and losses—whether from the scene, through interviews or stringers, or through releases and stories from the Associated Negro Press—was my first priority. Eventually, we were permitted access to such wire services as United Press International and the Associated Press.

Some people believe sportswriting is a sop. It's not. Often, a writer must assess the talent and conduct of major stars, some of them close friends, and at times, that conduct involves sensitive matters or questions that affect a person's ability to earn a living. To do it honestly, the writer must be as straightforward when dealing with the players as when challenging the personalities and institutions that refused for so long to open doors and opportunities for all talented athletes without regard to color.

For example, I spent years traveling with and writing about Jackie Robinson, and we became good friends, but there were occasions when I found it necessary to take him on in print. Same for Roy Campanella. Ditto Frank Robinson. Add Joe Louis. Throw in Arthur Ashe. There were times when family members of those criticized personalities responded as heatedly as the targets or more so.

That goes with the territory. Call 'em as you see 'em and accept the comebacks. Take it in stride, the same as other distractions. That's the way it was. Push forward or get pushed aside.

Regularly, black reporters faced special difficulties covering the organized minor and major league teams that had added black players, first in preseason games and later, during the regular season as the racial barriers were being attacked.

In some ballparks in Texas, particularly in Beaumont, San Antonio, and Galveston, I wasn't allowed to sit in the press boxes. So Branch Rickey, president of the Dodgers, got special dispensation from the National

League president, who told me I could sit in the dugout. All the players knew what was going on. They also knew I had permission to be there so no one said anything and I kept out of their way.

Because it's warmer in the press boxes than in the dugouts, especially in the South in spring, sportswriters often didn't pack heavy coats for spring training. But quite frequently, those Texas nights got extremely cold. I used to sit there wearing a Dodgers jacket, usually Jim Gilliam's or Joe Black's. Or it might be a jacket belonging to one of the other guys. Otherwise I would have frozen.

Early in Jackie Robinson's career after he joined the minor-league Montreal Royals, we ran into a situation in Sanford, Florida, when we arrived at a small stadium for a spring training outing. We didn't live in the same place as the other Royals, so there were just the two of us when we reached the stadium's gate, and we weren't allowed to enter. So there was this spectacle of a baseball player and a sports reporter walking outside the facility in search of a loose plank in the wall through which we could get inside to do our jobs. We found one and except for some name-calling and heckling, which Jackie pretty much ignored, there was no trouble.

Some of those stressful situations had interesting aspects. In New Orleans at the Pelican Stadium, I was refused entry to the press box. Usually it was an usher or someone at that level who had been advised to say the press box was off limits. So, I decided, if I can't work in the press box, I'll just go up on the roof. And I wasn't joking.

I had barely gotten settled up there when Dick Young of the *New York Daily News*, Gus Steiger of the *Mirror*, Bill Roeder of the *World Telegram* and Roscoe McGowen of the *New York Times* all came up on the roof with me, bringing their chairs. I said to Dick, "What are you guys doing up here?"

"We decided we needed a tan," Young replied.

Now they had just come from a month in Florida, where tans are plentiful. So that indicated to me they were just using that as an excuse to show support for me. I've never forgotten that. I've always been gung ho about telling that story.

The year Montreal won the International League championship, I was with Jackie Robinson and his roommate, pitcher John Wright, when they went to Kentucky to play the Louisville team that had won the American

Association championship. This time, I was directed to the far corner of the right field pavilion. Someone knew I was coming and had put up a sign there that said "Black Press."

When I asked one of the ushers where the men's room was, he pointed and said, "Any of those trees down there!"

Yeah, he was serious.

Understand now, these things weren't limited to the South. In Cincinnati during a regular season game, I could not get into the press box although I had the required baseball writer's card. Tom Swope was chairman of the Cincinnati chapter of the Baseball Writers Association and he told the ushers that I could not come into the press box.

Instead, he got a field box for my exclusive use—right on the first base line. I went down there and sat in this field box all alone. Nobody else was allowed in there but me. There were white paying fans who didn't have such good seats standing around gawking at me sitting there alone in that box surrounded by a number of choice empty seats, sort of a reverse discrimination situation. It was another personal humiliation, but at the same time, the irony of it was sufficient to allow me to be amused.

As recently as 1952, when the New York Yankees and the Brooklyn Dodgers played in the World Series, there was a problem when I showed up at Yankee Stadium. I had a baseball writer's card, but some flunky at the press gate wouldn't let me in.

He said, "Where did you get that card from?"

I said, "It's my card."

Just about then, Milton Richman, the UPI man, came by. He asked, "What's wrong, Sam?"

I said, "This guy said I couldn't come in."

Richman asked, "Why can't he come in? He's got the same card that I have."

That ended that confrontation.

There were many instances of this kind for all the black writers who covered sports in the years after the major leagues started integrating. Many of the situations involved housing or transportation of some sort. The color problems did not disappear just because the players and writers were in Cuba, the Dominican Republic, or elsewhere. But no place was as bad as certain areas of the United States.

Sometimes it depended on the kind of automobile you were driving. I found that out one day during spring training in Florida, when I decided to borrow Dodger pitcher Dan Bankhead's car and drive up to Orlando, where the Washington Senators were based. They had a training camp there and I wanted to see a black Cuban player named Carlos Paula. At the time, Paula probably knew that he wasn't that great a player, but he'd been hired as part of Washington's tokenism effort.

Bankhead's car was one of those long, luxury, Lincoln automobiles. It would get me stopped by the police. Close to Orlando, in a town called Kissimmee, the police pulled alongside and waved me over. That sinking feeling came over me—the one I always get when stopped by police—and with it came a heavy dose of apprehension. I knew the car was in good shape. I knew I had not been speeding. I did *not* know what kind of attitude these Dixie cops would have, so I also knew this was a time and place for me to be very careful.

First, they wanted the driver's license. Then they got to it. They asked me who owned the car I was driving. I told them it belonged to Dan Bankhead.

At that time in the South, it seemed a black guy had no business driving such a big car unless he was a preacher, or a school principal, or he was wearing a chauffeur's cap and some white folks were sitting in the back. Also during that period, to many, the Bankhead name meant only one family, that of John Bankhead, the United States senator from Alabama. To those with a certain mindset, casual use of the Bankhead name could be taken as a symbol of hostility, much like similar use of the names Beauregard or Lee.

"What are you doing with his car?" they asked.

I told them I was a newspaperman and showed them my press credentials. I told them why I was going to Orlando. Well, that didn't help any. So they asked me if I knew anybody in the vicinity. I told them I could call Burton Hawkins, who worked with the *Washington Star* and was the road secretary for the Senators. One of the policemen stayed with me and the other went to make the contact. They talked to Hawkins. He told them, "Yeah, he's a gentleman. I know Sam Lacy." That's the way I got out of that. They were affable and not overly aggressive; they just couldn't conceive of a black guy driving this big Lincoln Continental. Later, when I saw Burt, he gave me a good ribbing.

There was never any way to foresee when or under what circumstances something untoward might happen. On the very first Dodgers barnstorming tour north after Jackie Robinson joined the team, I was traveling with them when they landed at the airport in Macon, Georgia.

When the plane came down and we got off, two white girls ran out onto the airport strip to get Jackie's autograph. Now right away I'm scared to death. We got out of there and went to town, where Jackie and I stayed at a rooming house in the colored community. When we woke up the next morning, the Ku Klux Klan, or some other such group, had burned a cross on the lawn of the rooming house.

As I've said, these types of incidents happened to any black person; by no means were black sportswriters singled out for racial hardships. I wasn't on a writing assignment when I went to Hampton Institute in Virginia to referee the National High School Championship Basketball tournament, so I broached what I considered to be a good idea to my wife Barbara, who often traveled with me.

"Hey listen, we've ridden trains, we've ridden buses, done everything else, let's go down on the overnight boat." There was a tour boat then, just like those out of Baltimore—the overnight boat down to the Tidewater area. Barbara agreed it was a good idea.

We settled into our stateroom and after the boat pulled out, decided to get something to eat. We went into the dining room. The maitre d' came up and said, "Good evening, may I help you?" So far, so good.

I said, "Yes, we would like to have dinner."

He said, "I'm sorry but we can't serve you."

Barbara, who was extremely fair, with her feisty voice, asked, "What do you mean you can't serve us?"

He said, "Well, we can serve you, lady, but we can't serve him."

Obviously, the headwaiter mistakenly believed he was dealing with an interracial couple. No matter; Barbara Lacy wasn't about to take no for an answer.

"What are you talking about, damn it! That's my husband," she said.

"That's your problem, lady," the headwaiter rejoined.

Even I had to laugh at that one. Once the headwaiter was convinced he wasn't going to rid himself of the Lacys, he put up a curtain to hide us in a corner and served us dinner.

That "interracial couple" matter would come up later in a rather unexpected place—deep in the heart of Baltimore's black community. I was scheduled to present an award on behalf of the *Afro-American* newspapers to heavyweight champion Muhammad Ali at the Nation of Islam mosque on Wilson Street. The Muslims at the door thought my wife was white and refused to allow her to enter the mosque. They wanted to know who was with me. They said she couldn't come in, so I said, "Well, I can't come in either." We didn't have a bitter exchange, but I was not happy about this turn of events, to put it mildly. We got away from there, leaving the plaque at the door. Another *Afro-American* representative who had dropped by to attend the ceremony presented the award. The Muslims did not explain the problem, saying only that I had appeared, left the plaque, and departed.

Of all the racial incidents that cropped up in my years of covering sporting events, only once did I fear that a situation had the potential of turning into an ugly flap, and that one involved Jackie Robinson. You never knew how far a situation might go. Reading in my own paper about things like soldiers coming home from the war and being beaten until they were blinded for not giving up their seats on a bus, offered plenty of proof of how situations can deteriorate.

Still, I was always certain of one thing. I never let any of the indignities discourage me from taking on assignments I wanted to do. In fact, as time passed, in a more philosophical thought process, I looked upon them as mere annoyances, typical of what every black person faced in America.

The indignities came at you from all sides, not only making the job more difficult, but severely limiting economic opportunities. When I hosted a sports radio program on radio WINX in Washington, one sponsor canceled upon discovering that the host was black. Much later, as a pioneer black sportscaster on Baltimore's WBAL-TV, my experiences included what I considered to be an assortment of embarrassing incidents.

That television job, incidentally, was created as a result of the forethought of Kenneth Wilson, a Baltimore businessman who was a successful former advertising executive at the *Afro-American*. Wilson noticed that another former *Afro-American* editor, Robert Matthews III, was doing an excellent job as producer of the six and eleven o'clock news, but he was not then on the air at WBAL. Wilson gained an audience with the station's general manager, Brent Gunts, and recommended me to be the person to break the ice. He argued that I was one of the area's leading sportswriters.

This was during the period when Lenny Moore, Buddy Young, Big Daddy Lipscomb, and Mel Embree had been in the spotlight with the Baltimore Colts, and the likes of Frank Robinson, Paul Blair, Don Buford, Curt Motton, and Elrod Hendricks were with the Baltimore Orioles.

Wilson succeeded in his mission. WBAL sports editor Vince Bagli welcomed me. (We had met while covering a high school event several years earlier.) But while Bagli was friendly and a willing teacher, some other key personnel had reservations, and they did not hesitate to show them.

With no teleprompter available, I would read from copy while doing my segment in the limited time allotted to Bagli, who was a master at the extemporaneous. At points marked on the copy for camera change, I looked up at the monitor, expecting to see something related to my words, and instead, saw a blank screen because the booth director for some unaccountable reason had delayed several seconds in ordering the camera change.

On another occasion, while handling the weekend show in Bagli's absence, I prepared ten to twelve pages of copy and stacked them in order. Fearful of missing a page while shifting them (thus presenting a disjointed discourse), I disposed of each finished page by dropping it on the floor beneath my chair. To my utter amazement, on looking at the monitor, I saw that the cameras that normally took head and bust shots had shifted full length and were showing discarded pages strewn about the floor around my feet.

I was humiliated and thoroughly discouraged. Back in Washington later, I entered my apartment to find the bedroom door locked and a note from Barbara saying, "You can't come in here until you go back and clean up that mess you left in Baltimore."

The tension was lifted. She was a jewel.

CHAPTER 2

GROWING UP IN D.C.

I was born on October 23, 1903, in Mystic, Connecticut, and named Samuel Harold Lacy. When I was just two years old, the family moved to Washington, D.C., where we settled into a small frame house in the northwest section of the nation's capital. I never went back to Mystic. My father and mother were Samuel Erskine Lacy and Rose Lacy. My siblings were sisters Evelyn and Rosina, and brothers Erskine Henry and Raymond, who died at age five.

Older sister Evelyn became Mrs. Benjamin Hunton, a school principal who retired as assistant superintendent of D.C. public schools. Younger sister Rosina became Mrs. Lawrence Howe, a director in the school system's special programs, heading up the art and drama department. Brother Erskine was a government worker until he quit, deciding he could make more money hustling as a pool shark. His life came closest to matching mine.

I was in my fifties before Rosina told me that our mother was born a Shinnecock Indian, of the Mohawk nation. Rosina had been told by one of our mother's older sisters. That bit of information made me realize why I knew nothing about my maternal grandparents; the matter was never discussed around me, partly because there were no accurate records.

It also reminded me of the day in July 1910 when I was six years old and a fierce storm came up during funeral services for my paternal grandfather, Henry Erskine Lacy, who was the first black detective in the D.C. police department. The lightning was flashing and the rain was coming down. My mother stood there holding me at her side. She had slick black hair and the water was running off her head and seemed to be going right down her corset and into her shoes. That impressed me; I realized the strength of my mother. Later I came to realize why she was the dominant figure in my upbringing.

She took the lead in disciplining us children and was supported by my father. She got us off to school and did most of the shopping for the family. This was back in the early part of the century; none of us children got clothes unless she was able to pay for them in cash. In those days, parents bought things they could afford and then handed them down. I wore many of my brother's shoes with paper inside the soles to cover the holes where he had worn them out.

My father believed in reading newspapers and saving them. I don't think he ever threw one away. He had stacks of papers in his room. He also stashed a bunch of them out back in a woodshed.

One day when I was four and playing with matches near the shed, the inevitable happened. Papers started burning in the shed. Rosina, whom I called "Lolean" at the time, knew I had been making "mud pies" in the yard and thought little of it when I first came in and requested a glass of water. When I asked for another, and then another, Rosina asked, "What are you doing with all this water?"

Told the woodshed was on fire, she looked out and said, "Oh my God!" She called to my sister Evelyn and went out and started fighting the fire. I guess Evelyn didn't hear her, because the fire engines were coming while my older sister was still at the piano practicing her music lesson.

Rosina never let me forget that incident. She could tell that story, too. "Lolean, can I have a drink of water? Lolean, can I have a drink of water?"

At first we lived on Tenth Street between R and S, later moving to Thirteenth Street between T and U. The Young Men's Christian Association was a block and a half away on Twelfth Street and that YMCA was the site of a lot of athletic activities for me.

However, sports personalities and issues were not the only people or interests I grew up with. On Tenth Street, I was a neighbor of Duke Ellington, who lived just down the block, and of William Warfield, whose father was head of Freedmen's Hospital (later Washington Medical Center) and lived in a house on Eleventh Street with a backyard adjacent to ours.

My days at Garnet Elementary School were in company with Henry Robinson, later one of the city's leading physicians; Hilda Davis, a member of the famous military family; Raymond Glascoe, later a professor of dance at New York University; and Maurice Johnson, whose family employed a maid who prepared table-set lunches of pancakes and molasses for Maurice and his cronies to consume before rushing back to Garnet by the end of recess.

In high school, my classmates were Charles Drew, the blood-plasma specialist; William Hastie, later the first black federal judge; Otto Hardwick, for years a featured performer with the celebrated Duke Ellington Band; William George, a Harry Truman appointee to the foreign diplomatic service; and Allison Davis, professor emeritus at the University of Chicago.

Thus it might be said that my younger days were spent among the elite, but not as one of them. I was the stray. Actually, I have been considered antiestablishment. Maybe stubborn and impulsive would be a better description. I resented authority figures who behaved in autocratic fashion. That is something I tried very hard to avoid later in my own experience as captain, coach, manager, editor, and in other similar positions of authority.

I started working at about eight years old, and I worked at various jobs for all but two years of my life. That first job was for two dollars a week as a printer's helper in a print shop about two blocks from where the family lived. That's where I learned to set type and to run a rotary press.

In those early days after the print shop job, I displayed a little devilment and, to be honest, a little thievery. My two sisters had boyfriends who were willing to pay a price for peace. With Evelyn, the first was Cecil Gloster; later, she met Ben Hunton and eventually married him.

Whenever Cecil called, I made a point of dropping into the parlor while Evelyn was primping. With little hints, I'd let him know that I wouldn't hang around to interrupt whatever smooching he had in mind if he could spare a nickel. And when Cecil faded from the picture, the same little coercion was practiced on Bennie. It worked every time.

So, when Walter Adams came calling on younger sister Rosina, the nickels continued, although not as routinely, because Walter was a dental student at Howard and didn't have much extra money. After Walter came Lawrence Howe, who was to become Rosina's husband. The little demon inside me realized that this arrangement wouldn't last much longer, what with Rosina being the last available sister. So the bribe on Larry became a dime.

My knack for trying to turn an easy buck took a more serious turn before I learned a painful lesson. These early ventures as an entrepreneur (my euphemism for dishonesty) extended into my early twenties. An addiction to betting the horses kept me on edge for money. After resorting to some bad checks for ten or twenty dollars, I came close to becoming a jailbird instead of a journalist. It took all my wits to keep one step ahead of the police until I could manage to satisfy the various holders.

This experience taught me the fallacy of trying to get rich in one big hit at the tracks. Even today, I see a similar mentality prevailing among the hordes of unwitting gamblers seeking a fortune at the lottery windows.

Fortunately, as I realized in later years, my son did not inherit the horse-betting sickness that caused a low point in my life. I was convinced of this the day I took Tim and his wife Vernice to the races after a weekend at Atlantic City. Realizing they were buying a home and were burdened with the other financial responsibilities of a young married couple, I staked them to twenty dollars each for wagering as they wished.

Tim won sixty-six dollars in the first race of the day, cashed in his ticket, and returned to our box with a hot dog and soda. He took a magazine from his pocket and began reading. I asked if he had no intention of betting the next race, or any of the ensuing races.

"Nope," was the reply as he handed back the stake (twenty dollars) I had provided.

"Why not?" I asked. "You're betting the track's money, now that you're ahead."

"Wrong, Dad," he smiled. "This isn't the track's money. It's mine."

As a young man, I played a number of sports, particularly baseball, basketball, and tennis. I formed and coached men's and women's basketball teams. I refereed games, was a promoter, and tried my hand as a radio announcer. I even played in a band, without knowing much about music.

One sport I passed up was swimming; I was scared of water I couldn't drink. As the years passed, golf became my number one sports interest. For years, I was on the courses at least once a week. In my thinking, tennis didn't match baseball in those days, but while I never conjured the image of stars such as Arthur Ashe or MaliVai Washington, I was good enough to contend for the D.C. playground junior title, losing to Ted Thompson, a neighborhood pal who wasn't good at any other sport. Together, Ted and I won the D.C. playground doubles championship in 1920 at the old Howard playground in LeDroit Park. Ted went on to become the American Tennis Association (ATA) senior singles champion in 1925 and 1927.

That band gig was set up for me by friend Otto Hardwick. Hardwick (a saxophone player), Sonny Greer, and Arthur "Sheif" Whetsel were three Washington musicians the world famous Edward Kennedy "Duke" Ellington took with him on the road when he left Washington.

Hardwick was playing with the local Doc Perry band when the drummer didn't show up one day. Hardwick told Perry he had a buddy who could play the drums, and Perry decided to let me sit in. Well, I hung in for the first half. At intermission, Perry said, "Son, I guess you better get lost."

Probably the boldest and potentially most dangerous thing I did as a young man was to attempt a driving job, at age fifteen, without ever having had a lesson and, of course, without a driver's license. Tom Payne, who would later help me break into organized baseball, told a man at the Highlands Apartments on Connecticut Avenue that I could drive.

I drove him downtown, never shifting gears, staying in first gear all the way. When the man got out of the car, he told me to take it right back to the garage. By the time I got back, he had telephoned Tom and told him to give me five dollars and let me go.

Another example of my entrepreneurship cropped up in my early teen years on Thirteenth Street. Living in our house at this time was an elderly lady we kids were told to call Aunt Susie. Now Aunt Susie was really no aunt at all. We figured out she was a roomer, but my parents used the aunt reference simply to allay any curiosity we might have.

Meanwhile, my buddies and I were playing in the neighborhood vacant lot with old baseballs we were able to acquire from various sources. Naturally, covers would invariably break, and stitches needed to be sewed before we found ourselves with nothing but cord wrapped around a cork center.

That's when Mr. Turner came to the rescue. Mr. Turner was an aging bachelor who lived in the vicinity. He had a knack for sewing and, in kindness, took our wounded baseballs and restored them to life.

Aunt Susie and Mr. Turner became an unwitting partnership forged by me. I discovered that Aunt Susie had a taste for Old Orchard and always had a supply on hand in her room. Mr. Turner also could touch up a sip or two. So when Aunt Susie would leave the house on an errand, I'd sneak into her room and pour a little of her Old Orchard in a tiny receptacle and head for Mr. Turner's house with payment for his services on our baseballs.

Oh sure, Aunt Susie was probably aware that her Old Orchard was disappearing, but she wasn't about to mention it because she knew my mother would not abide a souse in her house. (Except for the small quantities of rum she kept in her cupboard for pies, pudding, and eggnog, Rose Lacy outlawed alcohol.)

By the time my buddies and I were in high school, we were playing pretty good baseball and basketball. There was Harry "Soup" Turner, Cornelius "Neagie" Ellis, Willie Hope, Hymie Curtis, James "Blip" Hundley, Francis Honesty, "Runt" White, "Red" Haywood, "Aggie" Riley, "Bill" Fauntroy, "Tom" Payne, "Mutt" Baylor, Johnny Pugh, "Jinx" Johnson, "Geechie" Williams, "Toots" Barber, "Pee Wee" Covington, Burrell Kenner, and "Lefty" Smith. The same group also played with YMCA teams.

I started secondary school at Dunbar High, making first sergeant in the school's cadet corps in the second year. However, when the weather turned hot and I found myself on the drill field in that uniform, I preferred to be somewhere else playing sports. I started taking the roll call of the cadets, reporting all present to the captain, and then cutting out. Principal G. David Houston learned of this and took away my stripes.

With that I decided to transfer to Armstrong High School. As team captain, pitcher, and sometimes third baseman, I got a kick out of beating Dunbar when the two teams squared off.

By this time, Armstrong had a basketball team coached by Edgar P. Westmoreland, a Springfield College graduate, who introduced our team to the fast break and zone defense. He was the first formal coach I ever had. Under his leadership, Armstrong beat teams from Philadelphia, Boston,

Richmond, and Norfolk but lost to Wendell Phillips of Chicago in the national championship match.

While still in high school but pitching for a Rhode Island hotel waiters team, I was invited to Norwalk, Connecticut, to pitch a game for an all-white team. The man who invited me had heard I was a good pitcher. He billed me as an Algonquin Indian in his publicity.

So there I was, pitching for this all-white team; there were no blacks on either team, in the stands, or anywhere else. My fast ball wasn't fast enough to go against that wind off the ocean. It was running up there and stopping. Batters seemed to be hitting off a tee. They were wearing the ball out.

I'd break my curve. The wind would get into that and take it out too far—nothing but two balls, three balls. I needed to come down the middle of the plate and they were knocking the stuffing out of that ball. They were hitting it all over the place. Finally, the guy who had invited me said, "Maybe you had better get out of here. This ain't no place for no Indian who can't play ball."

That took care of that situation.

To make extra money as sophomores and juniors in high school, some of my young Washington cronies and I would join others in places such as Watch Hill, Rhode Island, where we would wait tables and entertain the guests by playing baseball. The original black waiters team was for the Argyle Hotel somewhere in upstate New York and the idea caught on. Guests would pass the hat at the games and tip the players later.

Leroy Jeffries, who went on to become advertising director for Johnson Publications (*Ebony* and *Jet*) is one of the players I remember on those trips. He was a helluva glove at shortstop but couldn't hit a lick.

I had been a waiter on trains and at a Washington hotel in the 2400 block of Sixteenth Street, so the job was something I was accustomed to. I would have regular guests to serve all summer in Rhode Island. There was a man named Scott who was editor of the *New York Sun*, and there were the Pillsbury sisters. A lot of people don't know that the Pillsbury Flour Company was owned by those two sisters. These were my regulars.

Some of the young men I played baseball with were good at ambidextrous play, and one was an effective catcher although he had just one arm. The field where we usually played baseball was next to the Twelfth Street YMCA in D.C., and third base was on the side of the building. The batters, most of whom were right-handed, were breaking out windows. The YMCA officials and the police made it clear to us that we would have to stop breaking windows or find another field. It meant we all had to learn to hit left-handed.

On one of those summer trips to Rhode Island, I had won my mother's approval to go by promising to write to her three times a week. At the time, I couldn't know that promise would become a real challenge to write left-handed.

A holiday such as July 4 was always a good baseball day. On this trip, I landed behind the plate for the big holiday game when catcher Jack Martin, who would later officiate down in the Southern Intercollegiate Athletic Conference, shifted to first after the regular first baseman was hurt.

It wasn't long before a high foul ball came down and laid open a finger on my right hand. I shudder again even now—many, many years later—when I recall how the doctor, who'd been off on a family picnic, finally returned to his office and commenced to pour alcohol on that finger to start his treatment.

Now I was forced to write left-handed in order to get a letter off to my mother three times a week. And there was so much difference in my handwriting, she was concerned that I had taken up bad habits. "The boy has started drinking," she told my father, before learning the reason for the sharp change.

Recalling that incident brought to mind an earlier occasion when my mother showed how proud she was of my writing ability. For some unknown reason, I'd been blessed with beautiful penmanship, so it was a surprise when my first-grade teacher became critical, basing her criticism on the fact that I did not grip the pencil "properly."

Instead of placing the instrument between my thumb and index finger, I held it between the third and fourth fingers. The teacher, Mrs. Payne, became angry when I was unable to follow her instructions. She cracked my knuckles with a ruler and sent me home with tears in my five-year-old eyes.

The next morning, my mother went to school with me and told the teacher that "this child writes better than anyone in the room, including the woman in charge."

A transfer to the class of Miss Beason was immediate.

Decades later, that penmanship would prove valuable. Involved in a two-car accident in 1978 in which a young driver totaled my auto, I was forced to give up the typewriter temporarily. An injury I received caused an arthritis flare-up that prevented me from typing for a time, so I started writing my copy in longhand.

Even when I was able to type again, things were going very well with the typesetter, Elinor Parker Washington, who handled my *Afro-American* copy for years. I never went back to the typewriter, and I never challenged the computer. The arrangement made it possible for me to prepare copy anywhere without having to worry about lugging around a portable machine.

About that left-handed writing achievement of mine, it simply wasn't that impressive when compared to some of the guys I grew up with, such as the Dunbar High player known as "W.W.," who was truly ambidextrous. He played baseball, basketball, and football. "W.W." was so good that in doubleheader baseball games, he could pitch the first game as a left-hander, then come back in the next one as a right-hander.

Gary Mays was even more incredible. He didn't have a left arm at all. As a youngster, Mays had fallen while holding a shotgun; it discharged when it hit the floor, leaving him with a stump. But he was awesome behind the plate. He had a first baseman's glove that was made for the left hand but Mays wore it on his right hand. He took a lot of the padding out. He'd catch the ball in the glove, flip it into the air, shed the glove, catch the ball, and throw it. He had it down to a science. We're talking hardball here, no Mickey Mouse softball. A lot of runners tried stealing second base on him, assuming he had to go through too much to throw them out. They were often wrong.

Some of the more exciting athletes were not known outside of the Washington area. However, the teams I played on and coached were among the forerunners of the summer leagues that centered activities around Mott (later Howard) playground. That playground had three outdoor basketball courts. Cage stars the likes of Elgin Baylor, Dave Bing, and Marvin Webster, to name a few, came out of these leagues.

As a youngster, I wanted more than anything else to be a train engineer. My mother would take me down to the train station, and I would say that I wanted to drive one. That was my greatest ambition. (Later, my dreams included owning a grocery store, probably because I like to eat.)

Whether following my dreams or not, I was always a busy young man. These are some of the ways I kept occupied between that print shop gig and the eventual entry into journalism.

I set pins at the bowling alley in the basement of the YMCA for five cents per game, ducking pins sent flying by some flame-throwing bowlers who included local school teachers John Wilkinson, Jim Hunter, Clyde McDuffie, and John Cromwell.

I shined shoes and did other barbershop duties as a preteen at a downtown Bond Building shop that was operated by the uncle of Thirteenth Street buddy Sylvester Reeder.

I sold three-cent newspapers at Fourteenth and U Streets as helper, earning a penny of every sale.

I was a caddie at the Columbia Country Club, where I luckily got the bags of E.B. Eynon, then secretary-treasurer of the Washington baseball team, and Karl Korby, owner of Korby Bakery (later Wonder Bread).

I waited table at the House (congressional) Restaurant, where Phil Butler (my aunt's husband) was headwaiter; later I was a waiter on the Union Pacific Railroad, which ran the Challenger between Chicago and Los Angeles and the Mountaineer from Chicago to Rochester, Minnesota.

There was also the opportunity to pick up pocket change at the tender age of seven and eight, courtesy of Mrs. Christopher's backyard tree on U Street, located just across an alley from the right field wall at Griffith Stadium.

The tree afforded an ideal perch for watching major league baseball without having to pay fifty or seventy-five cents for a ticket at the park gates. Mrs. Christopher and her son Frank built little platform seats in spaces where the limbs branched out and sold them, fifteen to thirty-five cents, depending on how high up the seat was. We younger fans would get to the backyard early, buy the cheap seats, and sell them at a profit to the older, late arrivals. Then we would leap the fence to the stadium and get lost in the crowd.

In those days, I had no idea whatsoever of becoming a sportswriter or newspaperman of any type. The idea of journalism came about very gradually. Even in my sophomore year in high school, when I was writing some sports for the old *Washington Tribune*, it was not with any idea that it would turn into a career.

I credit Louis Lautier, then sports editor of the *Tribune*, William O. Walker, the paper's publisher, and Henry O. Scott, who later left the journalism field to return to real estate in Richmond, Virginia, with bringing me into what would be my life's work.

Lautier was to serve as Washington bureau chief of the Negro Newspaper Publishers Association and, in 1947, would be the first of his race to win credentials to cover the Congress from the Senate and House press galleries. Walker went on to become a giant in black journalism as editor-publisher of the *Cleveland Call and Post* newspaper.

These three men gave me the start in journalism, but it was not until I was out of high school and had been writing for awhile earning fifteen dollars a week covering local sports that the bug started to hit me. Still it was not uppermost in my mind, not a priority. Sometimes when I was away playing baseball, I'd think about going back to this field of journalism. When I came back to Washington permanently, I decided I would take that step.

Before giving up baseball, I'd played with some pretty good teams. By graduation time at Armstrong High School in 1922, I had played baseball with teams such as the Teddy Bears, the Washington Black Sox, and the Bachrach Giants in Atlantic City. It was unusual for a high school youngster to be playing with a semipro team like the Bachrach Giants.

In the 1920s, our home was about five blocks from Griffith stadium. I was among the young fellows who would shag balls out there for the Washington Nationals before they became the Washington Senators. I got to know a lot of the players by name. Also, I managed to get choice wares to sell at games, including programs during the World Series in 1924, 1925, and 1933.

Seeing what players the likes of Babe Ruth, Ty Cobb, and Pie Traynor could do, and comparing them to the black players I also watched inspired me eventually to go to Clark Griffith, owner of the Washington team, to encourage him to hire black players. At the time, Clark Griffith wasn't buying the idea.

After high school, I gave up football but continued with basketball and baseball as player, coach, or referee. I also organized some teams and spent time working as a promoter of matches. To please my mother, I went to Howard University for a year. After that, it was back to concentrating on the sports world.

As lovers of sports, my father and I were on the same beam. "Pop" Lacy attended most of my sports engagements. After I became a known writer, he would be thrilled when I brought sports figures such as Joe Louis and Jackie Robinson to his home to meet him.

One thing I never quite figured out about my father was why he refused to go see the all-white Redskins play but was a regular in the Jim Crow pavilion to take in games of the all-white Senators. He was a regular, that is, until he felt the team insulted him personally.

Here's the way that story was told later in one of my columns:

Faithful to the core of his being, my father proudly displayed a little white ribbon with the inscription, "I Saw Walter Pitch His First Game—1907."

It referred to the debut of Washington's revered Walter Johnson and Pop had received it in 1918 with a note from Johnson expressing appreciation for his presence. Johnson, of course, didn't know Samuel E. Lacy from one of the bulls back on his family's farm in Coffeyville, Kansas.

And evidence of what sort of influence his beloved badge wielded occurred at a parade when the Senators and the opposing New York Giants were marching triumphantly up U Street toward the stadium where they were to open the 1923 World Series.

Standing at curbside, waving a Washington pennant and flaunting his "I Saw Walter . . ." badge, my father had a dirty, wet towel tossed in his face by the first base coach and heralded clown Nick Altrock. That did it.

Pop went home, stored away his badge (which I have as a keepsake) and never went to another major league baseball game.

My own baseball career ran simultaneously with high school, college, and my writing career, starting, as I've indicated, at Dunbar and Armstrong high schools and continuing on into the years when I was writing for the *Washington Tribune* and the *Afro-American*.

When I was still pitching for Armstrong High, Andrew Allen, who was general manager of the LeDroit Tigers and a scout for the Bachrach Giants, asked me if I wanted to play for the LeDroit Tigers. I told him I didn't know if I could because I was still in high school.

I told Tom Payne about it; he was a player for the semipro Teddy Bears and a friend from my neighborhood. He had seen me strike out seventeen Dunbar batters and suggested I come play with the Teddy Bears.

The team was from the Foggy Bottom area, based on Twenty-third Street between Georgetown and the city proper. It turned out the owner/manager of the Teddy Bears, Ben Fels, and his brother also owned this bootleg place on Twenty-third Street. I found out the players would assemble there before and after games. It has been widely reported that most of the early Negro Leagues teams were run by bootleggers or numbers barons, and I know that a number of them were.

Anyway, I did not like the drinking, womanizing, and other carousing that was going on. I told Tom Payne that wasn't for me. "I understand," Payne told me. And that's when I went to the LeDroit Tigers.

Payne, a catcher, had taught me how to pitch to different batters, including such things as figuring out how to pitch a batter according to his stance at the plate. Payne wasn't all that pleased later to find me pitching for the LeDroit Tigers against his Teddy Bears.

I went to Atlantic City and played with the Bachrach Giants for a season and a half after finishing high school, but the same type of player boozing and bawdy-house carousing resulted in my returning to Washington. Anyway, I had become homesick up there.

In Washington, I played for the Washington Black Sox and for a local semipro team called the Hillsdales, different from the Hilldales (no "s" after hill) of the Negro Leagues. With these teams, as well as with the Bachrach Giants, I got to play against professional teams such as the Hilldales, New York Cubans, Philadelphia Stars, Baltimore Black Sox, the Cuban Giants out of Havana, and the House of David, a touring team connected to a religious group from Michigan, whose players had heavy beards and mustaches.

Among the professionals I played against were Dick Lundy, Pop Lloyd, Nip Winters, Stringbean Williams, Dick Seay, Pat Lloyd, John Henry Lloyd, Scrip Lee, and Jim West. Some of those guys were special. Scrip Lee had those big hands. He could squeeze a ball in his hands until he loosened the cover, deadening the ball. Winters was a tall, lanky left-hander who seemed to be handing the ball to the catcher when he took that stride off the mound. And Jim West—talk about Josh Gibson hitting home run balls, West couldn't hit as many as Gibson but he could hit them farther.

We didn't make a lot of money—ten, twenty, or thirty dollars a game, depending on the crowd and take. We were furnished good equipment, but you had to buy your own gloves and shoes.

We traveled in autos. The owners had these big cars they used for bootlegging, the phaetons, forerunners of the luxury limousines. The fields we played on were mediocre, many of them not even enclosed. But they were kept adequately. Later we got to play in some of the major league parks, a night and day difference.

My last team was the Washington Black Sox, and I was in my forties. Oddly, I ended up playing for William "Dofey" Jones, who played for me when I managed the Hillsdales. There's a field out in Bowie, Maryland, named for him: Dofey Jones Stadium.

For about two and a half years, radio broadcasting was included in my schedule. The stints on WOL and WINX, which became WMAL, consisted of sports reports along with music. I was my own commercial salesman for the shows. One advertiser who stuck with me throughout was the M.A. Leese Optical Company on Fourteenth Street. Others included Raymond Moseby, a small black-owned jewelry store on U Street, the Jarvis Funeral Home, and the Reid Clothing Store at Eleventh and U.

By the mid-1930s, married for several years and with the dream of a baseball career no longer a realistic option, I finally was ready to make the move into full-time journalism with the *Washington Tribune*, where I worked from 1934 to 1938.

It was in 1927 that I had married the former Alberta Robinson of Washington. We lost two children before our son Samuel Howe (Tim) Lacy was born February 8, 1938. Tim would later serve for a time as advertising director for the *Washington Afro-American* where I once worked, and would write a weekly sports column, "Another Viewpoint," which appeared on my sports page in the Baltimore and Washington editions.

My first wife and I divorced in 1952, and in 1953, I married Barbara Robinson, a government worker. She had a daughter, Michaelyn, now a teacher of dance in New York. Barbara was the best thing that ever happened to me. She calmed me down, taught me responsibility. She went with me everywhere.

In my early years as a professional writer, I looked back with pride at that job at the small printing shop. It helped that I knew my way around the shop. The *Tribune,* like many other black newspapers during the period, did job printing in addition to putting out a paper. For the *Tribune,* the Murray brothers, Norman, Morris, and Raymond, were in charge of that function. They owned the building in which the paper was located, and for a time, they were its publishers. Raymond Murray didn't stay with the business very long because he opened the Dunbar Theater at Seventh and T Streets, opposite the famed old Howard Theater.

The late Arthur M. Carter and I did sports for the *Tribune* and for the *Afro-American,* and remained good friends for decades. With another friend, Hal Jackson, we organized the Washington Bears, a basketball team that played Sunday games at Turner's Arena. I had previously organized a basketball squad called the Washington Bruins.

Harry McAlpin, a fellow *Tribune* employee who later became a White House correspondent for the black press, also was the head of Alpha Phi Alpha Fraternity. He had witnessed my success in coaching the Community Yellow Jackets to a city championship over the rival semipro Alcoes and Carlisles. He persuaded Alpha to hire me to coach its team in the annual D.C. Fraternity League made up of Alpha, Omega Psi Phi, Kappa Psi Phi, and Phi Delta Sigma.

For three years, 1935–1937, Alpha, Omega, and Kappa contested for the title. Alpha defeated Omega the first year, when games were played in the old Lincoln Colonnade, located under the Lincoln Theatre on U Street between Twelfth and Thirteenth.

In the second spring of the series, the Kappa team was strengthened by the addition of hyperactive Dennis Simpson from Chicago's national champion Wendell Phillips High School, and Harry "Freak" Wood, a deadly shooter for Howard University's high-profile team. My greatest concern was Simpson; he was tall, fast, and agile—the prototype of an early Michael Jordan.

My Alpha lineup included a converted fullback from Howard named Pete Tyson. He was not much as an offensive player, but he was strong, reasonably mobile, and fearless. I assigned him to guard Simpson. My instructions: "Don't worry about offense, don't concern yourself with where the ball is; just stay with Dennis. Every time he is looking for the ball, I want you to be in his face. Every time he looks up, I want you to be eyeball-to-eyeball with Dennis Simpson."

The strategy worked to perfection. Simpson became so frustrated, he began pushing, elbowing, and grappling with Tyson. The net result: Dennis Simpson fouled out (four fouls at that time disqualified a player), and Wood's efforts weren't enough to forestall Alpha's subsequent victory.

Coaching women's basketball teams was fun but tough. One team I considered quite good was a Young Women's Christian Association squad that included Anita Gant, Abby "Tiny" Johnson, Gertrude Offert, and Otero Tymous. Although good, they couldn't handle the Wissahickon women's team out of Pennsylvania.

The Wissahickon women, including the well-regarded Ora Washington and Lula Ballard, practiced against the men's team there and played the Downingtown team coached by Lester B. Granger. (Granger later gained national recognition as executive director of the National Urban League from 1941 to 1961.) I also coached the Freedmen's Hospital nurses team, but the nurses did not compete in organized leagues.

After Art Carter was transferred to the *Afro-American* headquarters in Baltimore to become sports editor for the chain, the Washington editor, Ralph Matthews Sr., lured me from the *Tribune* to handle sports for his paper. Matthews, who was to work many years in a number of capacities for the *Afro-American,* was known broadly for his wartime coverage, column writing, and interviews with entertainment personalities.

Sportswise and otherwise, the America of my first full-time stint as a writer with the *Tribune* (not then always doing sports) was not the America of the 1990s. I became sports editor for the *Tribune* in 1934.

It was in 1937, before moving to the *Afro-American* newspaper, that I went calling on the first major league baseball team owner to discuss the hiring of black players.

CHAPTER 3

THE 1930s

In the mid-1930s, black sportswriters kept tabs on what was going on in their own communities and in national sports involving blacks; at the same time, we tried to keep the heat on that period's racial segregation in sports. From time to time, white sportswriters joined in the battle and frequently I would reprint some of their material. Among the better known sportswriters focusing on the major league baseball issue were Wendell Smith of the *Pittsburgh Courier,* Joe Bostic of the *New York People's Voice,* and Frank A. "Fay" Young of the *Chicago Defender.*

All black sportswriters were doing their part in the ongoing war against racial injustice that was being waged by our newspapers on every front. For some perspective on the period, the *Tribune* was running stories in January 1934 concerning Walter White of the National Association for the Advancement of Colored People (NAACP), who was out drumming up support for a Democratic-sponsored antilynching bill. There would be twenty reported lynchings of blacks in 1935.

My regular sports page column at that time was called "Looking 'Em Over With the *Tribune*." In my column, I took on anybody and anything involved in any way with sports.

A "Sam's Scripts" piece on January 11, 1934, mused:

> Sometimes me thinks I'll write about white athletes who come uptown to play our colored teams, snatch the long end of the purse, the game and everything else that matters and run back downtown to wait for another invitation to come up and get some more money . . .

A week later, "Looking 'Em Over" spotlighted a high school situation:

> That this school (Cardozo), no longer modern enough for the use of white children of high school age and subsequently abandoned by them, should have a gymnasium far superior to either of those provided for the use of Negro children at the Dunbar and Armstrong buildings, is something to be looked upon with upraised brow if ever there was cause for such a thing.

One week later, Will Rogers was taken to task for using the term "nigger" in a radio program. Another column complained about the lack of a decent golf course for black golfers and the many unfulfilled promises of the Department of Public Buildings and Parks to do something about the problem.

A May 1934 column carried information from an article by Clifford C. Mitchell, author of "Digesting the News," in which Mitchell took up a subject some observers believe finally helped persuade major league baseball owners to integrate. Mitchell said such a move might help boost crowds. He linked his view to the fact that at a White Sox–St. Louis Browns game, about half the fourteen thousand fans in attendance were Italians, there to see the Italian player on the White Sox team.

Sports pages in black papers across the country would highlight stories such as the one the *Tribune* carried in September 1934, reporting that the Springfield, Massachussetts, entry in the American League Junior Baseball Tournament had withdrawn because the Gaston, North Carolina, hotel where reservations had been made would not accept the team's black pitcher-outfielder, Ernest Talliferro.

After Washington radio announcer Arch McDonald, in plugging a game between two black teams, said: "They are funny things, these colored ball games," it seemed necessary to fire back. I wrote that I was ready to bet McDonald had not seen a serious game between black teams in five years and didn't even know about the existence of the annual game between the Baltimore Black Sox and the white major league All-Stars, and added:

> I dare say the WJSV sports announcer would laugh in your face if you attempted to tell him that a colored baseball team played "ring-around-the-rosey" with an outfit composed of Lefty Grove, Hack Wilson, Joe Hauser, Kiki Cuyler, Monte Weaver, and a host of others.
>
> But Arch says, "They will keep you laughing, these colored baseball games." Haw, haw, haw . . .

My first column in August 1935 asked, "Why not give baseball a little color?" and went on to take up the likelihood that integration would increase attendance in major league parks. It noted that other teams were contemplating the lead of the Cincinnati Reds in adding night games in an effort to boost crowds.

By this time, former heavyweight champion Joe Louis, who started out being called "Baby Face" but by now had defeated Primo Carnera in June 1935 and was known as the "Brown Bomber," was involved in a column that brought me a sharp rejoinder.

Actually, the column was about entertainer Bill "Bojangles" Robinson being in the Joe Louis entourage and it started off this way: "Joe Louis's managers did a good job until they let 'Bill Bojangles' Robinson in." The column took pains to praise Robinson as a great entertainer and a credit to his race in that role but suggested he was out of place in the Louis camp where managers John Roxborough and Julian Black, along with trainer Jack Blackburn, had been bringing Louis along as a fighter whose lifestyle was quite different from that of the first black heavyweight boxing champion, Jack Johnson. Johnson was a colorful character who paid little attention to the white-black barriers of the day. He was the best of his time and probably the most hated world heavyweight boxing champion of all time.

The column described Louis and Robinson this way:

[They are] . . . two different types. Robinson belongs to the minstrel world. Louis is part of our athletic life, a life we are anxious to raise from the slough of burnt cork performance.

Bill Robinson's chair dance in front of Dr. W. A. Goodloe's home (where the party made its headquarters), his tapping act atop a table in the office of the District Commissioner, his truckin' in the street outside the District Building and his moss-covered joke from the ring at Griffith Stadium during the proceedings incident to the supposed honoring of Louis and Jesse Owens by the Elks, were discordant notes in the Louis local rendition.

And they were about as pleasant as a decayed tooth.

Well now! Someone sent a copy of the column to Bill Robinson in Los Angeles and he "promptly threw it in the wastebasket as so much trash," according to Mrs. Bill Robinson. She retrieved the letter, read the column, and decided to shoot back.

Mrs. Robinson suggested I was hiding behind a few Judas words of praise, and that if I knew Bill, I would know he would not be "putting himself on anyone for publicity or other reason." She noted that Robinson was widely respected in the United States and abroad before Joe Louis was born —and known for his charitable deeds, athletic ability, and other things in addition to his theatrical notoriety. As to my "burnt-cork" reference, Mrs. Robinson said her husband would be pleased to be linked with such stars as Al Jolson, Eddie Cantor, John Mason, Eddie Hunter, Swan and Lee. Then Mrs. Bill Robinson summed up her feelings:

Somehow, I feel that you should be pitied instead of being censured, so, if you don't mind, Bill still admires Mr. Louis with the rest of the world, as the greatest fighter of all times, and a gentleman, and so long as he (Joe) or his managers (whom Mr. Robinson has known for years, one of them before Joe was born) are not afraid of dragging Joe in the gutter, with his presence, etc., I think the right thing for you to do is try writing about something that is worthwhile, or truthfully explain your real reason for such silly trash in so much valuable space.

I ran the letter without comment, except to reprint the original comments "for those who tuned in late."

In August 1936, two stories ran in side-by-side columns on the front
page of the *Tribune*. One was a sports story about Joe Louis and the other
in many ways indicated how fragile race relations were at the time. The
sports story by my friend Art Carter was about how Joe Louis, sixty days after losing to Max Schmeling, would be taking on Jack Sharkey that Tuesday
night in Yankee Stadium. The story in the next column, out of Owensboro,
Kentucky, was about a mob of twenty thousand men, women, and children
"munching hot dogs and sipping pop" as they impatiently awaited the public hanging of one Rainey Bethea.

There was progress in some areas of the sports world with a story here
and there recognizing that black-sponsored competitions would suffer
when segregation ended in major league sports. Not everyone was happy
about the prospect. In October 1936, twenty thousand fans were expected
for the annual East-West classic in Chicago's Soldiers Field. Concern was
expressed in some quarters that the crowd's enthusiasm might be damp-
ened by the presence of black players on two football teams that would be in
action the same afternoon. Two black running backs were on the North-
western University team that was meeting Ohio State in Evanston. And
downstate in Champaign, Iowa would have two black stars going against
Illinois.

Racially, things could change in a matter of months. In November of
1936, a D.C. YMCA team of boxers went to New York to participate in the
All-American tourney after the D.C. Amateur Athletic Union refused to
sanction fights between blacks and whites for Golden Gloves matches held
at Catholic University under sponsorship of the *Washington Herald*. Months
later in February 1937, interracial boxing was initiated unofficially as a
Twelfth Street YMCA team defeated a Philadelphia team made up of representatives of the white Shackamaxon Club and the black Benezet Club.

The history of sports has shown that changes in attitudes and rules
were not always of a progressive nature. In some major sports that had featured blacks earlier, changes resulted in reverses that banned blacks from
competition. Thus there was concern when reports circulated in the summer of 1937 that the National Semipro Baseball Congress was considering
barring mixed teams from competing after the tournament in Wichita that

year. Honus Wagner, commissioner of semipro baseball and former Pittsburgh shortstop great, denied such action was contemplated.

Ironically, this was on the eve of my first meeting with the owner of the Washington baseball team to take up the matter of hiring black players. Also, on September 25, 1937, my column carried a lengthy letter by John L. Clark, secretary of the Negro National League, that bitterly attacked certain teams for launching a world series tour not sanctioned by the league.

So there I was, ready with recommendations to major league owners regarding the hiring of black players, and Negro National League teams were seemingly running amok. It led to this column comment:

> What with petty jealousies, cut-throat aspirations and willful disregard for rules and agreements on the parts of promoters and club owners, and team-jumping and general wrangling on the parts of players keeping so-called organized Negro baseball in perpetual chaos, it makes one ponder the advisability of entering the breach to submit recommendations.

Of course, there was no way I would have ended my quest for opportunities for black players in major league baseball because of wrangling in the Negro National League, but I didn't get a chance to belabor the discussion of the issue after finding myself smack in the middle of a national story. That developed when I disclosed that a young football player who had been advertised as the only Hindu in college football actually was a black youngster. The ruse was intended to make it possible for Wilmeth Sidat-Singh to play with Syracuse University against a college, the University of Maryland, that otherwise would not take the field against a black player.

In stories about the game, the Baltimore, Washington, and New York newspapers had been referring to Wilmeth Sidat-Singh as the only Hindu playing football until my story in the paper dated October 23 (but on the streets before that) exposed the trickery. Sidat-Singh, Syracuse's top passer and running back, earlier had rejected his school's public relations suggestion that he don East Indian attire.

My story was headlined: "Negro To Play U. of Maryland: Boy Called Hindu By Papers." An editorial in the issue declared: "There is much speculation as to what the University will do when it learns that its lily-white team must rub shoulders with a Negro."

The response came quickly and was what might have been expected. No white college in Dixie had played at home against a team with black members. (In 1936, North Carolina had gone up against New York University—which played Edward Williams—in a game hosted by NYU.)

I reported that after a "lengthy debate" with Maryland officials, Syracuse coach Ossie Solem broke the news to Sidat-Singh and his teammates, after the youngster already had dressed for the game. Teammates first sought to protest, then they tried to console their black teammate. Unhappy campers, they then went out and dropped the first game they had lost that season.

My lead for a front-page, postgame story said: "An unsullied football record went by the boards here today as racial bigotry substituted for sportsmanship and resulted in the removal of the spark-plug from the machine which was Syracuse University's football team."

The four-deck headline read: "Gridiron Star Ousted From Maryland Game; Wilmeth Sidat-Singh Removed Following Discovery By Maryland Authorities That He Was Not Hindu; Solem In Huff But Won't Comment; New York Team's Record Spoiled; Tribune Exposes Foreign Ruse; Players on Orange Eleven Sulk As Coach Is Compelled To Comply With Demands Of Hosts."

In exposing the attempt to pawn off the young man as a Hindu, I explained that Wilmeth had been born in Washington to black parents, Elias and Pauline Webb. After his father's death, his mother married an East Indian, Samuel Sidat-Singh, a Howard University–trained physician. Sidat-Singh legally adopted Wilmeth and changed his last name.

Wilmeth was also good at basketball and baseball. In fact, after his first year in college, Sidat-Singh was a premed student studying on a baseball scholarship. He landed on the football team after one of the assistant coaches spotted him playing quarterback in an intramural pickup game.

I took some flak from a number of critics who felt it would have been better to have kept quiet about the Hindu sham and let Wilmeth play. Reacting to those charges of indiscretion, I argued:

This department has what it, in its humble estimation, considers an iron-clad defense against charges that the act of publishing the true story of Sidat-Singh's racial connection was premature. This writer does not concur in the opinion that waiting until after the boy had played would have been a better "joke" on Maryland University.

To me such a contention seems only to be a weak-livered admission that we are willing to see our boys progress under any kind of masquerade; that we agree with the Nordic observation that ANYTHING BUT A NEGRO is okay.

As for Sidat-Singh, he continued to be involved in sports in the Washington area, participating in football, basketball, baseball, and tennis. In August 1939, he upset seeded Todd Duncan and beat Waldo Webb to reach the semifinals of the city tennis tournament. Sidat-Singh didn't live long enough to see the dramatic changes that were to occur in college and professional football. During World War II, 2d Lt. Sidat-Singh was killed in May of 1943, when his single seat pursuit plane went down in Lake Huron near East Tawas, Michigan.

Sometimes I would dash off a letter to big or little people, whether they were in sports or not. An example of this was a March 1938 letter to the distinguished president of Howard University, Dr. Mordecai W. Johnson.

The day before, in Rankin Memorial Chapel, Johnson had suggested that "some of the more thoughtful Howard students would provide seats for the Honorable Mister Mitchell of the Congress of the United States, the representative from the *Evening Star* newspaper, and some older graduates of the University" who were standing in the rear of the auditorium.

I wrote that in my personal observation "that reference to an employee of a daily newspaper was entirely out of place, especially in view of the fact representatives of the *Afro-American, Flash Magazine, Pittsburgh Courier,* and *Washington Tribune,* as well as several young women, were standing close by the representative from the *Star.*"

As 1939 was fading into history, and while then working for the *Washington Afro-American,* another story hit the sports pages indicating how frequently black players helped their teams reach lofty heights only to be humiliated by having to sit on the bench or remain at home when southern tradition prevailed.

Boston College's sensational running back Lou Montgomery, who had been forced to warm the bench when Boston played Florida and Auburn, decided to avoid some of the pain and remained at home while his team-mates went off to play Clemson in the Cotton Bowl in Dallas.

Although I took myself to be a serious critic of injustices in sports and else-where, often my writing took on a lighter note. Going into 1940, one of my co-lumns noted some things I planned to do for sure: "Eat regularly, sell Josh Gibson or Buck Leonard to Clark Griffith, and either obey Tim (my young son) or make him mind me." Among the things sworn off: "Any derned kind of eggnog, slow horses and Jim Crow boxing, which is D.C. boxing."

Back on a more serious note, there was a look at some of the questions put on the table regarding the integration of major league baseball. This June 1940 piece harked back to a 1937 two-and-a-half-hour discussion with Clark Griffith of the Washington team:

> Since then I have begun to wonder whether there is any weight in the arguments advanced by some of our players, the very men in whose in-terest the fight is waged.
>
> The Homestead Grays Jud Wilson, a veteran in the baseball wars, would argue that when baseball finally accepted black players they would be segregated when it came to hotel housing and "we will be madder than we are now."

Others took the position of Felton Snow, manager of the Baltimore Elite Giants, 1939 Negro National League champions, that major league moguls might pick the wrong player or players to break the ice, the result being "the opposition forces would have strong support for their disap-proval of colored diamond talent."

Griffith's position was "that this was not yet the right time and that in-tegration would kill black organized baseball." Also, Griffith supported setting up a league of eight bona fide clubs of black players. He said success of such a league would "surely guarantee eventual recognition by the solons who run the paying sport."

After considering these views, I took this posture:

> I, for one, would certainly like to see some definite move in the right di-rection. If we should act to correct the impressions of Snow and Grif-fith, who can tell but that Wilson's point may take care of itself.

Over the years, one galling realization for me was that regardless of talent, people of every other race and nationality on the earth's broad surface had been able to play on a major league team but blacks. I wrote:

"There have been Italians, Jews, Germans, Frenchmen, Irishmen, Indians, Spaniards, Mexicans, Slavs, name-what-you-want-and-you-can-get-'em, wearing the uniforms of major league teams within the past decade. But no colored."

At another point I summed it up this way:

Baseball has given employment to known epileptics, kleptomaniacs, and a generous scattering of saints and sinners. A man who is totally lacking in character has turned out to be a star in baseball.

A man whose skin is white or red or yellow has been acceptable. But a man whose character may be of the highest and whose ability may be Ruthian has been barred completely from the sport because he is colored.

Months before being assigned to the Baltimore office of the *Afro-American* in early 1941, I witnessed the falling of racial bars in one Washington sport. The story's lead on June 8, 1940: "Mixed boxing comes here on June 17."

The D.C. boxing commission "after six long years of wringing and twisting" had approved the application of Joe Turner to match Louis "Kid" Cocoa and the winner of the Steve Mamakos–Phil Furr welterweight match.

A few months later, "Looking 'Em Over" would exonerate both the D.C. boxing commission and the *Times-Herald* newspaper for the "maintenance of 'lily-whiteism' in the local Golden Gloves tournament."

The blame, I had found, rightly belonged to E. Joseph Aronoff, chairman of the registration committee of the D.C. Amateur Athletic Union and a white collar employee of the Interior Department who called himself the "bull-headed Dutchman." Aronoff wasn't "the least bit reluctant about taking the blame for the bigoted policy in force" when reached by telephone at the government agency.

He said he did not intend to permit colored boys to enter the tournament "because sentiment here is against it." Asked what evidence he had to support that statement, Aronoff said he had been approached by white parents and told that if he let the colored boys in the tournament that they would take their sons out.

There came the time when I found myself in the throes of two conflicting columns on Josh Gibson, regarded as baseball's best black player.

The first time around, Gibson, then twenty-eight and the highest paid player in black baseball, was described by me as reticent but congenial, a lover of the game who was back with the Homestead Grays after four months playing in Venezuela. He got six hundred dollars monthly there compared to the five hundred he would have received from the Grays. So now Gibson was telling me in a lengthy interview how the love of playing the game had brought him home before the end of the season:

"They play down there only once a week and that's not enough for me. Just sitting around waiting for Saturday or Sunday to come will drive a man nuts if you take it long enough . . . But the money is good and, after all, you know, that's something."

Gibson also thought a group of twenty players could be drafted from among the black teams to form a team that would be able to hold its own over the length of the season against major league teams.

For the next Gibson column, I said I had just read something about "one of my ex-favorite baseball players" and was groping for a way "to rid myself of the nauseous sensation that is gripping my stomach."

What chilled my respect for Gibson was his decision to jump from the Homestead Grays to Mexico without so much as consulting with the Grays coproprietors Cum Posey and Sonny Man Jackson. To me, Gibson was treating his contract with a colored business enterprise as no more than "a scrap of paper." I judged the action to be a blow to the struggle to move black players into the majors:

By his action, Josh, who by the way is one of the leading players in the world, throws those of us who are interested in the fight, back about five years in the campaign to get colored performers into big-league baseball. By such a crude display of his unreliability, Gibson retards us in any progress we may possibly have been making in that direction . . .

For all of me, Gibson can keep going—southward.

Meanwhile in college sports, with the Wilmeth Sidat-Singh matter in its recent history, the University of Maryland (after some haggling at top levels) avoided another flap by allowing varsity lacrosse player Lucien Alexis Jr., a Harvard University junior from New Orleans, to play. But a week after Alexis played against Maryland, the U.S. Naval Academy at Annapolis refused to permit him to play in an April 5, 1941, match.

That stirred an uproar on the Harvard campus. The *Afro-American* sports section devoted more than half a page to a story on the matter. The daily *Harvard Crimson* accused Harvard officials of "kowtowing to the intolerable jim crowism of Navy bigwigs" and accused the Naval Academy of practicing undemocratic principles. Protests went to the Naval Academy, to President Roosevelt, and to Harvard's athletic department.

The story said Harvard coach Robert Snibbe and team manager Robert B. Seidman, a senior student, were called in by Commander Davis, the academy's athletic director, and told Alexis would not be permitted to play. Eventually, they were taken to see Admiral Willson, academy superintendent, just as the week before, they had been taken to see University of Maryland president Curly Byrd (who left the decision up to the coach who left it up to the players).

The admiral called Harvard officials, touching off a series of telephone and telegram exchanges. Eventually, Harvard athletic director William J. Bingham was reached in another state. He insisted that Alexis be allowed to play. However, later that evening a wire came from Bingham advising the coach that Alexis was not to dress and not to play. The young man took the evening train back to Boston.

As time passed, my active involvement with sporting activities, especially the sponsoring and promoting of teams, did not meet with the approval of *Washington Afro-American* editor Ralph Matthews. He said I could not be committed to any outside enterprise while I worked for the paper. I felt a responsibility to players on a team I backed, and I did not think my work was being unduly affected.

A February 19, 1941, story in the old *Washington Daily News* reported that I had been running my own professional basketball team, the Bruins, with games on Sundays at Turner's Arena. The team was made up of former Central Intercollegiate Athletic Association (CIAA) players and had won twelve of thirteen games at the time the story appeared. The Bruins were attracting an average fourteen hundred paying fans. Twenty percent off the top went for arena rent. Yet, as the story reported, I was doing well enough to put up my out-of-town players at the Whitelaw Hotel and pick up the tab for their meals.

The team was built around such players as Tarzan Cooper, a veteran of basketball wars as a member of the famous New York Renaissance, and Soup Campbell, twice captain of the CIAA champion Virginia Union University. Cooper was the top paid player, the others being paid according to their experience. I coached the team and also handled its business matters, and was getting ready to play the Heurich Brewers, champs of the white Industrial League, when the story ran. I'd planned to become the first black team to join the all-white American Basketball League, to which the Brewers belonged.

Instead, I had another problem. As a result of my disagreement with Matthews, I was about to meet Carl Murphy, publisher of the *Afro-American* newspapers, for the second time. I had spoken to "Mr. Carl," as he was known, when he hired me on Matthews's recommendation.

Murphy was the power behind one of the nation's largest and most influential black-owned newspaper chains. The *Afro-American* had always been in the forefront of the struggle for equal rights and fair play. Murphy not only hired good reporters and sent them wherever stories were breaking, he put the influence and financial power of his publication at the forefront of the crusade by blacks to win first-class citizenship. That included the filing and support of federal suits aimed at ending racial segregation and discrimination. At one time, the *Afro-American* printed thirteen different editions on its presses at 628 North Eutaw Street in Baltimore. That included twice weekly papers for Baltimore and Washington, weekly papers for Richmond, Newark, and Philadelphia, plus a national edition and other state and regional papers.

Carl Murphy wanted me to come over to Baltimore to discuss both the problem and the possibility of a move to Baltimore. I told him I was already committed under contract to these players and to advertisers and couldn't just pull out and say I don't want to play any more. I said that if Mr. Matthews could show that my work had deteriorated in any sense, in quantity or quality, then I would be happy to withdraw from the promotion. But he was unable to do that and I knew it.

Carl Murphy told me, "I like to have my editors responsible. So, suppose you disassociate yourself from the *Afro-American* until such time as the season is over. When your season is over, you come on back over and see me." That's what I did, and that's when he put me in Baltimore.

That first stint in the Baltimore office would not have forecast my long history with the paper. First, my friend Art Carter was the sports editor, so I did other kinds of stories. Second, I wasn't terribly keen about some of the story assignments from my boss, who happened to be one of Dr. Carl Murphy's five daughters, Elizabeth (Bettye) Murphy Phillips. Later, of course, we became best of friends.

One of those stories in July 1941 ran under the heading, "How Aircraft Manufacturer Plans To Flout F.D.'s Executive Order." Glenn L. Martin, president of the firm by that name, had testified as to why the company could not abide by President Roosevelt's executive order outlawing discrimination in national defense industries.

It had a similar ring to some of the excuses I'd heard in the effort to integrate baseball. There were no black workers, there would be a work stoppage by whites if he brought in blacks, and there were also Maryland laws that prevented integration.

The Murphy daughter who gave me some of my early assignments became Mrs. Elizabeth Murphy Phillips Moss, a respected journalist who over the decades did some of everything at the *Afro-American* newspapers, filling some of the top editorial and administrative positions. Known widely as Bettye, her "If You Ask Me" column became one of the Baltimore-based paper's most popular features. She died in April 1998.

After a few months, there was an abrupt interruption of that first stint in the *Afro-American* home office. I was driving out Orleans Street on an assignment from Bettye that made no sense whatsoever to me. I just swung the damn car, made a U-turn, and the next time anyone from the paper heard from me, I was in Chicago.

I made one brief, working stop to earn some money en route to Chicago. I stopped briefly in Cincinnati and did some copy for radio station WJLW, but that wasn't for me. It was just a stopgap to get enough money to get to Chicago. I went straight to Marshall Field's newly organized paper, the *Sun,* and was hired.

Eventually, I went down to see Lucius Harper at the *Chicago Defender.* I had been staying clear for awhile because I had left the *Afro-American* under a cloud, having just bolted from the headman's daughter.

Right away, Lucius Harper suggested to John Sengstacke that they put me on. John Sengstacke, a member of the family of *Defender* founder-publisher Robert S. Abbott, was the top man at the paper. Under his leadership, the weekly *Defender* had newspapers in several cities and would publish the most successful black daily in the nation. He took Harper's advice, and I was with the *Defender,* but still not doing sports.

I worked under Ben Burns, one of the editors. Burns also did some work for John Johnson, who had a desk at the *Defender* on the way to becoming a magazine magnate with such publications as *Ebony, Jet,* and *Ebony Jr.,* in addition to other successful business ventures.

While spending much of my time on the desk at the *Chicago Defender,* there was talk in the spring of 1943 that the loss of major league baseball stars such as the DiMaggios, Ted Williams, Red Ruffin, and others to the military services during World War II might hasten the arrival of black players into the major leagues.

Meanwhile, I kept busy with editing chores and handling some writing assignments. One of the features I wrote was on concert artist and lecturer Paul Robeson. In August, there was a three-part series on the "shocking abuse of Jamaicans" working at farm-labor centers in the United States. I traveled nearly three thousand miles visiting the work centers. By October, there was a *Defender* headline saying the "U.S. Jails 600 Jamaicans" because they refused to accept contracts calling for them to buckle under to racial discrimination on farms in Florida.

There was also a bylined political story by me featuring inch-high type on the front page of the September 18, 1943, *Defender:* "Mitchell Warns Democrats: Aid Negro Or Lose To GOP." The story was based on an interview with former congressman Arthur W. Mitchell of Chicago. There was another on the investigation of the treatment of black soldiers at Fort Huachuca in Arizona.

Restricted largely now to desk duty and without a sports column and beat, my mind was still focused on this baseball desegregation business. I was closer to baseball commissioner Judge Kenesaw Landis in Chicago, so I tried to get the judge to let us talk to him.

He broke down and said, "Okay, you can talk. You can come on in."

This 1943 invitation was my long desired opportunity to go before the baseball commissioner and the owners of teams in the American and National Leagues to make the pitch directly. They were to meet in Cleveland at the Hotel Hollenden. I considered this something of a breakthrough and looked forward to participating in this meeting. But it was not to be.

The invitation went to the Negro Newspaper Publishers Association. Speakers were to be the *Defender*'s John Sengstacke, Ira Lewis of the *Pittsburgh Courier*, and, apparently at the encouragement of Commissioner Landis, internationally famed singer-actor Paul Robeson.

I was not included in the contingent to meet with the owners because it was believed that handing a speaking role to Robeson would have a greater impact on the moguls of baseball. I knew that was a kiss of death because at that time, Paul was considered by many to be a communist.

As Christmas approached in 1943, I was in Washington to visit my family and some friends. I dropped by the *Washington Afro-American* to see longtime friends, John H. Murphy III (who would head the newspaper chain years later) and William "Scottie" Scott.

Carl Murphy was there. This third talk I was about to have with the *Afro-American* publisher would turn out to be the most important. He always called me Sam. He asked, "What are you doing in Washington, Sam?"

"Looking for a job," I replied.

He said, "Are you?" So he took me into this ante room, just off the entrance way, and asked again, "Are you serious?"

I said that while I was happy in my present job, I wouldn't object to being closer to my family—but there were some stipulations concerning working for the *Baltimore Afro-American*. I really didn't know how they would affect Carl Murphy, but wanting to be absolutely clear, I tossed them on the table.

"I can't come back at the same salary and I can't come back working under your daughter." I told him this, to make it clear at first.

He said, "That's all right. When can you start?" I told him I would have to give notice and he asked, "How about right after New Year's?"

Would you believe, I came back making twice the salary? And he also paid my way back. I returned to the *Afro-American* for good on January 4, 1944.

Art Carter had been sent overseas as one of the war correspondents the paper had placed in the various theaters where large numbers of black troops were serving. That was the final matter to be clarified, as I was taking Art's old job as sports editor. "What happens when Art comes back?" I asked.

Dr. Carl Murphy told me, "We'll find a place for Mr. Carter." Art Carter was named associate editor when he returned from his war coverage.

After returning to the *Afro-American*, the very first "Looking 'Em Over" column I did was devoted to the meeting with the baseball owners that I didn't get to attend. I declared I was going to tell "the real story—if it gets past the censors," a warning that I was about to blister the Negro Newspaper Publishers Association of which the *Afro-American* was a prominent member:

> . . . A delegation which was originally supposed to consist of the president of the newspaper publishers' body, the only colored congressman in Washington, and a representative of either the Urban League or the NAACP, turned out to be a committee much too large and unschooled on the subject at hand.
>
> . . . The major league club owners are almost fanatical in their dislike of communism. His (Robeson's) presence on the occasion under discussion, and at the [insistence] of Landis, reminds me of a cartoon I once saw of a man extending his right hand in a gesture of friendship while clenching a long knife in a left hand concealed behind his back.
>
> In other words, by this clever little maneuver, Landis told the gullible colored folks, "Here's how I feel. This is your chance to put it squarely up to the men who control the purse strings of the game. I'm with you, now go to it."
>
> But on the other hand, he said to his owners, "Use your own judgment in this matter, but remember, here's a communist influence along with the torchbearers."

That out of the way, I resumed efforts to meet with commissioner Judge Landis, offering to travel any time to any place in the country. Before anything was arranged, Landis died late in 1944. Afterward, I struck up a relationship with Leslie O'Connor, who was chosen as chairman of a council named to oversee baseball until a new commissioner could be voted in.

In March 1945, I wrote to each team owner in both the American and the National Leagues, suggesting that a committee be set up at their next meeting to examine the desegregation issue. In what I considered a tactful letter, I urged formation of a committee to address the best way to go about integrating major league baseball. In conceding that achievement of the goal could be a slow and tedious process, I added:

"This is sort of a compromise for me as a colored man, in that it embraces certain elements of appeasement, but if it accomplishes anything I shall feel compensated in some measure for suggesting it. Certainly it will be a step in the right direction."

This time, I received an invitation from baseball's high echelon that I'd be able to keep personally. It was to be an eventful meeting, held at the Cadillac Hotel in Detroit.

I spoke to the owners on April 24. There were only sixteen of them then. They met in one of the small conference rooms. I was directed to wait in the hallway until they summoned me. After maybe an hour, during which time I snacked, browsed, and read, a young man, a waiter I suppose, came out of the room and said they were ready for me. No one showed any rancor or anything of that nature. Leslie O'Connor introduced me, and I handed out copies of my proposal. I made a brief statement, answered a couple of questions, and left.

As a result, the owners set up a committee on major league baseball integration, and I was approved as one of the members. Branch Rickey of the Brooklyn Dodgers, representing the National League, also was a committee member. The others were Larry MacPhail of the American League New York Yankees, and Philadelphia magistrate Joseph H. Rainey. A week or so later, Harold Parrott, the Dodgers road secretary, called to give me a date for our first committee meeting.

During the Detroit owners meeting, Senator A. B. "Happy" Chandler, former governor of Kentucky, was chosen as the new commissioner. Chandler's selection came as a surprise to most observers and drew a negative reaction from supporters of baseball integration. Filing my story from Detroit, I wrote: "It appears that his choice was the most logical one to suit the bigoted major league operators, of which there is a heavy majority on hand."

Chandler denied he had antiblack leanings. Actually, he didn't attract a lot of negative publicity on that issue at the time. Decades later in 1988, he was picketed at the University of Kentucky, where he was a trustee. During a meeting on university investments in South Africa, he reminded a finance committee, "You know Zimbabwe is all nigger now. There aren't any whites."

Shortly after I spoke for five minutes to the owners in Detroit (and I didn't learn this until much later), Branch Rickey stunned everyone by saying he planned to sign a colored player. The rest of the owners tried to stop the move by adopting a resolution that opposed hiring colored athletes for major league teams. Of the fifteen owners there, fourteen approved the resolution; Rickey abstained. But no matter the thinking of the baseball team owners at that 1945 meeting, the tide was turning against them. Rickey's decision was the beginning of what became both a social revolution and a boon to the big business of professional sports.

Elsewhere that same year, Jackie Robinson, who had left the army in 1944 after waging some battles of his own against discrimination in the armed services, joined the Kansas City Monarchs of the Negro National League, where he would play for a season.

A new day in the national pastime was dawning sooner than almost anyone had good reason to believe possible.

CHAPTER 4

BLACKS AND SPORTS

Realization that the dream of making a living as a professional athlete wasn't going to materialize—a story still being repeated every year for untold numbers of young men with similar aspirations—helped me make the decision to try a writing career.

Be it due to injuries, lack of talent, or too few professional slots being available, thousands of young athletes wake up from their dreams of hitting the big time in sports to the specter of facing the real world unprepared for any career. For me, the career choice came at a time when it was possible for me to join others in making a significant contribution as black Americans stepped up their national campaign for racial equality in the country. Sportswise, I was in a prized location.

Sports has always been important in the black community. During the 1930s and 1940s (and since), talented black athletes helped spearhead the drive for equal opportunity through their successes as competitors. Sports is a merit-focused competition through which individuals and teams seem

49

to have, as a result of their highs and lows, an emotional impact on people that enhances respect and tempers certain prejudices.

Additionally, at the time I started writing, sports probably represented a significant recreational and social outlet for blacks because of the racial restrictions all of us faced and the income restrictions a large percentage of us faced.

My geographic location was about as good as it gets. While there were no strict criteria, black sports thrived best in cities with large black populations, two or more high schools, black colleges, and semipro or professional quality facilities for whites where semipro or professional black athletes (for a rental fee) could play. Black colleges also made use of these white-owned facilities for many of their major attractions. In that era, great locations would have included New York City, Chicago, Pittsburgh, Philadelphia, St. Louis, Richmond, Kansas City, and my home bases of Baltimore and Washington.

With something like forty miles between them, Washington and Baltimore could boast of Howard University, Miner Teachers College, Morgan State, and Coppin College, as well as baseball, basketball, and football teams organized by various federal agencies—just for starters. Track and field events, tennis, and bowling were popular, and of course, boxing was a top favorite for many fans.

Up the road from Baltimore-Washington, there was New York City, with some of everything; to the west a bit was West Virginia, and down the road were Virginia, the Carolinas, Georgia, and Florida.

High schools, colleges, and the pros didn't create all the competition. Particularly important were the Young Men's and Young Women's Christian Associations, both as sponsors of athletic activities and providers of facilities others could use free or for a relatively modest fee. Groups that included the Elks, fraternities, sororities, hospitals, and companies also sponsored teams. Recreation centers likewise played a role.

Oddly, while relatively few major white college or professional teams were integrated in the mid-1930s, there were numerous matches featuring whites-only on one side and blacks-only on the other. When a black basketball team was to play a white one in Washington, the routine was for the black team to go to the other's place. Once in a great while, a team like the Epiphany Roses or Gonzaga would come uptown; Joe Holman was responsible for breaking that traditional "you come to us" pattern in Washington.

Unquestionably, the major sporting event for blacks in the nation's capital for years was the Capital Classic, featuring college football teams. Clashing in Griffith Stadium would be teams like Morgan State, Lincoln University, Howard University, West Virginia State, Tennessee State, and North Carolina A&T. The Capital Classic was bigger than the homecoming games or the city and state championships that also drew loyal fans.

One column I remember listed these upcoming classics and bowls: Old Dominion Classic, Richmond; Fish Bowl, Norfolk; National Classic, D.C.; and a Frontiers Club–sponsored charity game in Baltimore.

The big Thanksgiving Day matches usually featured same-state or same-conference foes, although that was not always the case. A 1949 lineup pitted Arkansas State against Philander Smith and Georgia State against Paine. Other matches paired Benedict/South Carolina State, Claflin/Allen, Morris Brown/Clark, Alabama State/Tuskegee, Tennessee/Kentucky, Shaw/Smith, A&T/North Carolina State, Hampton/Union, Lincoln/Howard, Morgan/Virginia State, and Dillard/Xavier.

Big crowds turned out for these games. More than a few fans dressed up for the occasion because they would often take in a dance or visit a night club or stage show before they returned home. Local entertainment centers planned to have special entertainment on tap to attract customers.

On a national level, the biggest event, once pulling in more than fifty-one thousand fans to Comiskey Park in Chicago, was the East-West All-Star baseball game. Black professional teams included the Chicago American Giants, Kansas City Monarchs, Birmingham Black Barons, Memphis Red Sox, Detroit Stars, St. Louis Stars, Indianapolis Clowns, Indianapolis ABCs, Cleveland Buckeyes, Baltimore Elites, Pittsburgh Homestead Grays, Pittsburgh Crawfords, Washington Homestead Grays, Philadelphia Stars, New York Black Yankees, New York Cubans, and the Newark Eagles.

For individual sports stars, the top draw was Joe Louis, who turned pro in 1934 and in 1937 knocked out Joe Braddock in Comiskey Park to claim the world heavyweight title at the age of twenty-three.

Fans and sportsmen from across the country would gather in New York (or wherever) to see Louis fight and to wager and party. Millions would gather around radio sets in their homes or in public places where proprietors knew they'd lose their customers at fight time if they couldn't pick up the broadcast of the fight.

Other surefire attractions wherever they played were the basketball Globetrotters, the Renaissance squad out of New York and later, for a time, the Harlem Magicians. The Globetrotters and Renaissance often claimed the national basketball championship. Both played and defeated their share of white all-stars teams.

For instance, the *Tribune* sports pages reported in March 1934 that an overflow crowd was expected to see the famed Renaissance team and the white professional Rinaldi five tangle at the Colonnade beneath the Lincoln Theater in D.C.

This was the same year we were spotlighting Jesse Owens, a Cleveland high schooler gaining fame, and Ralph Metcalfe posting exemplary times in track and field events at Marquette University. Owens would become world famous for his feats in the 1936 Olympics in Germany. Also in 1934, a black promoter in Washington put on a game in Griffith Stadium between the white Industrial League champion Heurich Brewers and the black Winston-Salem Twins.

Meantime, baseball's black leagues teams regularly played against white teams that sometimes were made up of big league stars—and the black teams won their share of those games. The better known of the leagues were the National Negro Baseball League, considered the most successful, the Negro American League, and the Negro National League. Frank Thompson, a headwaiter for a New York City hotel, is credited with having formed the first black professional baseball team in 1885. His team eventually became the Cuban Giants.

As the games featuring black players usually were played in major league parks, the major league club owners not only made hundreds of thousands of dollars renting their facilities for the matches, but because of this, everyone associated with the sport knew these owners were quite aware of the black talent available and the drawing power of these players.

At one point, I wrote about the Negro National League (NNL) and Thursday nights and Sunday afternoons in "colored town":

> They came to live by Thursday nights and Sunday afternoons, integral parts of the success story in early black baseball. Other games in the transient schedules of the teams were played in wayside stops like Bohunk and Yippety Switch and Rum Gulch, but Thursday nights and

Sunday afternoons were saved for the bigger parks—whenever they could get into them.

Thursday was laughingly referred to as "domestics night out," and it was assumed that the swains would begin the evening with beer and hot dogs at the ball game, then on to more serious entertainment.

Sunday was in-town respite from the crowded highways to the beach, and a haven for those without cars who were looking for something to do.

Most of the cities with major league clubs had their ball parks in the heart of, or bordering, colored neighborhoods—Griffith Stadium at Georgia and Florida Avenues; Yankee Stadium, a short walk across a bridge from Harlem; Comiskey Park on Chicago's Southside, among others . . . And minor league operations in Birmingham, Memphis, Kansas City and Toledo likewise were within a stone's throw of the ghettos.

During World War II, some games between the NNL's Homestead Grays and the Kansas City Monarchs (and others) would draw more fans than would the American League team in Washington.

Pitcher Satchel Paige of the Monarchs (at that time) was the best known of the NNL stars, but he did not figure in the biggest league trade in 1937. The story was reported this way:

"NEW YORK—The biggest player deal in the history of Negro baseball was completed here Saturday morning when (catcher) Josh Gibson of the Pittsburgh Crawfords and third baseman Judy Johnson of the same club were sent to the Homestead Grays in exchange for 'Pepper' Bassett, third baseman Henry Spearman, and $2,500 in cash."

A sports page piece in April 1941 reflected the problems the NNL was having with some of its top players going to better-paying opportunities in foreign countries. It said the Newark Eagles had signed pitcher Leon Day of Baltimore, one of the "outlaw" stars who had gone abroad to play. Day was beating the May 1 deadline for these players to return to their NNL teams in order to avoid a one-year suspension.

Two years later during gas rationing and the related restrictions imposed in the war years, the Office of Defense Transportation turned down a request from black baseball teams for permission to operate twelve buses after owners complained they could not afford to travel by train.

Sizing up the baseball picture in 1945 when Branch Rickey would sign Jackie Robinson to a minor league contract, actions and events were occurring in a manner that would help set the stage for astounding change. The Baltimore Elites would down the Newark Eagles on a ninth inning blow by Roy Campanella. The world champion NNL Homestead Grays would beat the New York Cubans before twelve thousand in the first night game of the Negro leagues to be played in a metropolitan major league park. And the Baltimore Elites would take two games from a team of International Leaguers made up mostly of Baltimore Orioles. So, it easily could have been said that the nation already was tolerating low-level, off-beat doses of baseball integration—and that there were enough quality black players around to make it a successful experiment.

CHAPTER 5

BRANCH RICKEY, JACKIE ROBINSON

The same month that I would appear before the commissioner and baseball team owners (April of 1945), other black newsmen were taking bold action under legal provisions.

President Franklin Delano Roosevelt had signed the federal Fair Employment Practices Commission legislation in 1942 and by early 1945, New York had its Quinn-Ives antidiscrimination law that called for an end to hiring discrimination by firms employing more than six workers.

Joe Bostic, the sports editor of the *People's Voice* in New York, took Terris "The Great" McDuffie and Dave "Showboat" Thomas to the Bear Mountain camp of the Dodgers and demanded a tryout for them. He reasoned that the team would be in violation of the law if it refused the players a tryout.

I certainly was supportive of the move but questioned the quality of the players Bostic chose. First baseman Thomas, thirty-four, once was the classiest at his position but never was much at the plate. Pitcher McDuffie, thirty-two, had won five and lost six for the Newark Eagles and won two against three losses for the Santurce Crabbers in Puerto Rico in his last outings.

Elsewhere, my friend Wendell Smith of the *Pittsburgh Courier* decided to test the Boston Red Sox. Both the Red Sox and the Boston Braves needed a license to play games on Sundays. One of Boston's city councilmen, Isadore Muchnick, had publicly announced he would block the licenses for the two teams should they refuse to give blacks equal opportunity to make the teams.

Oddly enough, Jackie Robinson of the Kansas City Monarchs was one of the three players on whose behalf Smith arranged tryouts with the Red Sox. The other two were Marvin Williams of the Philadelphia Stars and Sam Jethroe of the Cleveland Buckeyes, who later became a major league star, starting his career as National League rookie of the year in 1950 at age thirty-three.

Much later, in 1996, Jethroe would lose a federal court suit in which he sought pension benefits from major league baseball, contending racial discrimination prevented his getting into the major leagues earlier so that he could play long enough to qualify for benefits. However, in January 1997, major league baseball announced it would fund a pension plan for Negro Leaguers and other pre-1947 players (the year the major leagues' pension plan went into effect). Jethroe would be one of those eligible for the annual $7,500 to $10,000 in benefits. The pension plan covers players with at least four years in the Negro Leagues or combined service in the Negro and major leagues. National League president Leonard Coleman called the move "the very least baseball can do."

None of the three players Smith took for tryouts got a second look by the Red Sox. As noted, the Red Sox would be the last major league team to hire black players.

The day I was in Detroit making my pitch for the integration of major league baseball, the *Afro-American* carried a story saying Branch Rickey of the Dodgers was giving the newest (and weakest) of the black leagues, the United States League, exclusive rights to use his Ebbets Field when the Dodgers were on the road. Some saw this as retaliation against the Negro National League because the two NNL players had forced his hand on those tryouts with the Dodgers.

In talking to the baseball moguls I urged two key steps: forming a committee to determine the best way to go about integrating major league baseball, and bringing the Negro leagues into the family of organized baseball as another Triple-A minor league.

After discussions, the owners agreed to appoint a committee and to invite an owner from the black leagues to take part. The black team owners wasted no time in saying they wanted no part in the arrangement. Not only that, but as things progressed, owners such as Cum Posey of the Homestead Grays would suggest I was off base and let me know, "We don't want to help you break up our league."

Our committee on baseball integration never held a meeting with all its members because Larry MacPhail never came to one. Rickey and I met twice in the Dodgers' offices in Brooklyn, but Larry MacPhail always had something else to do; he couldn't make it.

Rainey had told me, "The moment you have set up a definite time and date, let me know and I will be there." Unless Rickey and MacPhail both attended, there could be no formal meeting; as a magistrate, Rainey would not take leave of his duties if nothing could be done.

I don't know if Rickey told anybody about our meetings but I had to tell Carl Murphy. Evidently Rickey had told Clyde Sukeforth because he was the one who went out and brought Jackie in to be signed.

In my meetings with Rickey, I observed him going through some difficult times because of the historic change he set in motion; one had to admire him. We spoke of many things, including Rickey's thoughts about a Brown Dodgers team. Writer Wendell Smith had brought Jackie Robinson to the attention of Rickey and he was one of the numerous black players whose names came up.

The only view I had was that Rickey was really nice. I detected a sort of inner warmth, and it came out later that he was indeed a very warm person. This man must have been a real saint to deal with the things he had to deal with. At the time he brought Jackie in, when all this was going on, he was having problems with Leo Durocher (something about gambling) and also Laraine Day (Leo's actress wife). Laraine was complaining to Rickey about her relationship with Leo. He had left his apartment in California in the hands of actor George Raft, who was hosting gambling games or something.

Of course, the media were reporting all this. Plus, Rickey had health problems. He had an ulcer, he had a heart problem, and he was suffering with rheumatism. In addition to that, all those other owners in the leagues were sniping at him because of his activities regarding integration of the major leagues.

It seemed obvious MacPhail had no interest in being a member of the committee on integrating baseball; I received a call from Rickey sometime after our second two-person session. He told me, "I'm going to ask Larry if he would meet with us one more time, and if he gives me some excuse, or just refuses . . . we will just give up on him and let nature take its course.

Apparently he had already decided what he was going to do. In several months, Rickey would startle the nation with his announcement of the signing of Jackie Robinson to a contract with the Dodgers Triple A team, the Montreal Royals of the International League.

Meanwhile, my work kept me busy in other sports areas. One tactic was to keep in touch with Art Carter, other sports fans, and other Americans in the war zones by addressing some of my columns to them.

In a May 9 piece addressed to "Dear friend Art, war correspondent, Ninety-ninth Fighter Squadron," my comment was on a New York columnist's question asking "What made the colored boy drift away from the jockey profession, which he dominated at one time?"

The columnist had mentioned jockeys Isaac Murphy, Jimmy Winkfield, Monk Overton, Oscar Lewis, and Jimmy Lee. I wrote:

> It isn't difficult to answer this one. The colored boy has not faded out of the hardboot business through any choice of his own. He was forced out as he is in everything else where the white man's money and influence dictate the course of events.
>
> There is nothing strange about the rise and fall of the colored boy and man in horse racing. It simply follows a normal American pattern.

How good were the black jockeys? Between 1875 and 1902, they rode winners in eleven of the fifteen Kentucky Derby races, with Oscar Lewis winning the first "Run for the Roses" in 1875 aboard Aristides.

Other winners were Billy Walker on Baden-Baden (1877); George Lewis with Fonson (1880); Babe Hurd, Apollo (1882); Isaac Murphy, who scored his three victories aboard Buchanan (1884), Riley (1890), and Kingman (1891); Erskine Henderson on Joe Cotton (1885); Ike Lewis on Montrose (1887); Al Cayton on Azra (1892); James Perkins on Halma (1895); Willie Simms on Ben Brush (1896) and on Plaudit (1898); and Jimmy Winkfield on His Eminence (1901) and on Alan-a-Dale (1902). The last black jockey in the Derby was Jess Conley, who finished third in 1911 on Colston.

Sometimes, a chance meeting provided the subject for a column. In the lobby of New York's Theresa Hotel after the Sugar Ray Robinson–Jimmy McDaniels fight, I bumped into Satchel Paige, and the lanky pitcher wanted to get off his chest some of his feelings about integration of the major leagues.

First, on the matter of how many black players could make it in the big leagues, Satch thought, "None of them as individuals. But we could scrap together about two teams that would do all right as teams."

About the NNL team owners: "All they want to do is sit in their little pond and be the big fish. They don't have sense enough to see they could pool their resources and fight along with you newspaper guys to put two teams in organized baseball and still go on doing their own league business just the same."

Satch was rolling now, heading my way:

And here's something for you. You writer fellows stink. You keep on blowing off about getting us players in the league without thinking about our end of it . . .

You fellows don't understand what we have to go through. You harp on "give them a chance," without thinking how tough it's gonna be for a colored ballplayer to come out of the club house and have all the white guys calling him nigger and black so-and-so.

. . . It'd be more than a man can stand and nobody can play his best ball unless he's in good spirits, and who the hell could be in good spirits under those conditions.

Another thing, you guys cry about fellowship and goodwill. What I want to know is what the hell's gonna happen to goodwill when one of those colored players, goaded out of his senses by repeated insults, takes a bat and busts fellowship in his damned head?"

Our world was on the verge of seeing how it all would play out with the October 23, 1945, signing of Jackie Robinson, then twenty-six and a short-stop with the Kansas City Monarchs, to play in 1946 with the Montreal Royals.

Branch Rickey Sr. had forced down the color barriers for the first time in modern major league baseball history. I say modern because with the Robinson announcement came reminders of Moses Fleetwood Walker, who was a catcher with the Toledo Blue Stockings of the American Association for forty-two games in 1884. His brother, outfielder Welday, was with the same team for five games, but neither of them was back the following year. Also, old-timers recalled George Stover winning thirty-five games for the Newark Giants in 1887 and George Grant playing with the New York Giants during the second decade of the century.

Talking to the *Afro-American* after his selection, Jackie expressed confidence in his ability "to handle any racial situations that may pop up." He said:

> I know that my position was obtained only through the constant pressure of my people and their press. I owe this to the colored people who helped make it possible and I hope I shall always have their goodwill.
>
> I realize the responsibility—not so much to myself as to my people, and I won't let them down. I'll start swinging as soon as I get to bat.

In January 1946, the Dodgers announced that Johnny Wright, a twenty-seven-year-old right-handed pitcher from the Homestead Grays, also had been signed to play with the Montreal Royals.

That year marked the first time I would be in spring training with the various teams in Florida and Arizona. I would continue to focus on the black players' development through the 1956 spring training, including coverage in Mexico, Cuba, and the Dominican Republic.

In addition to the challenge of making the team, Robinson and Wright knew that they would face problems with certain teammates, opposing team players, housing and traveling arrangements, as well as with threats from nonbaseball opponents of mixed teams in the game.

For their first workout, they dressed at a private residence in Sanford, the home of Mrs. David Brock, where they were staying. The Dodgers were based in Daytona.

When Robinson and Wright went to play the Dodgers second stringers in Daytona, they lived with the family of Joe Harris, a local real estate operator.

I learned that when talking to his players on the Thursday before Robinson and Wright arrived, Branch Rickey told them, "It is my sincere hope that the color of these men will not influence your acceptance of them.

"My sole motive in bringing these fellows here was to help the Dodger organization. In signing them I acted on the recommendation of my scouts and not because I sought to appease any pressure groups."

Jackie did not hit lustily in the early games, but I cautioned his fans not to be too concerned, that he would come around. Everywhere Jackie went, black fans were overcrowding the Jim Crow sections set up for them.

After a game in Baltimore, a city consistently unfriendly to the black players, Jackie muffed a play, and I ran an open letter editorial in the *Afro-American* to Royals manager Clay Hopper, a Mississippian who not only did not want Robinson on the team, but questioned whether blacks were human:

> You, like Jackie, are on the spot, if for no other reason than that you come from a section of the country that is generally hostile to Robinson's people.
>
> The *Afro-American* appreciates your position the same as it understands Jackie's . . . Jackie muffed an easy putout at second base in that second game . . . another player would have been bawled out by you immediately the game was over.
>
> If you didn't give him hell, you should have.
>
> Jackie's people don't want him treated any different from the rest.

Different people would remind me of that same-treatment position as time went on. Once before, when I was criticizing the way some black leagues players deported themselves, I had written: "I am reluctant to say that we haven't a single man in the ranks of colored baseball who could step into the major league uniform and deport himself after the fashion of a big leaguer without having at least a season in the minors as do other aspiring players." Larry MacPhail and others would toss around that quote whenever it served their purpose.

At long last, the Royals rolled into Montreal, where Robinson received a thunderous, fence-rattling ovation. It was a day that brought tears from Jackie's eyes. The adulation he received in many places prompted Jackie to pass a message through me to his admirers, explaining why he could not always show how much he appreciated them:

> The manager read a letter to us the other day from President "Shag" Shaugnessy of the International League and it warned players we'll be fined $25 every time we're caught conversing or fraternizing with people in the stands.
>
> Gee whiz! It'd cost me plenty if I talked with my friends as much as I wanted to. I sure hope they understand.

In July 1946, I swung down to Mexico to report on how the black baseball players were making out down there. Scores of these players skipped to Mexico because they were able to make twice as much money as they'd gotten during hard times in the black leagues at home. Those who went included Satchel Paige, John Wilson, Sam Bankhead (Dan's older brother), Jim Crutchfield, and Willie Wells, the Homestead Grays third baseman who stung the ball on line drives that were as hard as any I've seen ever—until this day.

Interested in building up the Mexican Baseball Leagues, President Jorge Pasquel had brazenly raided the U.S. major leagues for a host of their stars, but I quickly discovered that black players had become the backbone of Mexican baseball.

Pasquel owned the Vera Cruz Blues. He also held a controlling interest in the Mexico City Red Devils. Vera Cruz, Pasquel's pet, was stacked with Max Lanier and Lou Klein from the St. Louis Cardinals; Danny Gardella, Ace Adams, and Harry Feldman of the New York Giants; Mickey Owen and Luis Olmo, Brooklyn Dodgers; Chilie Gomez, Philadelphia Phillies; and Bobby Estalella, Philadelphia Athletics. But these major leaguers hadn't helped the Blues to win a single series.

Watching from Vera Cruz, Mexico City, Tampico, and Neuva Laredo, it was obvious why the boss of baseball was so unhappy with the efforts of his major leaguers, some of whom blamed the high altitude for their failure to win as expected. I reported:

And here's the rub, the teams that are heavily loaded with colored players are the clubs that have been the hardest on the Pasquel pets.

Monterey, for instance, which has no white talent at all, has taken five of the six games played with the Blues. The Monties have Ed Stone (Philly Stars), Art Pennington (Chicago American Giants), Claro Danny and Ramon Heredia (N.Y. Cubans), and Johnny Taylor (Pittsburgh Crawfords), and are managed by Lazaro Salazar (N.Y. Cubans).

The Blues had taken only three of ten from Mexico City, the latter playing Ray Dandridge (Newark Eagles), Bill Wright (Baltimore Elites), Carlos Colas (N.Y. Cubans), and Theo Smith (Cleveland Buckeyes).

I suggested, "A glimpse at the situation down here could prove interesting to the American and National League magnates at home."

Because this was an election year in Mexico, I got caught up in an interesting situation. I got into a cab to go to Bill Wright's house. Bill had played in Baltimore with the Elites. We were getting out of the busy section and just passing a park when a huge black automobile pulled alongside and forced my cab to the curb. I had no idea what was happening, but I got a hint of what could happen when I saw a big fellow walking toward us with a shotgun hanging from his right hand.

Not a word had been spoken up to that point, but I didn't need talk to convince me that, for the moment, I was in the wrong place. In no time I was out the other side of the cab and sprinting across the grass toward a batch of trees. As quickly as he had stepped from his car and headed for us, the big fellow had turned and was retracing his steps to the hearse-like phaeton up ahead. At the same time, the cabbie was shouting to me in two languages, apparently thinking I was bent on leaving him holding his meter.

Finally, enticed back to the taxi, I listened as the driver explained that the accosting automobile was loaded with supporters of a political hothead who was in a hot battle for office with another hothead. They were patrolling the streets intent on cooling the heads of the opposition. Since he was something of a neutral, the driver told me, they had no quarrel with him.

"But why you run away?" he demanded. "You no need to be scared, I protect you. See, I keep thees under my seat." With that, he lifted from between his legs a club-like stick. Compared to the gun the other guy had, it resembled the pencil I had in my pocket.

That incident reminded me of another election scenario that involved the longtime president of the Dominican Republic, Rafael Leonidas Trujillo Molina.

Since the Dominicans were so crazy about baseball, Trujillo's challenger set up a baseball team to follow him as he campaigned, figuring he could become popular by trading on the popularity of baseball. Trujillo decided he would get a baseball team, too, so he sent to the United States for some black ballplayers. The first one he thought about was Satchel Paige, because he had heard more about Paige than anyone else. At that time, Satchel was jumping from one team to another; Satchel was one of those ballplayers who played for whichever owner showed him the most money.

These three henchmen of Trujillo's came to extend an invitation to Paige and a couple of other players. Satchel tried to evade Trujillo's men, running from one place to another because he didn't want to go with them. He said he'd had enough of that bad food. He went from Pittsburgh to Chicago and then up to North Dakota. Trujillo's men kept missing Paige for awhile, but they finally caught up to him in Dallas. Satchel told them he didn't care to go down there, but one of Trujillo's guys told him, "Mr. Trujillo would like for you to come. It would not be healthy for you to refuse. So get yourself some company and come down with us."

So Satchel took Sam Bankhead and Roy Matlock and they all went to the Dominican Republic.

Back home in Baltimore, I witnessed an outpouring of epithets and slurs hurled at Jackie Robinson, who, to his credit, still played flawlessly. Later in Louisville, where he faced more abuse and two obvious spiking attempts in the first two games of the Little World Series against the Colonels, Jackie confided to me that the nasty things in Baltimore had hardened him.

He said he'd expected what he received "down South" in Louisville, noting that he even heard some applause mixed in with the boos, "But that Baltimore, holy gee!"

For spring training in 1947, Branch Rickey took the Dodgers and his minor league teams to Cuba in hopes of avoiding some of the housing problems encountered in Florida. The contingent of blacks included Jackie Robinson, Montreal; catcher Roy Campanella and pitcher Don Newcombe of the Nashua, New Hampshire, New England League; and pitcher Roy

Partlow of the Three Rivers (Canada) club. Dan Bankhead would join them in Florida.

Rickey hadn't taken into account that the Nacional Hotel was American-owned. So they barred the black players. We stayed at the Atlantic Hotel, which was a fleabag. Jackie made the Dodgers supply a rental car for us and give us ten dollars a day for subsistence.

There were reports that Rickey had ordered the separation by race. Anyway, some of the Royals were housed at a military academy for sons of wealthy Cubans. Rickey would move on the next year to the Dominican Republic for spring training. We went to the Hotel Jaragua, where everybody stayed together in beautiful surroundings. Every apartment had a patio.

Talk was growing at the training camps in Havana about Jackie moving up to the Dodgers. Robinson alluded to the question in a two-part "as told to Sam Lacy" series. Many players and managers did that kind of article with me. Yankee manager Casey Stengel was the longtime, die-hard exception. For some reason, I guess because the Yankees didn't appreciate my criticisms, we never developed any kind of a relationship.

The *Afro-American* learned that a petition against Robinson's being promoted to the Dodgers was circulating among the players until Rickey got wind of it while they were in Panama. He told them if they expected to remain with the Dodgers, they'd best concentrate on their own efforts and not try to pick the personnel for the team.

Robinson was promoted to the Dodgers April 10, 1947, a day after commissioner Happy Chandler suspended manager Leo Durocher for a year. Jackie played in his first game as a Dodger on April 15 against the Boston Braves in Ebbets Field.

I was one of the passengers in a coupe car that waited twenty minutes after the game for Jackie to get away from about 250 well-wishers who mobbed him outside the gate. We had agreed to keep quiet and let Jackie unwind, knowing he was physically spent. As we drove onto the Brooklyn Bridge ramp on the way to Manhattan, the Dodgers new first baseman broke the silence, saying, "You know, that went along swell. There's nothing wrong with these fellows that I can see."

Jackie was pleased that acting manager Clyde Sukeforth hadn't talked about his promotion at their pregame meeting. He also was pleased about the help he had received from Eddie Stanky, the second baseman. Looking back at the reception Robinson received from his own teammates, I noted Rex Barney, Pee Wee Reese, and Gil Hodges as the Dodgers players who were the most friendly toward Jackie.

I think Robinson's first indication of how bad things could get for him came in Philadelphia where, led by manager Ben Chapman, the Phillies hurled insults one after the other. When I spoke to Chapman about it, he admitted his team had gone after Jackie. He told me, "You writer guys, especially you, keep on crying that you want Jackie treated like every other ballplayer. You say you don't want any 'special case' made of him. Well, the Phillies and Chapman took you at your word."

After Robinson started to get threats against his life, Rickey asked me to see if Jackie would give permission for his mail to be opened. Jackie sent back his approval.

There were denials, but I was in a position to report in a front page story May 6, 1947, that league president Ford Frick and St. Louis Cardinal owner Sam Breadon had put down plans for a strike against Robinson. Reportedly it had been instigated by a small bloc of Cardinals who had envisioned a general walkout.

Frick not only told the players their friends in the press box would not support them, but that any strikers would be suspended, and that one citizen had as much right to play as any other. He summed up by telling the players, "The National League will go down the line with Robinson, whatever the consequences. You will find that if you go through with your intentions that you have been guilty of complete madness."

Frick also admonished Chapman of the Phillies for his part in the scurrilous hammering of Robinson. Chapman later posed for a photograph with Jackie, but neither man indicated there had been a change in their feelings at that time.

While the opponents of baseball integration were still hoping to trip Robinson, the Cleveland Indians bought second baseman Larry Doby from the Newark Eagles. He made his debut July 5, 1947, becoming the first of his race to play for an American League team. The next month, the Dodgers announced the purchase of pitcher Dan Bankhead from the Memphis Red Sox. Doby would recall in later years that when Cleveland manager Lou Boudreau introduced him individually to his new teammates, many of them refused to shake his extended hand. "It was one of the most embarrassing moments in my life," said Doby, when he looked back on his 1947 entry into the majors. In 1998, Doby was employed by major league baseball as a special assistant to American League president Gene Budig.

By 1948 spring training, all the Dodgers players stayed together in a quality hotel in Ciudad Trujillo, Dominican Republic. I remember Dodgers catcher Bruce Edwards going out early one morning to the swimming pool at Hotel Jaragua, jumping in, and hurting his shoulder. That accident enabled Roy Campanella to come up to the Dodgers earlier than he normally would have.

Gil Hodges was brought up to catch with Bobby Bragan as the backup. However, when neither Red Sanders, who was brought in from the St. Louis Cards, nor Chuck Connors, later "the Rifleman" on TV, satisfied the brass, they shifted Gil Hodges to first.

Bobby Bragan and Dixie Walker were two of the most rabid opponents of bringing up Jackie Robinson. Bragan didn't want to play with the team if Jackie would be playing so Mr. Rickey got rid of him, sending him down to Waco, Texas, to manage a farm club. That's when Campanella moved up to take over as catcher. Walker would later deny he opposed Jackie's promotion. Later, Bragan would change his views; he became a good friend of Jackie's widow, Rachel.

When we got back to Florida, Rickey provided integrated quarters for us all at "Dodger Town" in Vero Beach. The way he did that was through Bud Holman, a close friend who was a stockholder in Eastern Airlines as well as in the Dodgers.

There was an old air base at Vero Beach that had been used during World War II. When the war was over, Eastern Airlines had used it as a training facility. Bud Holman made arrangements for the Dodgers to lease that place. Later on, I suppose, the Dodgers bought it.

It was a great facility for training. The Dodgers were able to have their own policing. Even though they were in Florida, the city police couldn't come up into Dodger Town to enforce segregation. That's the reason I say Rickey was a smart cookie.

There were separate barracks for the press, but I was in them only one-fourth of the time. I preferred to stay with the colored players so that I could get inside stories.

When the Dodgers made the trek up through San Antonio, Houston, and Beaumont, we stayed in the Pullman coaches overnight. We would go to bed, for example, in Houston, and wake up the next morning in San Antonio. That's the way we avoided the housing problem there. As we traveled north, we had to stay in separate quarters in Richmond, Danville, Washington, and Baltimore.

I got a special thrill out of the playing of the "Star-Spangled Banner" at the Polo Grounds for the National League opener in 1948. I was there to look at the Americanization of the so-called great American game—and there it lay before me. The all-colored Fifteenth Regiment band rendered the music as Old Glory was raised in center field.

Lined up on either side were the two opposing teams, the Brooklyn Dodgers and the New York Giants. In the group, at long last, were black men who had been selected on their merits as ballplayers. In the stands, as always has been the case there, persons of all races sat together. In the field boxes, Mrs. Rachel Robinson and Mrs. Ruthe Campanella occupied seats with other players' wives, near Mrs. Laraine Day and Mrs. Branch Rickey.

Yes, it was different. I can't recall ever having felt quite the same about the playing of the national anthem.

For me, there were many other heartwarming aspects to covering the major leagues in the early years. One that I considered interesting enough to write about involved a group of student fans of Jackie Robinson. They were fourteen white seniors from the Lynn Grove High School in Murray, Kentucky. They had come to St. Louis, riding a bus for nine hours, and when I saw them, all were wearing Jackie buttons except for one girl; the vendor had sold out before she could get one. Principal Burton Jeffrey and his wife had escorted the youngsters.

The big crowds coming to see the black players helped to change things. At the same time KKK Grand Dragon Samuel Green was threatening to halt three exhibition games scheduled for Atlanta in April 1949, a number of southern cities wanted to make certain the black players in the Dodgers lineup came with the team for exhibition games.

For example, in January 1950, Branch Rickey confided: "When our club first signed a colored player, there was no town in the South that would accept us for exhibition games. Now we're swamped with requests for spring showings and in every case, they make it clear that we're not wanted unless we have our colored players."

As integration moved along regarding the hiring of black baseball players, I was stepping up my part of the campaign to get all the teams to find a way to house their players together.

The Cleveland Indians brought five black players to Tucson for the 1949 spring training: Larry Doby, Satchel Paige, Orestes Minoso, Artie Wilson, and Jose Santiago. When I talked to Indians president Bill Veeck about the refusal of the Santa Rita Hotel to accept his black players, Veeck told me:

> They won't accept our colored players. I don't want to wrestle with 'em about it. I feel I shouldn't throw a wrench into the training plans of 45 of my players on account of one, two, three or four other fellows. I believe that in tackling this thing, it shouldn't be done belligerently. Last year when we went to California, the Hotel Biltmore wouldn't take certain of our players. This year we're going there and they say they'll take everybody . . . In due time the thing will work itself out."

Those segregated living quarters were extremely distasteful to me, but the situation did provide me greater access to the black players because I lived where they did.

In addition to interviews, I could get to know the players better. Out in Arizona with the Indians, Monte Irvin kept me awake until three in the morning talking baseball and the prospects of various black players. Irvin predicted that in two years, Larry Doby would be one of the game's top hitters. He also told me he was glad he ended up with the Giants instead of the Dodgers because the Dodgers had so many black players they didn't know what to do with them.

Every player was different. Larry Doby and I were reasonably friendly, but Doby was quite moody. In Tucson, Doby and I would occupy beds in the same room. We would go to bed at night talking about baseball, having a general conversation. He would wake up the next morning and wouldn't speak. It wasn't a case of him being disrespectful or anything, he just had those moods. That's the reason I said that Doby would never have made a good manager, because of the various moods. Doby did manage the

Chicago White Sox for the last eighty-seven games of the 1978 season, posting a 37-50 record.

My son Tim traveled to training camps with me when school permitted, and he made a lot of friends among the players. While in Florida, Tim and Dan Bankhead became close. Sometimes, I would go to Florida alone. By staying in St. Petersburg, where the Yankees and Cardinals were based at the time, I would get to see all the teams that came in to play against them. Then I would leave there, and Tim would join me out in Tucson where I would cover the Indians (Tucson) and the Giants (Phoenix).

Out in Tucson, Tim and Minoso were just like that. If I was looking for Tim, all I had to do was find Minoso. He sort of adopted us as family. Once when we were leaving Arizona at 2 A.M., he got up and came to the airport to see us off.

I always believed that Minoso, a colorful, outgoing person, probably admired Jackie Robinson more than any other of the black players who entered the majors early. Some of them used to refer to Jackie as "the black prince."

On one of our trips out of Chicago heading for Arizona, I couldn't locate Tim on the train. Mickey Vernon was with the Indians at the time, and he and Mickey got all hooked in together. He had no business up in the bar car with Mickey Vernon. I was looking for him back in the Pullman car.

More than a decade after the first interview with Clark Griffith about integrating the major leagues, I talked to him again in March 1949 and reported that "he finally has seen the light."

We would talk on the subject again in the future, but I did see a degree of change in that now Griffith was saying the Senators may have overlooked opportunities to strengthen the team "and you can say I'm definitely interested in signing a good young colored player."

The reason why I and others had to devote so much time to racial matters in baseball (in the face of progress in certain other areas) could be explained by this excerpt from an April 19 newspaper story that year out of Texarkana, Texas:

Anyway, last week when the Cleveland Indians were in town with their three colored stars, Larry Doby, Satchel Paige and Orestes Minoso, the taxi cabs refused to haul them to the ball park. Since there were no colored cabs available, and since the Indians were expecting them to play in the game against the New York Giants that afternoon, the three players set out to walk.

It was a distance of a mile and a half from the hotel in which they stayed to the ball park and Doby, Paige and Minoso walked it. Also, since they were advised that they would not be able to use the clubhouse at the park, the trio walked it in their uniforms . . .

As the 1949 season waned, I did a piece from Cincinnati calling it "truly an antisocial town." I didn't stop at blaming just the fans:

At least one sportswriter here, Tom Swope, veteran *Cincinnati Post* baseball man, is still a long way from the acquiescent stage. He makes no secret of his reactionary attitude. Swope's antiracial feeling is so well known among his fellow writers that they frequently play jokes on him. The other day, for instance, he was the recipient of an autographed postcard bearing the pictures of Jackie Robinson, Roy Campanella and Don Newcombe. It bore a New York postmark and a fuming Swope challenged each of the Brooklyn baseball writers as he entered the press box at Crosley Field. All pleaded innocent. Later, out of Swope's hearing, they agreed on a leading Philadelphia scribe as the one who mailed the card.

From time to time, I would remind my readers not to let reports of progress blind them to the fact that the South was still the South.

In March 1950, I headlined a story, "Integration in Dixie Halts When Players Leave Field." I cited a few examples. A rental car picked up by Dodgers traveling secretary Harold Parrott was ordered returned immediately when it was learned that Robinson, Campanella, Newcombe, and I had been using it. Campy had gone with a squad of players to West Palm Beach; en route back to Vero Beach, while the others had dinner at a roadside inn, Campy sat alone on the bus, eating from a tray that had been brought out to him. A few days later, to avoid the same thing after a game in West Palm Beach, Campy ate there and took a train back to Vero Beach. Unfortunately, there was a slipup in instructions at the base. No one met Campy, and white cabs wouldn't accept him, so he walked the two and a half miles.

Near the bottom of my "From A to Z" column on March 21, 1950, I slipped in this line: "Breach is widening between Jackie Robinson and Roy Campanella."

By April 11, the story had landed on the front page of the *Afro-American* under my byline. It developed that the rift grew out of a 1949 barnstorming tour arranged by Ted Warner of New York, which Jackie helped to plan. Jackie negotiated a deal for himself calling for a guarantee plus a percentage of the gate. Campy's deal was for a guarantee only.

The tour was hugely successful, reportedly netting $92,000. Because he had a percentage deal, Jackie reaped considerably more than did Campy, and the catcher felt Jackie did nothing to protect him and the other players. Jackie took the position they all negotiated their own deals.

Newcombe was also on the tour; he and I tried several times to bring the two players to accord, but without success. As the opening of the season loomed, I reported, "Robinson has begun to show signs of being receptive but Campanella continues in his extreme coolness."

Looking back at that situation years later, I realized some of the problem was that Campanella resented Jackie's popularity. Their families lived near one another before Jackie moved up to Stamford, and their wives, Rachel and Ruthe, used to ride to ball games together. When I wrote the story, Campy stopped it.

Campy had a little trouble getting over the fact that I was the one who reported he was jealous of Jackie. The main reason was because people used to run past Campy to go to Jackie for his autograph. Campy always resented that. He didn't seem to realize that Jackie was a symbol.

Campy got angry with me when I said there was this estrangement between these two guys who had been pioneers. Even when we discussed it and Campy relented, he still said I didn't have to write it that way.

Jackie took it, just as he did when I criticized him in 1948 for coming to camp overweight. He came to camp bloated from the banquet circuit after the 1947 season. He had been making all those dinner testimonials and whatnot and he came in looking about fifteen to twenty pounds overweight. I wrote a story saying that.

Durocher liked the idea. He said, "You are telling it like it is and I think Jackie will listen to you." Jackie got a little ticked about it, but it did not last long. That's one of the reasons I say Jackie was a real classy guy.

I closed out the account of that Robinson/Campanella feud in July of 1950, with an update saying, "Reliable sources tell me the relationship between Jackie Robinson and Roy Campanella is greatly improved."

Jackie was fortunate to have a wife like Rachel—she never criticized. She was the person who kept Jackie in tow and kept him on an even keel. She filled the role beautifully, helping him control the emotions he would bring home from a stressful situation.

I would fall back on some of her words to her husband when he would feel down and express his frustrations to me. From time to time, we'd be having breakfast or something together, and Jackie would be in a somber mood. He'd say something like, "Sam, sometimes I get to thinking about all the things going on with me, and around me, and I wonder if it's worth all the punishment and sacrifice."

I would remind him that "Rachel told you when you got into it, even before you went to see Rickey, what you were getting into and not to start if you didn't intend to go through with it. If you give it up you're going to have to answer to her and to yourself."

We would talk about what the success of his breakthrough would mean to other players and to progress in the country. It was a tough road he had to walk, out there by himself often among hostile fans and opposing players. But he always came through like a champ. You had to admire his guts.

Through the years, Jackie maintained a close relationship with me and when his book, *I Never Had It Made,* was published, he included this note to me: "To Sam with thanks and appreciation for helping make our career possible. I'll always be appreciative. Jackie Robinson."

Years later, when Rachel Robinson was in Baltimore to receive an award made posthumously to Jackie, I closed a column on the event this way:

Looking at her sitting next to me on the dais Saturday night, I recalled with a glow a remark she once made to me when I was writing a series on the wives of top black athletes: "Whatever happens to us, I shall always cherish the memory of our days together. Jackie Robinson is the kind of man who will never need cheering crowds and headlines and newsreel cameras to make him a hero to his wife."

I was touched in 1997 when we participated in the opening of a new wing on the role of African-Americans in the sport at the Baseball Hall of Fame and Museum in Cooperstown. Rachel, who was the keynote speaker, referred to me as a counselor to Jackie when he was going through rough times while traveling on the road with his team.

Robinson died in 1972, and in 1973, Rachel Robinson started the Jackie Robinson Foundation to provide scholarships for deserving minority students. In 1997, when acting commissioner Bud Selig formally announced a season-long baseball tribute to Jackie Robinson to honor the fiftieth anniversary of his breaking the color barrier in major league baseball, he also announced a million dollar donation to the foundation. The celebration was kicked off at the April 15 game between the Los Angeles Dodgers and New York Mets in Shea Stadium, during which Selig also announced the retirement in perpetuity of Robinson's old number 42 by all thirty National and American League teams. Players wearing number 42 at the time could keep the number until they left the game. After the April 15 game, a number of teams contributed to the foundation.

Participating in the "Jackie Robinson Night" celebration in New York, President Clinton praised Robinson both for his role in breaking the baseball color line and for his efforts in opening other doors for African-Americans after he retired from the game. Standing alongside the president, Rachel Robinson said the finest tribute Americans could pay Jackie Robinson would be to give new support for a more equitable society. Jesse Simms, Jackie's grandson, threw out the ceremonial ball for the game.

Back in the spring of 1950, when I had talked to Connie Mack, owner of the Philadelphia American League team, Mack said he would take a black player "if we can find one like Doby for instance, who can hit the ball out of the park."

Prodded as to whether he might be interested in a good player who will hit fairly well and field satisfactorily, or perhaps a good pitcher, Connie Mack answered, "I'm thoroughly satisfied with my defense. I wouldn't be interested, I'm afraid, in anyone who can't help me with the long ball." I didn't expect to see the team add a black player in the near future.

When Clark Griffith graciously greeted me for another interview in April 1951, he had something to add to his insistence that his team was interested in "any player who will help the team, color notwithstanding." This time he added: "The colored people shouldn't try to press this thing. They should be patient, let it take the natural course . . ."

Hank Greenberg, general manager of the Cleveland Indians, was steaming over a story I did about living conditions and segregation at the Indians Daytona Beach base. He termed the story untrue. Still, Greenberg conceded his black players "live in separate barracks but Lacy seemed to think we had these boys in quarters that are unsanitary on account of the toilets near their rooms."

My comeback was that I never called the quarters unsanitary but factually reported that the players' beds were directly opposite open toilets, and that they could lie in their bunks and look into open commodes not fifteen feet away.

Greenberg's response was that the players "can't see the toilets if they close the doors." Greenberg said he felt everyone should go along with separate quarters in Tucson because the only hotel in the city that would take ballplayers refused to accept the black players.

Meanwhile, during a couple of games, Jackie had some run-ins with Giants manager Leo Durocher and the team's pitcher, Sal "the Barber" Maglie. Jackie told me he was ready to call off the feud "but I'm not going to be a sitting duck." The upcoming Maglie incident was one that shook me up. The Dodgers were playing the Giants on Labor Day in the Polo Grounds. Maglie brushed Jackie back. You know, Sal was one of those who could throw the ball and cut your whiskers off. They called him "Sal the Barber" because he believed in shaving you.

On the next pitch, Jackie laid down a bunt on the first base line, making Maglie field it. I hoped I was wrong, but I could see what was coming and I didn't know how the crowd would react to it. Jackie ran right up Maglie's back. That's when I got scared. I got on him after that. I said, "Man don't ever do something like that again."

He said, "Sam, I had to do it. I'm sorry, but I had to do it. It's just in my blood to get some revenge when they do that to me."

Durocher (then the Giants manager) called Jackie's action a bush-league trick. "Then you're a bush-league manager, because you taught me to do things like that," Robinson yelled back at Durocher.

Situations that could get out of hand might crop up without warning. There was the time, probably Don Newcombe's first spring in Vero Beach with the Dodgers, that I had to grab him and get him away from a white Cuban when they were having a heated argument. The situation was that white onlookers were mumbling and taking sides—not Newcombe's. This was serious enough for a predawn meeting with Branch Rickey and others about whether it would be necessary to slip Big Don out of town for a while.

I wasn't in Havana the previous fall when trouble first brewed between Newcombe and the Cuban, a catcher named Fermin Guerra. Anyway, when Guerra came in with the Philadelphia Athletics, Newcombe, apparently forgetting he was in the Deep South, seemed to want a piece of Guerra. I had to step in and lead him away.

Although not too much was made of it in the media, I do know that friction existed between some Latinos and American players—black and white—during the 1930s, 1940s, and 1950s.

When fellows like Newk, Roy Campanella, Satchel Paige, the Bankhead brothers (Sam and Dan), Henry Thompson, Josh Gibson, and others would go down to Cuba, Mexico, Puerto Rico, or the Dominican Republic, pockets of friction festered.

Many of the local Latin American players regarded the Americans as intruders who were taking jobs the natives had held for decades. This involved white players as well as blacks, although there were fewer of the former on the scene. That subsurface animosity seemed to continue on several occasions when paths crossed in the majors.

Frank Robinson experienced a taste of this attitude when he was manager in Cleveland in 1975, and Cuban Rico Carty was one of his openly rebellious players.

In the case of Newcombe, I witnessed another verbal confrontation involving him as late as 1957—another round of the age-old battle between pitchers and umpires, the latter seeing a ball when a pitcher is thinking strike.

In a spring exhibition game in Washington, Newk became irate over the ball-strike calls of umpire Joe Paparella, but the ump displayed open disdain toward the pitcher's complaints. As Newcombe was heading toward the Dodgers dugout at the end of an inning, he threw a scornful look at the umpire. Paparella immediately took the bait, demanding that Newk should shut up. "You're lucky to be here," he barked.

Seated above the (then) Brooklyn dugout, I heard the remark and immediately questioned it in my mind. I wondered how it could be that a man could be described as "lucky to be here" in the spring of 1957, following a season in which he had won twenty-seven games and had taken the Cy Young and National League most valuable player (MVP) awards. Unless there was another reason Paparella felt Newcombe didn't belong.

I spoke to Jock Conlon, an ump with whom I had excellent rapport, to get his opinion of the comment. Jocko said he was not present, had not heard the exchange, and preferred not to try an explanation. Not to be considered a nitpicker, I dropped the matter at that point, but it wasn't something to forget quickly.

Away from baseball, I spotlighted the National Celebrities golf tournament in Washington after a columnist friend at the *Washington Post* did a piece on how easy it was for celebrities to become invitees. It was the fifth year of sponsorship of the charity event for the *Post*.

There was some question about who was responsible for the easy selections—Bus Ham, *Post* sports editor and tourney director, or the Army-Navy Country Club where the celebrities played. I called some celebrities worthy of invitations to ask if they'd ever been invited. I called Nobel Peace Prize winner Dr. Ralph Bunche, federal judge Bill Hastie, entertainer Cab Calloway, singer Lena Horne, Olympic gold medalist Alice Coachman, Congressman Adam Clayton Powell, Congressman William Dawson, football star Marion Motley, and boxer Joe Louis. Not one of them had ever been invited. That confirmed what I knew about which "celebrities" got invitations, so I wrote:

> No matter who is at fault, there's one thing quite obvious. My friend, the columnist, made an excellent point in his yarn when he wrote that to get into the Celebrities, "You don't even have to be an American." . . . To all his points, he should have added—you just have to be white.

During a single car ride with ballplayers, I could find something to be happy about, and something to be unhappy about. In 1951, when Roy Campanella won the MVP award in the National League, my "A to Z" column on November 6 would point back to a July 27 car ride. I was up front, squeezed between the taxi driver and Campanella, who'd just had a big game against the St. Louis Cardinals. Jackie Robinson and Don Newcombe were in the back. After I suggested Campy had a good chance to be the MVP if he continued having the kind of year he had been enjoying, Campy scoffed at the idea, but both Jackie and Newcombe agreed. That was the happy part.

The column said:

> But there also was an unpleasantness about what I was witnessing. For there on July 27, 1951, were three of the world's finest ballplayers, riding a Jim Crow taxicab to a colored hotel, far removed from the plush quarters of the Chase, where the rest of their Brooklyn teammates were lodged . . .
>
> In Dixie-bound St. Louis, it matters little that men like these, approximating a half million dollars in market value, are human beings and American citizens . . . Because their skin is of a darker hue, they must take themselves off into the racial hinterlands while a dozen or more $5,000-a-year ballplayers are extended a welcome hand by the ultra-exclusive uptown hostelry.

En route to Arizona in February 1952, I swung by Nashville to cover the first black national collegiate basketball tournament, held at Fisk University. I had the pleasure of presenting the *Afro-American* trophy for first place winner to Tennessee State. The *Courier, Defender,* and *Atlanta Daily World* also presented awards.

I regularly mentioned the baseball players' wives in my columns. In March, talking to Hank Thompson's wife, Maria, and Monte Irvin's wife, Win, I learned why their favorite cinema was a drive-in theater between Phoenix and Flagstaff:

"The city theaters are hard to figure. One will admit you, another will put you in the gallery and still another will refuse to sell you a ticket. Rather than play a guessing game with them, we go where we are made to feel we are welcome."

Remembering previous discussions with the Indians Hank Greenberg about housing his players, I credited him for insisting on housing everyone at Hotel Santa Rita in Tucson. Also, in Chicago, the Indians would switch from the Del Prado to the Sherry, which accepted all the players.

In nineteen spring exhibition games in the 1952 spring season, I had not heard the "Star-Spangled Banner" played until the Dodgers hit Mobile,

Alabama. Ironically, it also was the first town where antiracial remarks were made. The music had barely died out when boos were aimed at Sam Jethroe, and cries of "hit him in the head" were directed at Jackie Robinson. Both in Mobile and Montgomery, at the first appearances by the Dodgers in those cities, the Jim Crow colored bleachers and the white grandstands vied in extending greetings to the black players.

In March 1953 in San Francisco, I didn't understand why Cleveland, whose officials I'd confronted on the housing issue previously, could house all its players together at the St. Francis Hotel, but the Giants selected the swank Palace for its white players and the Olympic for the black players.

I spoke to Eddie Brannick, the Giants traveling secretary, about the situation. Not satisfied that change was in the making, I decided to take the issue up with Charles S. "Chub" Feeney, vice president of the club and nephew of Horace Stoneham, president and owner of the Giants. We had a good relationship, so when he came out to the park I said to him, "Chub, do you realize that up here in this Olympic Hotel you have Monte Irvin, Hank Thompson, Ray Noble, Reuben Gomez, and Bill White?

"Now you've got over $2 million worth of talent up here and you don't know what they're doing. They're up here isolated. You have no way of controlling what they're doing.

"Yet you have downtown at the Palace a lot of white ballplayers who won't even make Class B, but you've got them staying down there simply because they're white and you got us staying here because we're colored."

He said, "You know, I never thought about that." I think what happened was he realized that these guys were up there having fun. So he said, "Let me get back to you. Let me talk to Horace tonight." He called Horace Stoneham that night, presumably, and the next day everybody moved down to the Palace. (However, the next spring in Florida, nothing had changed; the Giants black players, with me along, stayed at the home of a shoemaker named Alex Williams in St. Petersburg.)

Before heading east from Phoenix, one of those outrageous Satchel Paige stories came my way courtesy of Ray Watts, then a Giants catcher and witness to an exchange between Paige, a relief hurler for the St. Louis Browns, and National League umpire Lon Warneke, a former pitcher.

When Paige came to bat in the top of the ninth inning, he was still seething over Warneke's 3-2 call in the eighth that gave Monte Irvin a walk.

He glared at Warneke, and then came this incredible umpire-player exchange.

Lon: "What's the matter little man, you trying to steal the show as usual?"

Satch: "No sonny boy. I was just thinking and wondering how a guy, who once was a pitcher, could turn into such a pancake as an umpire. Why you're even blinder than they say you are in the other league."

Lon: "All right, you've showed your rump now, come on, get up at the bat. I don't care anything about 'the great Paige.' One more word and I'll throw you outta the game."

Satch: "Now don't talk like a fool, sonny boy. You know you ain't gonna put me outta no game. Those people up there (in the stands) would tear you apart, rump to elbows, for throwing Satch out of an exhibition game. So pipe down and try being good, which you can't, in no way, shape or fashion."

Probably more than any other of the guilty clubs, the New York Yankees didn't appreciate criticism of their failure to employ black players. In some circles, it was said that the successful Yanks seemed to get special treatment from some of the media. I alluded to that in a story in April 1952 after no pictures were published of American Labor Party pickets at Yankee Stadium protesting the Yankees being the only New York team with no black players.

I reported that photographers from the major services showed up but took no pictures. A Harlem photographer snapped several and a representative of the news picture service bought the negatives. The service told me the quality of the prints they'd been able to obtain was too poor for handling.

My story said, "The powerful influence of the Yankees could be behind the picture-grabbing stunt . . ."

Still, when Roy Campanella and other Dodgers players insisted that manager Casey Stengel had called for Campy to be beaned in a World Series game, I found it difficult to believe such a serious charge. But I did note that, "In seven years on the major league beat, in which this reporter has enjoyed intimate contact and amicable relations with every manager in both loops, he has yet to obtain a civil answer to any question from the New York pilot."

I expressed doubts that Vic Power and Elston Howard would remain with the world champion Yankees when it was first revealed that they had been added to the roster. Power was soon traded to the Philadelphia Phillies.

In March 1954, a column about the Yankees started on the front page under a banner headline. The piece said Elston Howard was "perhaps the most unfortunate young man in all of sportsdom." The Yankees were trying to turn the twenty-four-year-old outfielder into a catcher. Plus, another newspaper had quoted Howard as having said uncomplimentary things about Vic Power. My column termed Howard "a very unhappy boy." I said he had written a letter to Power, denying the remarks attributed to him. Also cited were names of reporters I suggested were pro-Yankee writers helping the team with its "knock-em-down" campaign against Howard.

The following week, Elston Howard, discussing my article in front of Yogi Berra, Yankee catcher, observed, "You sure had all the facts in there." Jackie Robinson had talked to a number of reporters, agreeing with the piece. Other reporters asked for copies.

A March 30 "A to Z" said the Yankee brass—general manager George Weiss, manager Casey Stengel, and coach Bill Dickey—called Howard in and demanded to know if he was guilty of telling the *Afro-American* he was unhappy and dissatisfied or if he thought he was being given the runaround by the switch from the outfield to the catching position. Howard told them he didn't say those things.

"For the Yankees to take a story which in no single instance purported to quote Howard and convey to him the impression that this was what would kill his chances, is typical of their petty, narrow-minded behavior," I wrote.

By this time, Stengel was telling Howard he would get tryouts at catching and also at first base, both with several good players ahead of him, as well as outfield, the position Stengel had said he didn't think Howard could handle in the majors.

Reacting to a report that Casey Stengel has "loosed another blast against this corner, branding 'A to Z' as the agent who broke the spirit of Elston Howard . . . and thus reduced his chances of making good," I noted that "Stengel and Co. within the past year have engaged in wordy combat with Bill Veeck, Frank Lane, Chicago White Sox general manager, and Jackie Robinson. I'm at least moving around in Cadillac company."

Although Elston Howard did not stick with the Yankees in 1954, as I had predicted, he was brought up for the 1955 season with Stengel calling him "my three-way man."

Some sports announcements of interest in my home area took place in 1954: The Washington Senators announced that two Cubans, outfielder Angel Scull and Carlos Paula, would be with the team when the season opened; the University of Maryland announced it would welcome colored football players; and the Navy said it would ignore "for use of Caucasians only" ticket restrictions in disposing of its thirteen thousand tickets to the Sugar Bowl in New Orleans.

From my home base in Baltimore, I had to report that in May of 1955, Baltimore was the only American League city that offered no hotel option to visiting teams for housing all their players together. My report May 17 on visits by the White Sox and Cleveland Indians showed the main body of the Sox went to the Emerson while Minnie Minoso went alone to the black-owned York Hotel. White players for the Indians stopped at the Lord Baltimore while Larry Doby, Al Smith, and Dave Pope went to the York.

What was happening with the Yankees continued to get attention in "A to Z." One off-the-mark position I took was that as long as Casey Stengel was manager, the Yanks would never have a black player.

Before the end of the season in 1954, I asked the managers of all sixteen teams and their senior assistants to pick the top three black players for me. The Yankees Casey Stengel and Frank Crosetti did not respond. Incidentally, the top winners were Willie Mays, Jackie Robinson, Minnie Minoso, Larry Doby, Ernie Banks, and Roy Campanella.

Late January the next year, "A to Z" disclosed that Zip Brooks, popular athletic trainer, had joined the ranks of folks who harbored a peeve against the New York Yankees. As head trainer of the Richmond Virginians of the International League, Zip was the only black person employed at the Triple A or major league baseball level—until the Yankees took control of the Virginians and dropped him. Brooks didn't like being lost in the shuffle, but his main beef was that he hadn't caught on with another team because the Yankees had "assured" him he had no reason to seek employment elsewhere.

Brooks told "A to Z":

What I dislike most of all is the way they (the Yankees) tried to cheapen me. After acting as they did, they attempted to keep down public resentment and square things in the eyes of everybody by offering me the same money I got in Richmond to go to Binghamton (Class A). This they probably felt would keep me quiet.

I immediately declined, pointing out that I was the only colored head trainer in the upper circles of baseball last year, and that I had no intention of becoming the first Triple A trainer to be demoted to Class A baseball, simply because of my complexion.

For several weeks, word reaching me in St. Petersburg was that Stengel was admitting that Elston Howard likely would make the team as an out-fielder, not as a catcher, as long as Yogi Berra was around. I observed that I'd "almost got run out of Florida" the year before for saying that Howard couldn't make the team as a catcher, would have to make it as an outfielder, and for adding that Stengel was giving the Yankees best colored prospect the proverbial runaround by switching him to a position he had hardly any experience playing.

When the Yankees general manager complained about criticism concerning the team's housing Elston Howard separate from the other players, he said, "I do feel it is unfair to single out the Yankees in this situation since the Yankees do just what all the others do in baseball."

I talked to high officials of other teams who agreed that George Weiss "may not be fully aware of the fact that the Yankees actually are not doing what 'all the others' are doing." It was pointed out that for American League teams, only in Baltimore was it necessary to accept separate housing.

Two weeks later, regarding the housing of Yankee players, I wrote, "This writer, Weiss intimated, again was trying to stir up trouble." Nonetheless, I was able to kick off that column by reporting, "Whether or not it was coincidence is up to you to decide, but the fact remains that the New York Yankees are now lodging Elston Howard right along with the rest of the team in all cities except Baltimore."

Because I spared no one in challenging views and actions, my critics could always get a shot at me. J. Wilkins of Baltimore took a hard swipe in a column leadoff piece:

Dear Sir: I'm writing you just one more time to see if I can get you to give up on trying to be a sports editor. I can't see why the AFRO keeps letting you [embarrass] the paper year after year.

If you had the least idea what the baseball fans think of your coverage and predictions, I believe you would call it quits. If not, you're dumber than I think. After the boner you pulled predicting the last World Series, you should never open your big mouth again.

But to the contrary, you've got the nerve to come right back and try to run the Giants' and Willie Mays's business. You say you can't begin to figure why owner Horace Stoneham and Leo Durocher consented to let Mays play winter ball. Well, listen stupid, no one expects you to figure that out because if anyone looks at your figures for the World Series ALL the Giants need to play winter ball.

Don't you ever sit down sometime and look over your old records and see just how wrong you have been all the time? If you insist in trying to predict baseball, let me give you a good tip for next year: It will be the Giants and the mighty Yankees and I don't follow "no" team to spring camp.

Before that blasting, I took on "some unthinking colleagues" for recommending that "colored fans vote under the influence of race" in making their All-Star game picks:

"A to Z" implores its readers not to vote in this manner. It urges you, as it has in years passed, to cast your ballots for the men you honestly believe to be the best at their respective positions . . .

Suppose all the fans who vote made a point of adhering to racial lines in their selections, wouldn't it be a long time before we'd again have a colored face in the midsummer classic?

"A to Z" got caught flat-footed in one of its chidings of a friendly colleague early in 1955, resulting in the following column notice:

Postcard from AP's Joe Reichler: Dear Sam . . . Same day I read your column saying how anxious you were to see me to give me 'out' about not knowing the Chicago White Sox had disposed of Connie Johnson to the Orioles, I also read Frank Lane's announcement that the Sox had signed Connie for 1955. Still anxious to see me Sammy? . . . Two word reply: N-O."

Months later though, Connie Johnson was in Baltimore.

It may have seemed so to many, but "A to Z" was not always being critical. Here was one of the many positive assessments the column made of sports figures, this one of Monte Irvin:

> Monte is the quietly efficient type . . . not easily rattled and unusually philosophical . . . he is one of the real gentlemen of the sports world . . . never speaks disparagingly of an opponent and defends wrongdoers with the casual observation, "We all make mistakes."

In July of 1955, I commented on Irvin's fate in being shunted off to the minors by the Giants after having played so brilliantly only a few short years before. It was an effort to answer some of the questions of fans who were wondering what had brought about the decline.

> Actually, it was nothing really unusual about Monte's case . . . surprising and a little disappointing perhaps, but not unusual.
>
> His was the tragedy that is shared by a great majority of the colored players in professional baseball today. He, like a number of others around him, was denied the chance to play by a stupid prejudice that persisted through the first 167 years of the organized game.
>
> Monte, as were many of his counterparts, was bypassed by big league teams until he was well past his prime. Have any one of you readers ever taken into consideration the fact that, of the 31 colored players in the major leagues, 10 are over 30 years of age? . . . that six others have passed their 29th birthday? . . . that only seven of the 31 are under 25?
>
> For reasons that are all too apparent, the colored players who finally have made the grade were not considered until they had matured far beyond the age of the white recruit.

A bit over a year later I could update the record thusly:

> The fact that the future of the colored player (by then a total of 38) in baseball is so very bright is because 12 of the leading tan performers of today have youth on their side. Elston Howard, believe it not, is the "old man" of the lot and the New York Yankee entry is just 26.

Here's the way they line up: Frank Robinson of Cincinnati is 20; Roberto Clemente of Pittsburgh is 21; Sandy Amoros of Brooklyn, Henry Aaron and Wes Covington of Milwaukee, and Vic Power and Hector Lopez of Kansas City are all 24; and Willie Mays of the Giants, Ernie Banks and Solly Drake of the Cubs, and Charley Neal of the Dodgers are all 25.

The Washington Senators got around to adding black players in 1954. Manager Bucky Harris announced in March that he planned to keep Angel Scull, an outfielder from Cuba, and Carlos Paula, also Cuban.

Years later in 1978, when Calvin Griffith was running the team in Minnesota after the death of Clark Griffith, he denied in an interview with me that he had intended any racial connotation when he told a Minneapolis audience he'd moved the team there when he discovered the city "had only 15,000 blacks."

Calvin Griffith told me he was only trying to be funny and what he said may have been misconstrued after *Minneapolis Tribune* reporter Nick Coleman quoted him saying: "Black people don't go to ball games, but they'll fill up a rassling ring and put up such a chant it'll scare you to death. We came here because you've got good, hard-working white people here."

Some of Griffith's black players let it be known they didn't consider the statements funny, including Dan Ford, who said, "If he said them, I'm pretty sure he meant them."

Shortly thereafter, first baseman Rod Carew, having just won his seventh American League batting crown, announced, "I will not ever sign another contract with this organization."

The Boston Red Sox, the last major league team to add black players, did it in the summer of 1959, first promoting infielder Elijah (Pumpsie) Green, after having kept him in the minors for six years, then bringing up pitcher Earl Wilson, having kept him in the minors for seven years.

I recalled in the column what Branch Rickey had said in 1947 when Jackie Robinson was signed by the Dodgers—that in ten years, he expected every team in the majors to have at least one colored player.

"The Mahatma was wrong. It took over 12 years for the Boston Red Sox to see the light."

CHAPTER 6

SEPARATE HOUSING, OTHER ISSUES

I realized early on that for many and often rather different reasons, there was not total agreement among black baseball players on the matter of pressing the issue of integrated housing.

We were at breakfast one morning in the spring of 1957, and I said to Elston Howard that I would like to talk to Jerry Coleman and would like Elston to be there too (Coleman was second baseman and player representative for the Yankees at the time). He said, "Okay."

So when we went out to the ballpark, the players were warming up on the sideline. I asked Jerry if he had a few minutes he could give me. He said, "Sure, Sam."

I called Elston over. I said, "Jerry, you are the player representative of all the ballplayers not just the white players, but the colored as well. Would you have any objections to presenting at the next major leagues meeting the idea that all players should live together? That we should get rid of this separate living?" Elston turned and walked away.

Jerry said, "You see what colored ballplayers think of your idea?"

As I continued my pitch, Coleman and I went through this exchange:

Coleman: "We can't become involved in politics."

Lacy: "But it has nothing to do with politics; there are no ordinances or statutes of any sort requiring hotel segregation in Baltimore."

Coleman: "We can't dictate to the owners what they must do."

Lacy: "The proposal is not meant to pressure the owners, only to let them know your organization is interested in solving the problem."

Coleman: "Well, what about the other cities, Kansas City and St. Louis?"

Lacy: "Howard stays with the club in Kansas City and the National League (Dodgers and Giants) broke down the bars in St. Louis. The National League Clubs are not affected by the Baltimore situation. But it is surprising to learn that you didn't know Howard lives with you in the hotel in Kansas City—everywhere in fact but in Baltimore."

Coleman: "Elston's a good guy, we all like him. But I have no right to crusade for him."

Lacy: "Neither Howard nor anyone else expects or wants you to crusade for him or any other player. He is a Yankee and he has a grievance. Inasmuch as you are the Yankee representative on the committee, it was assumed you'd be willing to air his problem at one of your meetings."

Coleman: "Personally, I think the element of time has to be considered."

Lacy: "How much time is needed? Colored players have been an integral part of baseball for eleven years. Shouldn't that be enough time for their representatives, at least, to come to the realization they're here?"

Coleman: "That's not the point. The point is that time is erasing a lot of ills. It must be admitted things are a lot better than they once were . . . I'm going to have to loosen up for the game now. I'll have to leave you now . . . I promise you, though, I'll speak to Mr. Weiss (Yankee general manager George Weiss) about it."

I didn't write a story on the Howard reaction at that time, but somehow other colored players in St. Petersburg—Curt Flood, Ernie Wilkes, Milt Smith, Bob Gibson, Harry Simpson—knew about it.

Also, Brooks Lawrence of the Cincinnati Reds approached me one day and said, "I heard about your little incident in Florida with Elston." I don't know how he heard about it. He didn't hear it from me.

The day after talking with Coleman, I broached the proposal to Sherm Lollar, player representative for the Chicago White Sox. Sherm endorsed it without hesitation. I credit Lollar, Eddie Yost, then of the Washington Senators, Carl Erskine of the Dodgers, and Joe DiMaestri of the Oakland Athletics with doing a "highly commendable job" in helping end the barrier against black baseball players in Baltimore hotels.

As the last major league city to act, Baltimore had been pounded by local and state agencies, along with the *Afro-American* and other groups, but the Baltimore Hotel Owners Association held tight to its discriminatory policies until the bitter end.

Another housing situation, this one involving the Dodgers, was covered in "A to Z" in May 1954. It happened in St. Louis. My first column remarks were based on quotes from stories by writers traveling with the Dodgers, as I was not there when the event happened, although I later interviewed some of the involved players for a follow-up story. The column said:

According to reports, Jackie Robinson was the only one of the Dodgers six colored players to accept housing at the Chase Hotel, where the main body of the team stays, when Brooklyn was in the Mound City last week.

. . . Roy Campanella and Joe Black, the reports state, persuaded the others (Don Newcombe, Junior Gilliam and Sandy Amoros) to refuse the Chase offer.

In previous years the tan Brooks stayed at the Adams Hotel because the Chase management did not want colored patrons. Last year the Chase acquiesced and the New York Giants housed Monte Irvin, Hank Thompson and Ruben Gomez along with the rest of the squad. This year, the Dodgers planned the same thing but the actions of Campy, Black, et al., balked them.

Two things apparently influenced the refusal: (1) the Chase people reportedly asked that the colored players have their meals in their rooms, and (2) the Brooklyn players felt they didn't want to go where they are not wanted.

Robinson, however, is always an independent thinker. His contention is that presence in the hotel, even under ground rule conditions which are not pleasant to take, is important as an icebreaker.

"Other players coming along behind me," declares Jackie, "will benefit by this opening wedge. If you don't get your foot in the door, you'll never force it open," he asserts.

Argues Campanella: "The Chase is not for me. As I see it, they didn't want us down there for seven years. So, as far as I'm concerned, they can make it forever."

Only flaw in this position, as "A to Z" views it, is that Campy (and the others) won't be around forever." There are times when issues are bigger than individuals.

Black revealed that he had talked with Irvin, Thompson, Gomez and Willie Mays and these Giants have decided to bypass the Chase when they visit St. Louis . . . This comes as a real surprise to "A to Z."

Campanella, in a later interview with me, denied he gave the quotes the reporters attributed to him or was responsible for the players not staying at the Chase. Campy told me any blame for their not staying at the hotel belonged to the Dodgers. He said:

We were told we would have to stay out of the lobby, eat in our rooms, etc. And we felt that if we were to be Jim Crowed inside the hotel, it would be just as humiliating being Jim Crowed (through separation) . . .

As far as I am concerned, personally, I will be glad to live at the Chase any time the management assures me the same privileges accorded my teammates . . .

You know how major league teams operate. You know we couldn't have stayed at another hotel unless the club gave us permission to do so."

At first, some of the players didn't particularly care for my efforts aimed at having all team members stay together because, if successful, that would take away a lot of other freedoms they enjoyed. Some said, "What the heck are you doing, Sam?" When I told them it was something we had to think about for the colored ballplayers coming later, most were all right with it. Some still didn't care for it. Living together would cramp the style of a fellow like Sam Jethro, because Jethro stayed out all night long, all the time. It wasn't anything to see him coming across the compound at five o'clock in the morning.

Meanwhile, pressure was building on the hotels in Baltimore. The Maryland Commission on Interracial Problems was one of the groups demanding change. Personally, I questioned the Interfaith Day planning committee, a supporter of brotherhood and fair treatment for all, for scheduling its meeting in the segregated Lord Baltimore Hotel at a time when the campaign was seeking to bring pressure on the hotel to drop its discriminatory practices.

In April 1957, two Howard University professors—W. Montague Cobb and M. Wharton Young—were publicized when they refused to attend a meeting at the Lord Baltimore of the American Association of Anatomists.

For a player like Minnie Minoso of the White Sox, who had been voted best-dressed player, it meant "terribly lonely" stints when his team came to Baltimore and he landed at the black-owned York Hotel while his teammates went to the Emerson. I did a front page story in 1955 quoting Minoso saying that during a three-day stay that included two rainouts, "I've been to every movie in town. I have no one to visit with, no teammates to play cards with. It is terribly lonely. I wish Baltimore was not in the league, I do."

By this time, American League team officials were also speaking out against the separation practices, particularly those from the Cleveland Indians and Chicago White Sox.

Finally, in July 1957, it was announced that downtown Baltimore hotels would accept professional players and integrated conventions—but not black citizens who did not fall within those categories.

For perspective on this period in American history, a 1952 report from Tuskegee said that for the first time in seventy-one years, no lynching had occurred; in 1954, the Supreme Court ruled segregation in public schools unconstitutional; in 1955, Mrs. Rosa Parks refused to give up her bus seat to a white man in Montgomery, prompting a boycott call by Dr. Martin Luther King Jr.; in 1957, President Eisenhower called out paratroopers to enforce the desegregation of Central High School in Little Rock; and Henry Aaron was voted the National League's most valuable player and won his first home run title with forty-four. The lunch counter sit-ins would come

in 1960, the Freedom Rides to test bus station compliance with desegregation orders of the Interstate Commerce Commission were in 1961, and by
1964, the civil rights bill against racial discrimination in public accommo-
dations and employment was enacted with the major backing of President
Lyndon Baines Johnson.

With hotels in every major league city at last accepting all players, the
housing situation in the states where the teams worked out in the spring
was coming under closer scrutiny. Many of the black players had been quietly seething about this situation.

In February 1961, I wrote that as far as I knew, only Jackie Robinson
had openly protested the spring training housing separation. He did it the
last seven years of his twelve with the Dodgers.

When he could do nothing about the situation, Jackie would insert an
extra item in his customary expense account. Along with the usual items
such as meals, rent, and transportation, he added "humiliation" without
specifying an amount. Jackie left it open and suggested the club fill in the
amount "in accordance with what it thought should be paid to a man for
suffering indignities that were not included in his contract."

The closest thing involving other players that I would describe as a re-
bellion against the dual treatment occurred in 1956 among members of the
Milwaukee Braves. I handled that situation this way in the column:

> George Crowe, Billy Bruton, Hank Aaron and Humberto Robinson
> were to take a team plane from Mobile, Alabama, to Houston, Texas.
> Because they had to make their way through a maze of traffic to a col-
> ored home on the other side of Mobile, then line up single file for use of
> the private bath tub, they missed the plane.
>
> Their white teammates, many of whom did not last two weeks after
> the season began, had a police escort for their chartered bus to a down-
> town hotel. They bathed in their separate rooms (not more than two to
> a shower), then reboarded the bus and went, behind police sirens, to the
> airport. After a while, the team's plane took off . . . without the entire
> team.
>
> On their arrival at the airport, Crowe, Bruton, et al. discovered that
> they had been left behind, with instructions to take the next flight.
>
> They refused to do so.

They returned to the place where they had been staying and let the club know. Arrangements were made for them to fly out the next day.

Oddly enough, it was a statement by the Braves vice president, Birdie Tebbetts, in early 1961 that resulted in colored players openly protesting the housing situation in training sites.

The NAACP president in St. Petersburg, Robert Wimbish, said he would no longer assist the New York Yankees and St. Louis Cardinals, who trained there, to locate housing for their black players. Several teams got turned down when they asked hotels if they would accept their colored players.

When Tebbetts was asked what reaction his club got, he said the club had done nothing, indicating his players seemed satisfied with their plight. At least ten players—including Hank Aaron and Wes Covington—spoke up immediately, with Hank insisting: "We most certainly are displeased. At least I am. And I know Wes and Billy Bruton, who was with us until he was traded this winter, also resented having to live away from the rest of the club."

My story identified some of the others who spoke out as Al Smith of the White Sox, Frank Robinson and Vada Pinson of the Cincinnati Reds, Bill White, Curt Flood, and Dick Ricketts of the St. Louis Cardinals, and Bob Boyd of the Kansas City Athletics.

Boyd, who was the only black player with Kansas City after having been the only one the previous year in Baltimore, told me: "I don't like it any more than they would in my place."

White Sox outfielder Floyd Robinson probably sounded a theme supported by all the players: "He (Tebbetts) says the players haven't complained. All of us have been hurt by the condition. It could be nothing but their indifference that kept the owners from understanding how we felt. You don't have to be told that you're digging a pin in a man's face."

Reached at his home in California, Pinson of the Cincinnati Reds told me: "They shouldn't have to guess whether we like it or not. Nobody enjoys being regarded as something inferior—not good enough to live with his brothers."

In 1961, of the thirteen major league teams training in Florida, only one had all its players living together. The Dodgers, since 1949, had owned their facilities at Vero Beach.

In my last February 1961 column, I reviewed some of what Branch Rickey had done over a fifteen-year period to keep his team together—training in Cuba and the Dominican Republic, using the Vero Beach facility, and traveling through much of the South in chartered Pullman coaches. I wrote:

> And for 15 years, the other clubs have gone along living in the shadow of a dying ideology, ears cocked apprehensively for the noises they knew would some day be coming from the closet.
> If only they had possessed the guts of Rickey, their headaches would by now be forgotten.

The Milwaukee Braves played in a municipal park and had a contract giving the team the right to use the park as it wanted. To show that the club indeed was concerned about the feelings of its players, the Braves told city manager Martin Casale they would immediately put an end to separate seating in the park.

General manager John McHale told me, "The Braves do not have two standards—one of complete integration in the summer and another for the winter and spring." He said it was "unfortunate" if anything said by any club official had been construed that way.

McHale continued, "When Henry Aaron and Billy Bruton (since traded to Detroit) expressed a distaste for the situation in spring training, we felt we owed it to them to do what we can to improve matters . . . We assured Billy when he was in Milwaukee for his send-off (given by citizens) that we'd put all our energies into correcting the situation, not only here in Bradenton but throughout Florida. This (desegregation of the park) can serve as an indication of our feelings about segregation."

With movement on the spring training housing matter, I found myself knocking on the door of room 219 in Miami's Sir John Hotel (for blacks) to talk to Earl Robinson, who was seeking to make the Baltimore Orioles.

I expressed my disappointment to him that he had chosen the Sir John Hotel when he could have stayed with other members of the team at the Hotel McAllister. I told Earl, "Other colored players throughout Florida are protesting separate housing, not because they have any driving urge to live with other races, but because they think their contribution to the game and their citizenship entitle them to equal treatment. It is unfortunate that you didn't wish to make their aim logical and their road easier."

In my next column, March 21, I carried a response from Earl Robinson, some of which is reproduced here:

It is true that Mr. (Lee) MacPhail told me I could live at the team's hotel if I so desired, and that I told him I preferred to come here . . . As I've already said, my first objective is to make the club. That is why I came to spring training. I am convinced that my best chance to win a job rests with my ability to relax, in an atmosphere in which I'm completely at ease.

That doesn't mean to say that I don't feel comfortable in any company. Rather it is intended to point out that here I am at liberty to go and come and do as I please. At the Sir John I room with Mickey McGuire. We have friends in to watch television and we talk and play cards. At the McAllister, I would have roomed alone because Mickey is not on the Oriole roster.

If I were downtown I would have spent most of the time in my room, isolated so to speak. Another thing, it would cost me money. If I were downtown and felt the need of some social life, I would have to pay taxi cab fare to get across town where I am to find my friends; even if I desired a haircut, I'd have to take a cab to find a barber who'd be willing to wait on me.

. . . I'm still a rookie looking for a job. Established players like Hank Aaron, Minnie Minoso, Ernie Banks and others, are in a position to embarrass their teams. When fans show up outside their hotels and ask for them, it would be embarrassing for the officials to have to say "they can't stay here with us." My case may be different at some future time. Another year, even possibly next year, might bring another decision by me.

During May of 1961, two of the most outspoken of black sports figures spoke in Baltimore—Jackie Robinson and Jim Brown, the great Cleveland Browns running back. When I sought their views on the simmering housing situation in the South, they were adamantly opposed to team players being separated by race.

Jackie lashed out at the owners who had gone along with the status quo in Dixie: "They were so convinced that Branch Rickey's experiment with colored ballplayers was a hair-brained scheme that wouldn't last, they decided to make the best of it and let matters ride."

Brown was speaking to me after it was learned his team would be going to Texas to play the new Dallas franchise, and hotel and motel operators already had said separation would be in vogue. Speaking for himself and his black teammates (halfbacks Bob Mitchell and A. D. Williams, fullback Prentice Gault, and guard John Wooten) Brown said: "You can be sure we have no intention of accepting it."

Brown added, "It just wouldn't be right for us to do so in the face of the daily sacrifice being made by students all over the South in their sit-in demonstrations. We're together on this thing and I'm sure (coach) Paul Brown understands that we mean business and will do something about it."

There were reports in August of 1961 that the three major professional sports were zeroing in on racial discrimination in housing in Dixie.

Bill Bruton of the Detroit Tigers and Bill White of the St. Louis Cardinals acted as consultants for a letter drafted by team player representatives of the American and National League baseball players to be presented to owners meeting in Boston. (Years later on April 1, 1989, White would become the top ranking black in professional sports when he took over as the first of his race to serve as president of the National League. The former first baseman, who broke into the majors with the Giants, announced before his term ended March 31, 1993, that he did not want a second term, but agreed to remain in the post until 1994, when a successor was named.)

Although unable to reach all the football players on the six National Football League (NFL) teams scheduled to meet the Cowboys in the upcoming season, I was told that many had publicly taken the position that they would not accept unequal treatment.

On the basketball front, Bill Russell, the Boston Celtics defensive specialist, and Elgin Baylor, star of the Los Angeles Lakers, said they had been assured of concerted National Basketball Association (NBA) action against Dixiecrat insults. Baylor informed me, "Owner Bob Short told me that the league is guarding against any possible repetition of Charleston (West Virginia)." In 1959, Baylor had staged a one-man strike and refused to play in an exhibition game when the team's hotel refused rooms to him, Tom Hawkins, and Alex Ellis.

Russell, along with several teammates, had suffered humiliating racial bans before and after a game in North Carolina three years before; he told me Celtics owner Walter Brown had issued strict orders that no game should be scheduled where assurance of equal treatment for players wasn't guaranteed.

During the World Series, I had polled the various baseball teams about actions they would take to bring about change in Florida in 1962. The first to announce dramatic change was the White Sox. General manager Ed Short had told me the team would definitely take action. The White Sox bought the Sarasota Terrace Hotel in the fall of 1961, spending a half million dollars.

This move forced me to check back with other teams before I had planned to do so. Milwaukee still had not publicly disclosed its action but Don Davidson, road secretary for the Braves, let me know the club had pulled out of its Bradenton hotel and leased a motor court in nearby Palmetto, Florida. The Orioles would be returning to Miami, where the McAllister already had agreed to accept all players. Those were the most positive results.

The New York Yankees, which had announced it would move from St. Petersburg to a more tolerant Fort Lauderdale, took over a motel there but with a catch—Elston Howard, Hector Lopez, Al Downing, et al., would live in an annex and would eat and sleep there.

Early on, in the 1930s and 1940s, although all the sports editors on all the black newspapers were strongly backing the effort to bring about fairness in the world of sports, few had the financial strength to keep personnel on the front lines as did the *Afro-American* and the *Pittsburgh Courier.*

Both Wendell Smith of the *Courier* and I were credited with boosting the circulations of our publications as a result of our coverage during the early years after Jackie Robinson broke the modern era ban on blacks in major league baseball.

Smith, whom I always spoke of as the better writer, often traveled in the South with a friend, Billy Rowe. As he had more contacts and friends to call on in areas where we went with the teams, Smith did not go through some of the experiences I endured. But I felt that with its vast network of stringers, the *Courier* provided its writers access to more contacts in Dixie locales.

Some of the scholars who have researched our work and noted my feelings about Smith's work have come up with differing assessments. One of them wrote to me in the summer of 1996. Chris Lamb, assistant professor of journalism at Old Dominion University in Norfolk, Virginia, became familiar with some of our work in connection with a series of pieces he wrote regarding the way the black and white media handled coverage of the baseball desegregation issue. He wrote me:

> I really like Wendell Smith's writing. With no disrespect toward him, I still think you're the better writer. Wendell would get so angry about the situation—something he had every right to be—and sometimes his anger would get the best of him. Your writing, or what I've read of it, is controlled. The frustration is there but you always seem focused. It's clear and sharp and heartfelt. You write from the heart and head.

Anyway, Smith (who later would cover baseball and boxing for the daily *Chicago American*) and I frequently worked together in the field. In a 1973 column, I discussed the meeting places where we planned ways of being more effective in getting action from the National and American Leagues:

> We talked deep into nights in ghetto hotels, at his house in Pittsburgh, at my house in Washington, at dimly lit ballparks where our paths would cross covering Negro National League games, in lunchrooms in Harlem and over counters in greasy-spoons and hog-maw joints of Memphis, St. Louis, Baltimore and Philadelphia."

On one occasion when we were working together, several writers on the Dodgers beat were gathered on a bus waiting to shove off to the city where the team would be playing. A question arose concerning the true quality of black players and whether they really could measure up to Triple A or major league standards. Wendell mentioned that the same year Babe Ruth hit his sixty homers (1927), John Beckwith of the Harrisburg Giants had hit seventy-two.

Rud Rennie, a *New York Herald Tribune* writer who rarely had much to say to either Wendell or myself, quipped, "That's colored playing only against colored."

I had a quick retort for him. "Your leagues have been only whites playing against whites."

That level of jousting took place now and then but on the whole, I remember the writers getting along on a professional basis, with some of them being quite helpful and becoming good friends. One of the helpful newsmen was Bob Considine. He and I knew each other from our days growing up in Washington, D.C. Considine played with the basketball Epiphany Roses, a team my cohorts and I played when we were young.

We were playing tennis one day when Considine said to me, "Sam, you know it's a shame. When we grow up, I'm going to be able to go a lot further than you."

A similar conversation occurred years later when I was working part-time at WBAL-TV channel 11 in Baltimore. I was playing golf at the University of Maryland with Jim Wittemore, a friend who had worked at the station and had access to the courts. Wittemore expressed regret that I was handicapped as to what I could do in television due to lack of opportunity.

I told him not to worry about that because the only reason I took the television job was to show people that blacks could do it, that there were blacks who know something about sports. That was my glory in going to WBAL-TV.

One spring training season, when I arrived in Florida to join the Dodgers, the manifest was full and Harold Parrott, who was then traveling secretary for the Dodgers, told me, "Sam, we don't have space for you on the train."

Bill Roeder of the *World Telegram,* one of the classy guys on the baseball beat, spoke up, telling Parrott, "Well, I have an upper berth. He can use mine." It was unheard of, in those days, to share a train compartment with a black guy.

Dick Young of the *New York Daily News* was a very good friend. Another early close friend was Francis X. Flaherty, who went to the West Coast to the *Los Angeles Examiner.* We communicated from time to time but eventually lost contact.

The best of all throughout was Kenny Smith of the *New York Mirror.* As mentioned earlier, it was Smith and Joe King of the *New York World Telegram* who in 1948 sponsored me for membership in the Baseball Writers Association.

I became a member of the association in April 1948 and it was not too long before my friend Wendell Smith also was accepted by the organization.

Milton Gross of the *New York Post* was another classy guy, and Milton Richman of UPI was also a very friendly person.

Most of the white writers on the baseball beat were OK to work with. Rud Rennie of the *Herald Tribune* was friendly but distant. Once I had my picture taken with Roscoe McGowen of the *New York Times*. Al Laney was also with the *New York Times* and in those days, they were referred to as "the gentlemen from the *Times*." Among the other reporters I found to be friendly were Gordon Cobbledick of the *Cleveland Plain Dealer* and Hal Leibovitz, then with the *Cleveland Press*, later with the *Sporting News*.

Dan Parker was another one of those who accepted me but was distant. Yet, he quoted me every chance he got, especially if it was criticism over something. I criticized boxer Sugar Ray Robinson when he came to Baltimore and complained about the lack of an elevator or something. It so happened that he was in a building downtown and the elevator had gone out. Sugar threatened to get in the car and go back to New York. If it hadn't been for his trainer, George Gainford, he probably would have done it. I wrote a piece saying I felt he should have shown a little more courtesy to his hosts because he knew it was something out of their control. Dan picked it up right away.

Jimmy Powers, a columnist for the *New York Daily News*, was another one who liked to pick up stuff that was critical. Parker and Powers were the two who picked up the flap about Shirley Povich.

The incident with Povich referred to a flap that developed when Povich, of the *Washington Post*, carried part of a statement I made, leaving readers with a different view than that conveyed by the entire statement. I had said at the time I couldn't say that there were any colored baseball players ready to move up to the majors without at least one year in the minors. Povich left off the qualifying portion about the year in the minors. Unhappy about it, I called Povich unfair in his treatment.

In the early years of baseball integration, the daily reporters were more likely to come to me for information than the other way around, because I was staying with the black players and had better access to them.

Locally in Baltimore, over the years I was closest to Vince Bagli, my editor at WBAL-TV; John Steadman, formerly sports editor of the old *News American* and later a columnist for the *Baltimore Sun;* and Bob Maisel of the *Sun.* In that group, while not in sports, I also include *Sun* columnist Michael Olesker.

Over the years, John Steadman, strictly on his own, had promoted me for inclusion in the writers' wing of the Baseball Hall of Fame. In a November 1989 column he wrote:

> Awards for excellence in his craft, citations for exemplary citizenship and contributions to humanity have come to Sam Lacy, but none would compare to being beckoned by the Baseball Hall of Fame. And what an appropriate, although belated, distinction for a pioneer who took a strong stance and never backed away in his pursuit to do what was best in behalf of the black player at a time when prejudice engulfed the field . . . and also the press box.

Among athletes, there were different degrees of public support for civil rights, some taking the position that it was not appropriate or wise for them to express their views on this issue. As a way to spur progress, some thought it more important to go out and succeed at their jobs rather than to be on a soap box.

To me, they were taking a shortsighted view of things and at one point I urged them to come together in one place to put their strength into the struggle for fair play for all. In a column in May of 1963, the year of the big freedom march on Washington, I reflected:

> Except for the tireless drive of others toward the goal of equal rights, all these fellows in today's pro world could have been government clerks, Pullman car porters, elevator operators, bootblacks, numbers writers or just plain bums . . . and they'd better believe it!

Jackie Robinson also was a prodder, and he and some of the other athletes got into public spats. I did a special column about how some of the black players felt about Jackie after hearing Willie Mays, the great Giants outfielder, pay tribute to Jackie. Asked about what I considered a change of heart regarding Mays's thinking about Jackie, Mays said no one had ever asked before. Mays said, "I know, and I'm sure the others do, too, that none of us might be here if Jackie hadn't delivered."

In 1970, I said it was difficult to believe that Orioles star Frank Robinson had told a *Look* magazine writer that a baseball diamond or clubhouse was no place for political discussion, that Jackie Robinson was taking pot shots at him for his failure to speak out in the war against racism, subtle or otherwise, and that the time had arrived when a man is no longer hampered by his complexion, among other things.

Frank Robinson told a Baltimore writer that the *Look* article was "not altogether accurate." *Look*, of course, sent Jackie Robinson a copy of the article. Jackie wrote to Frank suggesting he might have said some of the things quoted because he was seeking a manager's job. Jackie also wrote: "I was a bit surprised to read your comments, and concluded you must have a guilty conscience for I haven't taken pot shots at you or anyone else in particular.

"But, Frank, if the things I have been saying hit you where it hurts, if the shoe fits, then wear it. Only you know if you belong."

On another occasion Jackie had asked, "Has (Maury) Wills forgotten the color of his skin?" after the Dodgers shortstop had been quoted as saying he didn't want "to be involved in a controversy."

Noting that for several years I and others "have complained about the lackadaisical attitude that seemed to embrace several of the world's leading colored athletes on the question of civil rights," in a January 1967 story I called it "a most rewarding experience when Gus Heningburg of the NAACP's Legal Defense Fund announced the formation of a National Sports Committee."

Accepting posts as cochairmen were coach Bill Russell of the Boston Celtics, halfback Gale Sayers of the Chicago Bears, first baseman Bill White of the St. Louis Cardinals, and Frank Robinson of the Baltimore Orioles.

I paid tribute to Maury Wills, who was at the New York meeting at which the sports committee was formed as a stand-in for Bill White, saying he "plunged into the swim with both feet." Wills volunteered to turn over to the cause all fees from his speaking engagements for the year and to enlist at least ten other players to do the same. He also got ABC broadcaster Howard Cosell to pledge $250 when he went to tape a show with him.

Black stars in the American Football League (AFL) had made a dramatic statement in January 1965 regarding their growing concern about racial discrimination when they balked at playing an All-Star game in New Orleans because of the treatment they received after arriving in the city. For years I had been warning about the disaster awaiting professional teams that ignored the horrible treatment black players often received in the South. A rooter for the new AFL, I nevertheless expressed concerns about the league's going into Houston, New Orleans, and Dallas.

On January 12, 1960, I cited the Cotton Bowl experiences of Syracuse University's Ernie Davis, Art Baker, and John Brown, who vowed they "had never encountered anything quite like the treatment they received in helping defeat Texas in Dallas on New Year's Day." They were spat upon and generally insulted.

One of my columns warned in 1962 that AFL commissioner Joe Foss and the expected owner of an assumed franchise in New Orleans could be suspected of "winking" at the racial situation in the Crescent City—although they were making statements saying there would be no problems. Sources in New Orleans were reportedly convinced Dave Dixon, a promoter for the game scheduled in New Orleans, wanted to do the right thing, but was cowed by the White Citizens Council.

I pointed out that the NFL had made much progress in the fight against the Jim Crow bugaboo, partly by abandoning cities like New Orleans, Columbia, South Carolina, Jackson, Mississippi, and Birmingham, Alabama, as sites for preseason exhibitions.

Again in 1963 I predicted the AFL was playing with fire in moving to accept New Orleans. Shortly before the AFL "stars" game was to be played in New Orleans, the Sugar Bowl featured Syracuse and Louisiana State. Legal racial barriers had been dropped. But when the black AFL players arrived, in a matter of days, they found doors on Bourbon Street closed to them, had trouble getting cabs, and received other racial insults. They decided not to play and the game was moved to Houston.

Players who joined in the protest included Ernie Ladd, Earl Faison, Frank Buncom, and Dick Westmoreland from San Diego; Cookie Gilchrist, Ernie Warlick, Elbert Dubenion, and Butch Byrd of Buffalo; Bobby Bell, Mack Lee Hill, Abner Haynes, Junious Buchanan, and Dave Grayson from Kansas City; Willie Brown and Art Powell, Denver; Winston Hill and Clemon Daniels, Oakland; Larry Garron and Houston Antwine, Boston; Sherman Plunkett, New York; and Sid Blanks, Houston.

By November 1966, I had come around to saying that developments had dispelled some of the apprehensions about New Orleans becoming a football league city. Positive moves included the listing of C.C. Dejoie, publisher of the *Louisiana Weekly,* and Norman Francis, assistant to the president of Xavier University, among the family of stockholders, marking the first time blacks had infiltrated the ranks of owners in major-level professional sports.

In December 1955, my continued criticism of racial disparity in college athletics led me to accuse Georgia Governor Marvin Griffin of playing politics when he urged the regents of Georgia Tech to pull the school out of the Sugar Bowl because Pittsburgh would play a black fullback, Bob Grier. The storm Griffin provoked included his being hanged in effigy by Georgia Tech students. Georgia Tech played in the game.

Louisiana passed a law banning interracial athletics in August 1956, and as a result Notre Dame, St. Louis, and Dayton pulled out of the Sugar Bowl basketball tournament, leaving only Kentucky. Wisconsin and Pitt had canceled future contests. Marquette was on the verge of dropping its cage games with Loyola of the South.

In that kind of climate, "A to Z" in November could not understand why Buck Shaw at the Air Force Academy and coach Earl Blaik at West Point would schedule games with Tulane, even if they had no black players on their teams. I said Colonel Blaik's position in suggesting white boys on the Army football team "are not involved or affected" when they play Jim Crow games in this age of advancement was comparable to telling them lynching is all right, fellows, as long as it isn't happening to you.

As bowl game selection time was approaching in late 1961, "A to Z" reminded readers of the saying that "money isn't everything" as signs indicated that schools such as Louisiana State and Alabama were quietly hinting that they could live with a Rose Bowl bid.

Some elements of the South wanted its segregated games treated just like any other by the media, leading me to do a column on the position of the *Montgomery Advertiser* after the paper blasted NBC for deciding not to telecast the December 28, 1963, Blue-Gray game.

The paper's editorial termed the NBC action "a studied chastisement of the state of Alabama, a punitive expedition against a state's social order" and frothed, "NBC does not care if it destroys the institution of the Blue-Gray game if it cannot sit on Manhattan Island and dictate management of the game. If NBC cannot get a mixed roster of players in Montgomery, it does not hesitate to blight the game."

I reasoned that (editorial page editor Grover C.) Hall and his cronies "appear to feel that NBC shouldn't create this sort of problem 'on account of a few colored football players.'"

It also was suggested the "arguments are so full of holes that anyone who takes him seriously would insult him . . . Only die-hard local segregationists are expected to swallow it, I'm sure."

When in 1968, University of Florida president Stephen O'Connell and University of Mississippi chancellor Porter Fortune insisted during a meeting in Tampa that they couldn't find black athletes who could meet their entrance requirements, I felt compelled to comment: "When one considers the claims of O'Connell and Fortune, the inclination is to suspect that we're embracing a multitude of morons at Yale and Harvard and West Point and Annapolis and Michigan and California and the countless other top-drawer institutions which have colored athletes."

However, I think the record reflects that I never tried to cover up the fact that too many black athletes were permitted to skate through college as long as they could help win games. In 1984, after nearly two decades of harping on the issue, I had to discuss one of the saddest of "miseducation" stories. The story poured out before the Senate Subcommittee on Education.

Kevin Ross, with three years of basketball under his belt at Creighton University in Nebraska, told lawmakers how he left the school unable to read or write. He said the school was only interested in his playing ball; though supposedly a student, he was assigned courses such as "The Theory of First Aid" and "The Theory of Tennis" while school secretaries produced term papers for him. Ross reported that after an injury in his junior year virtually ended his basketball career, school officials told him to go to a grammar school and learn to read and write. At Marva Collins's school in Chicago, Ross ended up in the second grade. Later he was able to go to Roosevelt University.

My favorite whistle blower in all the world was Professor Jan Kemp, who won a $2 million-plus award from the University of Georgia in 1986, after she said she was fired for exposing a policy of special treatment for Bulldog athletes. Her contentions, and those of supporting witnesses, before the U.S. District Court were that athletes were admitted who could not read or write, and that some were promoted out of remedial courses so that they could participate in revenue-producing sports.

In a column on the matter, I also cited the case of the running back at the University of Virginia—star of the Cavalier offense and leading rusher in the Atlantic Coast Conference—who was not declared academically ineligible until the week before his final game of a four-year varsity career. The final game was of no importance to the university.

Other media played up the whistle blower story but my conclusion was that I have the dubious privilege of being more righteous than any of them, because in every single episode of hanky-panky, the central figure was black. My argument was that countless numbers of young blacks had been lured to major schools by a recruiter's hot-sell philosophy and had fallen victim to academic exploitation.

Some months later, I received a letter from Vince Dooley, the Georgia school's athletic director, (along with a new mission statement and a handbook) dealing with academic objectives of the University of Georgia Athletic Association and ideas relating to academic standards for athletes. The entire letter was published.

In December 1969, editor-publisher Roger Stanton of the *Football News* did a column entitled, "Blacks Are Ill Advised." He said, "The greatest tragedy of the 1969 football season is the revolt of certain black football players on some of our major campuses. It is tragic because they are hurting themselves, their schools and the entire race."

The way I saw it, if publisher Stanton felt that the entire colored race was hurt by young men standing up to protest what we (older members) had tolerated for more years than we were proud of, he should be informed that we could stand the hurt.

As recently as March 1997, the *Houston Post* reported that two Texas Tech players failed to pass a single course during the 1996 fall semester.

Often, and sadly, I had to look no further than my backyard of Baltimore and Washington to keep busy. Pimlico race track was a case in point.

As the Preakness Stakes approached in 1958, I suggested in a column that bigwigs of the Maryland Jockey Club could be embarrassed if asked: "How come a colored sportswriter is asked to vote in the Jockeys Hall of Fame balloting, and a colored rider (the immortal Isaac Murphy) is included among the murals lodged in the track's hall—yet no colored person is allowed to pay his or her money to get into the clubhouse to see the display?"

Although I devoted considerable attention to the race track problems at nearby Pimlico, the situation was much the same elsewhere. A March 1951 "A to Z" dealt with a situation in Miami, Florida, that created quite a stir, partly because it involved famous boxer Sugar Ray Robinson, known in his heyday as the best fighter "pound for pound" in the world. Here's something on that from my column datelined out of Miami:

Hold on to your hats! The ultimate was reached here last week when Sugar Ray Robinson became a daily visitor to the clubhouse of the Gulfstream Park race track. The world middleweight champion became the first colored enthusiast to "graduate" from the Jim Crow bleachers of Florida's horse-racing circuit.

Gulfstream officials didn't like the idea the first day Robinson showed up in the tow of Walter Winchell and they made their resentment quite clear, "explaining" it was regrettable and all that, but . . .

The next day, Sugar Ray was back again, this time accompanied not only by Winchell, but by Mrs. E. L. Hopkins, owner of a powerful racing stable headed by the handicap champion, Three Rings. It was then Mrs. Hopkins's turn to "explain" that Sugar Ray was to be her guest and was to have access to her clubhouse box as long as she was racing her string in Florida.

Track people don't like to cross folks like the Hopkinses, the Whitneys, the Vanderbilts and Calumets, people who run "big money" horses, so Robbie had another "kayo" to his credit.

In 1975, I reported positive things about Pimlico and Chick Lang, "the progressive general manager." It was Lang who approved "Soul Express," a tip sheet published by James "Biddy" Wood of Baltimore, a former *Afro-American* reporter and magazine picture-editor. It appeared on the peddler stands at Maryland race tracks for a time. Before the Wood venture it had been forty years since a black selector calling himself "Long Shot Red" had some success with a tip sheet before it faded away. Blacks were represented in various jobs at Pimlico.

A few years later, though, I found myself pounding away at the hiring practices of the state race tracks, saying blacks made up only 2 percent of the employees at the tracks but represented 15 to 25 percent of the customers. The specific beef was that none of the tracks, Pimlico, Laurel, Bowie, or Timonium, "has a black in the front office, in public relations, on the usher force, on the assistant starter crew, among receiving barn personnel, or among the horde of car parkers." That led me to complain there was "as much racism as racing" in the state's "sport of kings."

During Preakness Week in 1981, an official at Pimlico responded. Jimmy Dollar was described as an administrative assistant in the front office, working directly under general manager Chick Lang; Jimmy Powell was cited as an employee in a responsible position who'd just had a race named for him on his eighty-first birthday the week before; Calvin Myers was reported as serving as a supervisor of the jockeys room; Lee Vincent and Donald Graham were listed as overseers of the electrical system at Pimlico.

Also, Vivian Addison, Barbara Brailford, Celeste Ball, Delores Chambers, Andrea Bowser, and Charles Brown were termed important cogs in customer services, jobs not previously held by blacks.

At first I felt some gratification, thinking my complaints may have at least gained a toe in the door. But then I took a more studied look. When I did, I realized that, when applied to blacks, the title "administrative assistant" was little more than one who serves in any capacity from messenger boy to go-for . . . that the "responsible position" subterfuge covered one who had worked more than fifty years as a handyman in the private service of the track owner's family, not at a track job.

The closer look also showed that the man in charge of the jockey quarters was a state employee, not a Pimlico or any other particular race track employee. The electrical experts were not hired by Pimlico, but by an outside contractor named International Sound. And why was there no mention of the fact that all the valets working from the jockey room were white?

Finally, Addison, Brailford, Ball, Chambers, Bowser, and Brown could not be claimed by Pimlico. All were bartenders on the payroll of the H.M.

Stevens Company, the catering concessionaire. So, I concluded, under the light, the picture looked the same—not so good.

Efforts by delegate Walter Dean and state senator Clarence Mitchell III, both of Baltimore, to spur change through amendments, fell short. I was concerned after a member of the Legislative Black Caucus was quoted as asking a daily newspaper writer why Lacy was "the only one raising a ruckus" over the situation. Maybe, I retorted, it's because a major portion of the other writers, being themselves white, have no cause to notice it.

About a dozen years after initiating the campaign about the race tracks, I did a story in June 1988 noting that Governor William Donald Schaefer had named Ernest Colvin, a black Baltimore dentist, as chairman of the Maryland Racing Commission. Since 1986, there also had been these changes: the security force had been desegregated, the tellers' windows gradually had become occupied by an occasional black, Calvin Myers had been placed in charge of the jockeys' quarters, Robert Flournoy had been named to a swing post on the patrol judges' roster, and "Cocky" Johnson had been appointed stable manager.

Although changes had started earlier, when Frank DeFrancis took over ownership of the two major tracks, replacing the Cohen brothers at Pimlico and John Shapiro at Laurel, additional employment opportunities for blacks became a fact of life in the Maryland racing picture.

CHAPTER 7

'SKINS, COLTS, BIRDS

As owner of the Washington Redskins, the last National Football League team to include black players, George Preston Marshall could be as testy as any of his critics.

In January 1957, I sent him a telegram asking if radio-TV broadcaster Harry Wismer, a minor partner in the team, was accurate when he told a Capital Press Club audience that when he had proposed use of colored players, Marshall responded that Wismer should do the broadcasting and leave running of the team to him.

Marshall replied that Wismer "just simply isn't telling the truth"; as to the threat of a boycott hinted at by several black leaders, Marshall's comment was, "Any citizen has a right to avoid any event he does not care to attend."

After the Redskins were beaten by the Cleveland Browns in 1958 behind Jim Brown's record-setting rushing, *Washington Post* sports editor Bus Ham wrote: "Too bad . . . there's only one Jim Brown in professional football and the Redskins can't get him."

My column reminded that the Redskins "could have had him" as well as Jim Parker, the Baltimore Colts all-pro defensive lineman.

I wrote: "White-only-minded George Preston Marshall ignored both Brown and Jim Parker in the draft of college players. The fact that they were All-Americans didn't mean as much to the 'Skins owner as did the fact that they were colored."

Tackle John Thomas graduated cum laude from the College of Pacific in June 1958. He got a telephone call approving a workout as a free agent. But when he showed up at the Redskins Occidental College camp, assistant coach Mike Nixon discovered he was colored and explained there must have been some misunderstanding because there were no openings. The young man went on to make the San Francisco 49ers.

Year after year, the one thing Marshall's policy won him was a certainty that he would get an early pick in the draft—as losers do. What eventually provided the impetus for Marshall to make a change was his being notified in March 1961 by President John F. Kennedy's Secretary of the Interior Stewart L. Udall, that the team "will not be able to carry its discriminatory hiring policy into the new D.C. stadium, now being constructed on federal land in the nation's capital."

Marshall won a reprieve from Udall. Meantime, he wrote NFL commissioner Pete Rozelle, denying he practiced discrimination and adding his intention was to field a team that "would be representative of Washington." That got me wondering how he was to use a perennially lily-white football team to represent a city that was 54 percent colored.

No court test proved necessary in this case, but I could report in September 1961 that as part of the preparation for that possibility, Solicitor General Marvin Cohen and his assistant Bill McGlone had received permission to study the *Afro-American* file on Marshall and the Redskins.

Syracuse All-American running back Ernie Davis came under heavy pressure when the Redskins announced they would draft him. Many media people asked if he wanted to be the first black player on the all-white squad; some actually urged him not to be the icebreaker. It didn't develop into much of an issue as Davis's draft rights were traded to the Cleveland Browns.

Marshall welcomed me in for an interview for the December 12, 1961, *Afro-American*. I observed that Marshall had shown good faith in drafting three players and inviting two of them (Ron Hatcher and Joe Hernandez) to come in for contract talks. Marshall wanted to give me a scoop:

> This is something you can write which hasn't been written before. For years, I was this city's largest employer of colored persons.
>
> I was the first laundry operator to use all colored route men. How many do you see on laundry trucks now?
>
> I was first to use colored ushers and vendors at Griffith Stadium athletic contests, and at one time there were nearly 500 colored persons employed in this very building—when the (Palace) laundry plant was situated here.

The other thing that came out of the interview was Marshall's insistence that he would not pose for a picture with Hatcher as photographers had been requesting because he did not want to exploit the youngster since he did not pose with other rookies.

Early in February 1966, the Redskins named former Cleveland Browns quarterback Otto Graham as coach, and I could not avoid wondering about his attitude toward colored players. In 1964, Graham had said he would trade Jim Brown were he the coach of the team. He said the Browns would never win the championship with Brown because "he doesn't block and he doesn't fake enough." It seemed to me that was like saying the Chicago Cubs hadn't won a National League pennant because Ernie Banks didn't pitch. That, of course, was the year Jim Brown and the Browns defeated Baltimore 27-0 for the crown.

But my concern regarding Graham went further. Graham had called Charley Taylor, top player in the All-Star game, "lazy." Also, since his retirement, Graham had been "rashly critical of Brown, Taylor, Johnny Sample, and Gale Sayers," all black. Two of the players Graham had tagged as "lazy and indifferent," Sample and Taylor, were on the 1966 team he was to coach.

Though I questioned the leadership of the Redskins, I had nothing but admiration for that of the Colts. When Carroll Rosenbloom owned the Baltimore Colts and his general manager was Don Kellett, I rated the Colts among the best in the area of racial relations. So it did not come as a surprise to me in 1963 when Rosenbloom announced that the team would not be returning to Western Maryland College for preseason training if "racial bars which exist in the town of Westminster and the adjacent community have not been completely eliminated."

Rosenbloom said the club could no longer condone the indignities that were being visited upon colored members of the team and their families and friends. When the Colts were at the training facilities there during mid-July to late September, several restaurants and other places of business and numerous entertainment facilities were off-limits to Colts players the likes of Lenny Moore, Jim Parker, Joe Perry, and others.

For my money, Carroll Rosenbloom ranked on the highest rung as a leader of a sports franchise, along with Art Rooney of the Pittsburgh Steelers, Bill Veeck of the Cleveland Indians, and of course, Branch Rickey of the Brooklyn Dodgers.

One of the incidents I revealed in a column after Rosenbloom's death in 1979 involved the team owner and the Lord Baltimore Hotel, where a dinner was being held in 1954 to usher in the second season of the Colts in Baltimore. Buddy Young, George Taliaferro, Charlie Robinson, and Mel Embree arrived early. When they were refused service at the open bar prior to dinner, the four black players left.

When Rosenbloom arrived approximately half an hour later, he was informed of what had happened. He asked me if I had any idea where Young and the others might be. I suggested several places. Carroll sent his then general manager, Don Kellett, with me in his chauffeur-driven car to try to locate them. In a driving rain, we went to two spots on Pennsylvania Avenue, then to Charlie Burns's Club 10-17 on Madison Avenue, where we found the missing foursome.

Back at the site of the dinner, we stood by as Rosenbloom called up to his room and told wife Georgia to pack their things. "We're checking out tonight," he advised her. From that night until Carroll Rosenbloom left Baltimore in 1971, the Colts used the Belvedere as their hotel headquarters.

The difference that ownership of a franchise can make became apparent in Baltimore soon after Rosenbloom took over the Los Angeles Rams and Robert Irsay bought the Colts. Under a headline that said, "Racial Attitude of Colts Suspect," I kicked off a September 19, 1972, column this way: "The Baltimore Colts are showing unmistakable signs of deterioration on both the playing field and the racial front."

Questions were being asked about the Colts' lack of at least one capable black running back when every one of the other twenty-five teams had one or more. At the same time, the once recalcitrant Redskins were running up and down the field on the shoulders of Larry Brown, Charlie Harraway, and George Nock.

Back at work after convalescing from ulcer surgery, I wrote on September 25, 1973, that I had almost forgotten a promise to stop writing about the Colts situation "as much with my heart as with my typewriter." But then I admitted to having become emotionally involved in the shenanigans being practiced by the coaching staff of the Baltimore Colts and almost blew my stack (and my stomach):

> If they want to keep people like Lydell Mitchell and Roy Hilton on the bench while they play inferior white players, let them . . . And if they want to lose nine of the twelve games they are scheduled to play (as I predict), to teams which have no hang-ups on using black players, that's entirely up to them. No more ulcers for me.

Later that year, when general manager Joe Thomas was quoted by a daily paper's reporter as saying, "This is the first time I've been asked about the subject" of racial unrest on the team, I recalled asking him about the issue a year before and I reprinted the response Thomas had given. Thomas also was quoted by the daily reporter as suggesting that if any player on the club thought racism existed, "I wish they'd identify themselves." My reaction: "And give up playing football for Russian roulette?"

In early March 1980, the headline on my column was: "The light finally shines downtown." On one Sunday, both John Steadman of the *Baltimore News-American* and Cameron Snyder of the *Baltimore Sun*, writers with unquestioned belief in right, wrote pieces that fell in line with the *Afro-American* in its criticism of the lily-white hiring practices of the football Colts.

By the opening of the Colts minicamp in Owings Mills in May, the team showed some progress with three candidates covering two positions that were rarely filled by blacks in the National Football League at that time. One of them, Ray Donaldson, a center, became a star at the position. Two quarterback prospects, Matt Reed from Grambling and Mike Dunn from Duke, weren't with the Colts very long.

Ominous clouds were hanging over the Colts and in February of 1984, I was trying to warn Baltimore in fairly blunt language that unless something was done to make the team's owner happy, "Bob Irsay is going, believe it!" I wrote:

> Certainly, Irsay has provoked a number of critical columns in this space, but I would rapidly point out that there is some justification for the complaints he has uttered. The place he has to play in is outmoded, the conveniences he is compelled to offer his customers are atrocious, and the scheduling he is forced to accept (no Sunday games before 2 p.m. when NFL TV broadcasts start at 1 p.m.) cuts deeply into his revenues.
>
> Media do-gooders who cling like leeches to the argument that Memorial Stadium can be made adequate with a few improvements are mounting the sort of contention that monkey-back suits and blue suede shoes can be made wearable with minor alterations.

A headline pleaded, "C'mon, Ballmer, it's time to wake up."

I urged commitment to a new stadium and slam-dunking our esteemed legislators to the realization that the proposed $15 million to update Memorial Stadium was absurd; threw into the pot the need to satisfy Edward Bennett Williams, then owner of the Orioles; and warned of the futility of hoping to get someone to buy out Irsay because while he might sell part of the franchise, you can bet he'll keep the controlling share.

Not hearing or not believing, Baltimore kept posturing, even sliding to the level of speculating about whether condemnation under the right of eminent domain might be brought into play to force Irsay to stay.

So one snowy night while they all slept, figuratively speaking, the big Mayflower moving vans were rolling—and the once beloved Colts were off to Indianapolis. Baltimore and Maryland would begin one of history's longest and most bitter blame-the-other-guy crying spells over a lost professional sports franchise. Returning from vacation, I wrote in April 1984: "Time to quit crying and share the blame for loss of the Colts."

Taking note of Mayor William Donald Schaefer's view that Irsay "sneaked out under cover of darkness," I likened it more to a guy who kept ignoring his girlfriend's desire for marriage, or at least a commitment, until it was too late, "And she didn't even call to say good-bye."

In baseball, the Orioles often seemed to be flying into stiff winds on the racial front. Baltimore Orioles president Clarence Miles told a Frontiers Club audience in 1955, "We'd be the most stupid people in Baltimore if we didn't want a colored player." He informed his listeners that "even as recently as last week" the Orioles had offered the Cleveland Indians $25,000 and two players for outfielder Dave Pope.

That got me to scoffing. Pope, "as recently as last week was the hottest player in the American League," banging away at a .443 pace with five home runs in seven days as a stand-in for injured Larry Doby. I didn't think $25,000 would go very far in the baseball marketplace and figured the Orioles would have to look long and hard to locate two players they could afford to part with that any other major league team would want.

In addition, I thought Miles should check with manager Paul Richards before entertaining people with the notion the Orioles wanted Pope because shortly before, Richards had asserted the team was not interested in the left-handed outfielder as the team had plenty of left-handers.

In a June 1969 column, I had a chance to make sure a former white Orioles player received the credit he deserved for a "first" in player relations. The UPI's Darrell Mack did a piece about Curt Blefary, then a first baseman with the Houston Astros. Blefary roomed with Don Wilson, a black pitcher with the Astros, when the team traveled. Mack said, "It is the first time in major league baseball history that a colored and white player have roomed together, although it has been done in football."

Blefary told Mack, "It's time all this silly stuff that's been going on for 200 years stopped. What the hell difference does it make? We get along and that's what counts."

The additional credit I wanted to add concerning Blefary, a helluva person, was the fact that three years before, when he was with the Orioles, Blefary had roomed with Sam Bowens, another black teammate.

Another Orioles player I always felt a special relationship with was everybody's favorite on the team for both his talent and his image as a warm and sensitive human being—third baseman Brooks Robinson.

My off-field stories about Robinson included his working around an already busy schedule to be my first on-camera guest when I went on TV as a rookie in a new medium. Robinson also agreed to do a star-with-family interview for another *Afro-American* associate that might have been the first time he'd appeared in print with photos of his wife and children. The article was for a magazine slanted to children and Robinson did it "because I never turn down a genuine effort on behalf of kids." Mentioned also was Robinson's throwing out the first ball (with Don Buford) to get a Little League venture started in the ghetto; his showing up with Ellie Hendricks to talk at a hospital for the blind; and appearances at every hospital for children in the area.

Writing about Brooks in 1977 after the Orioles had announced plans for a day for him, "A to Z" told about Robinson's first visit to a race track: "Two years ago when Pimlico race track set aside a day to salute the old, popular jockey, Skeets Holland, a pair of 65-year-old eyes dropped happy tears when Brooks Robinson and Paul Blair walked up to shake his hand. Somehow word had leaked into the Baltimore baseball clubhouse that Skeets is an avid fan, a die-hard Oriole rooter, and that Brooks and Paul were his favorite players."

CHAPTER 8

LEADERSHIP BARRIERS

Leadership positions in the major league sports of basketball, baseball, and football were hard to come by for black coaches and managers, even after years of integration. My efforts to promote the hiring of blacks for these jobs over the years included providing *Afro-American* readers with running accounts of the hiring of whites, some over and over again even though they were consistently posting losing records—the old retread system.

The first black modern-era basketball coach in the pro ranks, Johnny McLendon, a veteran college cage coach with an outstanding won-lost record, was hired in 1961 by the Cleveland Pipers of the American Basketball League (ABL). He was hired by president Ed Sweeny, who liked McLendon's record and demeanor.

However, in a matter of months, McLendon was under fire from a different club president, George Steinbrenner, "for some unknown reason." People in Cleveland said one of Steinbrenner's peeves was that McLendon "does not go in for sideline histrionics." John Braucher, athletic director, St. Ignatius

118

High School, said, "Apparently the president of the Pipers does not want a Negro, a gentleman and a peerless basketball man to be his coach."

The Cleveland press, fans, and Pipers players came down on McLendon's side in the dispute. But under pressure, McLendon quit and got out as Steinbrenner desired. Pressure from the media and area fans led to Steinbrenner's selling out to Ralph Wilson of Chicago. Wilson immediately brought McLendon back as a vice president with duties that included director of player personnel, assistant director of public relations, and member of the board of directors. Steinbrenner remained with the team as the second of two vice presidents. I called it "a living example of the old saw about being kicked upstairs."

A head count of coaches, managers, and front office personnel for one of my April 1963 columns turned up a couple of black coaches in baseball: John "Buck" O'Neil of the Chicago Cubs, and Gene Baker of the Pittsburgh Pirates. In football, Buddy Young of the Baltimore Colts and Emlen Tunnell of the New York Giants held key instructional posts, and in basketball, Earl Lloyd of the Detroit Pistons was an assistant coach. At the time, basketball was 38 percent black; baseball, 24 percent; and football, 18.8 percent.

The few blacks in leadership roles prompted Dady Brown of Plainfield, New Jersey, a lettered four-sport star at Virginia State, to remind me of "a sort of blackout on tan coaches in the major colleges and universities," and especially the military academies. Colonel Raymond Murphy, athletic director of the U.S. Military Academy, had written Brown explaining that "as nearly as I have been able to determine, we (Army) have never had (colored) applicants for a position within our coaching staffs."

Professional basketball's leadership in sports race relations was advanced in April 1966 when NBA all-star Bill Russell was named head coach of the Boston Celtics. That prompted me to write:

> The Celts have always led the field in the NBA. They broke the color line 16 years ago with the hiring of Chuck Cooper, who had been a star at Duquesne University. For some time thereafter, Cooper was the lone pioneer. Then came the Nat (Sweetwater) Cliftons, the Don Barksdales, Davage Minors, et al. And it was the Boston bravery of Red Auerbach that dared condemnation by fielding a starting team of Willie Naulls, Tom Sanders, Sam Jones and K. C. Jones with Russell, all of

whom were just as tan as Bill. The thought was preposterous until Auerbach had it.

Cooper, of Duquesne University, was signed by Boston in April 1950. Clifton and Earl Lloyd joined the NBA the same year. Lloyd, a product of West Virginia State College, went on to become the first black coach in the NBA when he retired from the Detroit Pistons as a player after the 1959–1960 season.

Student protests at Michigan State University in 1968 brought about the hiring of the school's first black coach, Don Coleman, a former All-American at MSU, but Coleman gave it up after a season, saying football had changed too much for him since his playing days, which had ended seventeen years before he was hired. He took another job with the university. I provided names of several players who would have been better choices because they had been part of the game in more recent years, but I knew Michigan State had gotten the message, as did UCLA, which hired Earl Robinson, and Southern California, which added Willie Brown.

My 1969 review showed that Lenny Wilkens had become the second black coach in the NBA when he took over at Seattle, then became the only one upon the retirement of Bill Russell. For a couple of months, John McLendon coached the Denver Rockets in the American Basketball Association (ABA). This also was the year in which Hank Aaron of the Atlanta Braves went on record declaring that after their playing days, blacks wanted to become managers and get front office jobs.

In February 1970, when I again expressed concern about blacks not being picked as managers in baseball, I pointed to a previous column that listed the nine managers hired between the All-Star game and the World Series without a black person even being considered. The point, "That's what baseball has done lately, fellows."

Joe Reichler, a former AP writer, then director of public relations for major league baseball, would tell me later in 1970 that Bill White, former first baseman in the National League, had turned down the chance to manage the Seattle Pilots in 1969. At the time, White said he was happy with his broadcasting job in Philadelphia. The Seattle franchise was transferred the next year to Milwaukee—under new ownership.

An open letter to Frank Robinson took up all of my column in an April 1970 issue. It dealt with a *Look* magazine article on Robinson. I adopted the tactic of suggesting the magazine had been putting words in Robinson's mouth when it quoted him as saying things such as "I don't think the baseball field or a clubhouse is the place to discuss these things (integration of the colored player's role in society)." Tongue-in-cheek, I said it probably was okay for *Look* to say that Frank Robinson was careful not to follow the dialectic of pitcher Bob Gibson, who'd suggested it was time to stop all the bull and hire a black baseball manager, because it wasn't quoted. I went on to doubt *Look* was accurately quoting Robinson when he said other players critical of him "took the same stand when they were playing baseball. I mean Jackie Robinson . . . now he's taking pop shots at us for not being more active in civil rights . . . that's not right or fair."

I kept feigning belief that *Look* was behind F. Robinson's statements:

I know you didn't throw that dart at Jackie because it was at the Netherlands Plaza Hotel in Cincinnati where you played with the Reds, that Jackie took it upon himself to stop that business of "off limits in the dining room" for colored members of visiting teams . . . and Jackie put up with it those first two years that he was under oath to Branch Rickey to "take it easy," then took off the lid. He repeatedly presented himself at the Netherlands dining room and made them turn him away. When the Dodgers jumped him about "creating a scene," he calmly told them they were paying him to play baseball, not to sell his dignity. From that day forward, Walter O'Malley hated his guts.

Rickey left the Dodgers at the end of 1950 and went to the Pittsburgh Pirates. In 1956, O'Malley's Dodgers worked out a deal and traded Jackie Robinson to the New York Giants—but Robinson surprised everyone. Instead of accepting the trade to the Giants, he announced his retirement in an exclusive article in *Look* magazine. Robinson took an executive position as a vice president with Chock Full O'Nuts.

One of the baseball players who never dreamed of managing and didn't think much of managers, was Dick Allen. When we talked after he was the American League's MVP as a member of the White Sox, he declared, "All you have to do to be a manager is know how to write your players' names (on the lineup card) . . . There isn't anything such as a good manager. Take Walt Alston of the Dodgers. What gives him the authority to tell me if I'm doing something wrong? . . . He had one at-bat in the big leagues and he struck out."

Turning to the days when he played in Philadelphia where he was greeted with "go home nigger" signs and cruel racial taunts, Allen told me, "When they brought in Bob Skinner, one of the first things he said was he knew how to handle Dick Allen . . . Now how asinine can that be? . . . you don't handle human beings . . . you handle horses . . . And I handle my horses better than baseball treats its people."

The update on baseball coaches by April 1973, when the St. Louis Cardinals added Johnny Lewis, a former pitcher, as first base coach, was five in the National and two in the American. Lewis joined Ernie Banks of the Cubs, Larry Doby of the Expos, Jim Gilliam of the Dodgers, and Dave Ricketts of the Pirates. The two American League coaches were Elston Howard of the Yankees and John Roseboro of the California Angels.

I didn't get excited about every high-level appointment. When Joe Cronin, president of the American League, announced in July 1968 the appointment of Jesse Owens to a job on the league's public relations staff, I wrote him a "Dear Joe" letter asking him:

> Please don't do us any more favors . . . You can't convince me, Joe, that Jesse wasn't handpicked by you, mainly because he's been running around the country preaching the status quo for members of his race . . . Is a fellow like Monte Irvin too outspoken or ambitious? Or Joe Black, or Larry Doby, or Brooks Lawrence or George Crowe, all former major league baseball players?

I considered Cronin's choices of the two men "you picked in desegregating previously all-white baseball areas are alike in their thinking . . . both Owens and our first colored umpire, Emmett Ashford . . ."

A bit over a month later, I had a different view in the column to baseball commissioner William D. Eckert, praising him for an appointment to his staff:

> I don't think it is possible that you could have selected a better man than Monte Irvin, and I have little doubt that every colored person in the

land shares my view. The former New York Giants outfielder qualifies in every respect. He is personable, intelligent and articulate, he knows baseball and baseball people . . .

Basketball, relatively speaking, continued to set the pace in utilizing black talent, "A to Z" said, in commenting about the appointment in 1974 of Lenny Wilkens as coach of the Portland Trail Blazers. The column said neither football nor baseball "can match the cage sport in its awareness of the equal opportunity concept." Basketball would open the 1974–1975 season with two black general managers and six head coaches.

The general managers were Wayne Embry of the Milwaukee Bucks, and Bill Russell of the Seattle SuperSonics. Russell also was coach of the SuperSonics. The other coaches were Al Attles, Golden State Warriors; Ray Scott, Detroit Pistons; K.C. Jones, Washington Bullets; and Wilt Chamberlain, San Diego Conquistadors of the ABA.

Hank Aaron loosed a baseball bombshell in Atlanta when he unexpectedly was brought into the managerial picture and had a surprising reaction. Along with announcing the firing of manager Eddie Mathews from the Braves, Eddie Robinson, executive vice president, informed the press Hank wasn't interested in the job and the younger Aaron, Tommie, was doing an acceptable job as coach of the Braves minor league team in Savannah. Hank then stepped to the plate saying he would, indeed, be receptive to any offer made to him that would serve to break the ice for a black manager. That got a lot of publicity. I had talked to Aaron in Atlanta a few days before the exchange and was certain Hank didn't actually want to manage.

I did think the manager who was eventually hired, Clyde King, a personal friend of mine, had been a flop at San Francisco when the team had the likes of Willie Mays, Willie McCovey, Gaylord Perry, Juan Marichal, Bobby Bonds, and Ron Bryant. This was another occasion for me to list a number of managers I put into the retread category: "This column could go on and on reciting cases in which stubborn, complexion-conscious ownerships have operated on the theory that they can convert brass into gold."

A black coach had to win the NBA crown in 1975 when Al Attles's Golden State Warriors defeated the Washington Bullets and coach Bernie Bickerstaff. Bill Russell had coached the Celts to titles in 1969 and in 1970, but this was the first time a coach who had come out of a black college,

North Carolina A&T, had accomplished the feat—and he'd taken a down-and-out team in the 1969–1970 season and built it into a championship squad.

As much as I tried to spur the hiring of black baseball managers, one owner seemed believable in his decision to pass over a former star because "I like you too much to make you one."

The former player thus passed over was Ernie Banks of Cubs fame. Banks, who had played shortstop with the Kansas City Monarchs, joined second baseman Gene Baker with the Cubs to form major league baseball's first black "keystone unit." The passing was done by Chicago Cubs magnate Phil Wrigley—and because of my respect for Wrigley, I believe the reason given represented his honest view. Wrigley got battered by many in Chicago for skipping over Banks, some saying he didn't want to be the owner to hire the first black manager. When the criticism was rampant, Wrigley called Banks in from his job as a minor league batting instructor to talk with him about the decision. Wrigley told Banks if he wanted to manage, he'd start him in the farm system and work toward that goal, "But to be perfectly frank, I think you are too nice to manage. Being a major league manager is like being a kamikaze pilot. But if that's what you want, and you tell me that's what you want, we'll start working in that direction." He said Banks didn't give a flat answer either way, giving the impression he was not that anxious for the job.

Baseball finally lowered the managerial barrier on April 8, 1975. Frank Robinson took the field as manager of the Cleveland Indians. To me it was "a special day in the archives of organized baseball."

But almost immediately, I detected bad omens shaping. Ace pitcher Gaylord Perry, who'd asked to be traded within forty-eight hours of the Robinson announcement, got into a hassle with Robinson over a difference of opinion on conditioning, and general manager Phil Seghi had to step in to settle the dispute. That prompted a column reminder that "life in the boss teepee has lasted just over two and a half years, on an average," although there had been some illustrious names among the tribe's managers.

Seghi didn't wait until World Series time to rehire Robinson for the next season. I wrote that "Robinson is entitled to high praise for proving the point he had been trying to make for nearly five years: that a black man, and this black man in particular, can do an adequate job of running a big league ball club. Frank accomplished that beyond question."

I owed it to my readers to share this: "Regrettably, Robbie and I have not been on the best of terms since I criticized him in a 1970 "A to Z" for statements attributed to him in a *Look* magazine article and in national network television interviews."

I wasn't sure Robinson's success would change things drastically. The question, "whether it would have any effect on baseball's ongoing game of musical chairs remains to be seen . . . But in all likelihood, it will continue to use white retreads whenever a change of field leader is dictated."

Robinson was fired in June of 1977. When I reached him by telephone past midnight, Robinson said:

> I didn't doubt that my days were numbered, too many things were happening—on the field, in the clubhouse, with the media and in the front office. Really, I have no regrets. I can look in the mirror and see the face of a man who did the job the best he knew how . . . I don't feel sorry for myself.

It was ironic, I wrote, that "the first black manager in the major leagues was undone to a great extent by black players. His open feud with Rico Carty was just one of two bitter clashes in which his authority was challenged.

"Not so widely publicized was Robinson's continuing rift with infielder Larvell Blanks, who resented being benched after a dull start afield and at the plate this spring."

The team's second baseman, Duane Kuiper, told UPI, "Frank had a meeting with us. He shook everybody's hand and left like a pure man."

Another breakthrough came in 1978 when the Atlanta Braves named Bill Lucas, a former brother-in-law of home run king Hank Aaron, as general manager. He was in a wonderful mood when I interviewed him for my March 21, 1978, column. Despite the problems he had with a team that had finished at the bottom of the league standings the last two years, and his consideration of 20 percent cuts for many, this was one of the yarns he shared:

> I didn't really know whether I should laugh or cry when so many of the players came in to see me and demanded raises. I had one pitcher come

to me and say that the reason he had a losing season was because of the rest of the team. I pointed out that his won-loss record was worse than the team's . . . When I mentioned he had given up more than a hit an inning he blamed the defense. When I pointed out that he had more walks than strikeouts, he blamed the umpires.

Larry Doby, an outfielder for Bill Veeck in Cleveland and Chicago, was named manager of the Sox in 1978 by Veeck. Doby was unique among black players who came up from the old Negro National League in that when Veeck plucked him from the Newark Eagles to become the first of his race in the American League, he went straight to the Indians without spending a day in the minors.

Except for the National Football League, blacks had now penetrated into leadership roles to such a degree that the opportunity to serve increasingly meant firings also were rolling down the pike.

In February, I noted that the firing of Willis Reed as coach of the New York Knicks and the dismissal of Tom Sanders by the Boston Celtics had not affected results for what I termed "just . . . bad teams."

In 1986, Wayne Embry took over as general manager to lead the rebuilding of the Cleveland Cavaliers. At age forty-nine, he was moving into his third high-level front office post. He was the first black to obtain such a job in 1972, when he was named vice president and general manager of the Milwaukee Bucks. He moved on to the Indiana Pacers as vice president and consultant prior to accepting the Cleveland challenge.

When I updated the baseball managers' situation again in July 1986, there had been eleven baseball managers hired since the last black man held a manager's job in 1984. So far, I figured, the total number of years served as managers by three persons added up to fewer than eight: "Frank Robinson had approximately five and a half with the Indians and Giants, Maury Wills had less than one at Seattle and Larry Doby had a similar trial at Chicago."

I suggested, "Ask any of the 26 club owners why they have never gotten past the 'we're considering' stage, and they'll offer a variety of excuses which even they realize won't wash."

On the verge of the 1990s, the National Football League got the first modern-era black coach when Art Shell was chosen for the Los Angeles

Raiders by Al Davis, general partner. Shell had been a star player for the Raiders.

As a measure of how far colleges had come by 1993, Rob Evans was serving as head coach of basketball at the University of Mississippi in Oxford. Elsewhere in major Dixie colleges at that time, Nolan Richardson was the veteran, into his eighth year at the University of Arkansas. Wade Houston was at Memphis State, and Perry Clark was handling the basketball program at Tulane University.

In football, the quarterback is considered the field general, team leader, the boss; he's a guy who's intelligent, efficiently skillful, and cool under fire—and for the longest time, colleges and professional teams denied blacks who actually possessed all those attributes the opportunity to function at that position.

Professor John Dalton of the University of Maryland economics department summed up the picture in a letter I used in a December 1958 column.

There have been great strides in abolishing barriers in football (but) it seems . . . one particular spot appears to be reserved "for whites only"—the quarterback. No doubt (this is due to) rationalizations about confidence in leadership and the necessity for harmony. When a pro team or even a major college team entrusts the signal calling to a colored boy, then integration can be said to have been firmly established.

My research at the time indicated that George Taliaferro, a star at Indiana, had been the only tan athlete to fill the position for any length of time in the pros, when he played in 1954 for the Baltimore Colts. (The Colts regular quarterbacks weren't getting the job done.) Willie Thrower of Michigan State played a few minutes of two games for the Chicago Bears in 1952. At the college level, Bernie Custis of Syracuse ran the team the Orange fielded in the 1940s, and Sydney Williams was second string at Wisconsin. The Philadelphia Eagles took a look at Custis in 1951, but he ended up drifting into Canadian football. The Green Bay Packers in 1958 used Charley Bracken as a kickoff specialist and occasionally as a defensive back. Williams was named to the East squad for the East-West Shrine Bowl but as a halfback.

Here's how the procedure worked: A college or pro coach inheriting a star black high school or college quarterback simply switched him to another position, usually running back or defensive back.

Standout Florida A&M coach Jake Gaither, who was betting me that his quarterback, Jim Tullis, wouldn't be taken by a pro team, sized up the problem this way:

> The trouble in the pro league is that every team has some prejudiced players—not all from the South either. They'll play alongside colored boys but they won't take direction from them. Only lack of opportunity keeps colored athletes from playing quarterback with the pros, a lack of opportunity that stems from bias—nothing else.

In 1961, Sandy Stephens of the University of Minnesota led his team against Washington University in the Rose Bowl. Before that, the closest a black player had come to playing quarterback in the Rose Bowl was in 1922 when Washington and Jefferson would line up Charley West behind center but have tackle Russell Stein move out to end and call the signals from there. West, who became a dentist in Alexandria, Virginia, led his team to an 0–0 tie with California. Stephens ended up playing in Canada after his hopes were dashed by the Cleveland Browns.

The New York Giants seemed interested in using Pete Hall, a fine quarterback from Marquette, but with the team's acquisition of Y. A. Tittle, Hall had no chance. Eldridge Dickey of Tennessee State drew raves as a quarterback in 1966. He was one of the young quarterbacks who said they would not play any other position unless beaten out at quarterback; he wanted the opportunity to try out for the position.

One of the fanciest quarterbacks to see a bit of action was Marlin "The Magician" Briscoe, a 5-foot, 10-inch, 177-pounder who, for a time in 1968, thrilled Denver Bronco fans for coach Lou Saban. He was the first of his race to play the position in the AFL.

In February 1969, I reported the pros had drafted three black quarterbacks: Freddie Summers of Wake Forest, Cleveland Browns; Onree Jackson of Alabama A&M, Boston Patriots; and one who would be around for a while, James Harris of Grambling, Buffalo Bills. It was the same draft in which the Buffalo Bills plucked running back O. J. Simpson, who would turn out to be one of the game's biggest names.

Summers, who got converted to defensive back, was credited with being the first member of his race to play quarterback for a Southern school. Eddie McAshan of Georgia Tech was played up as having been the first for a "deep south" squad. He proved to be a big star but was dropped by coach Bill Fucher when he missed practice for a game in retaliation for being denied tickets to a game for his parents. For three years, McAshan had gone through hate letters, threatening calls, and the battering of the car his father had given him. He took the ticket turndown as proof that even the athletic department held him in disdain despite his contributions.

At one point in 1974, I would name Joe Gilliam of the Pittsburgh Steelers, James Harris, then with the Los Angeles Rams, and Karl Douglas, who taxied for two seasons with the Baltimore Colts before stepping into a starting job in the Canadian League, as the only "black quarterbacks to last longer than a cup of coffee in the pro ranks." I remarked, as have others, that they faced the "throw too hard" stigma. "Isn't it ridiculous," I asked, "to suggest that these fellows who compiled brilliant records passing to college boys throw the ball too hard for pros to catch it?"

Gradually, black quarterbacks were gaining respectability in the pros. In January of 1975, I observed that for players not supposed to be able to "get the job done," Joe Gilliam had led Pittsburgh to six victories before Terry Bradshaw resumed his starting role on the way to the Super Bowl, and James Harris had won the Pro Bowl MVP trophy for pacing an upset, come-from-behind win by the National Football Conference (NFC) team.

Another piece of 1975 news that made my column was the decision of John McKay, University of Southern California coach, to accept the coaching job at Tampa Bay. McKay had never shied away from using black quarterbacks, among them Willie Wood, Jimmy Jones, and Vince Evans, who later made a name for himself in the pros.

By 1976, when New York Jets quarterback Joe Namath was thirty-three and, from my point of view, "had been wooing (Carroll) Rosenbloom and the Rams shamelessly in the public prints," I suggested that Namath at the time was no better than James Harris, then playing first string for the Rams ahead of backups Ron Jaworski and Pat Haden. Namath was claiming he could take the Rams to the Super Bowl. Eventually, Namath would get the job, but the Rams wouldn't get the Super Bowl. Harris would be traded to the San Diego Chargers. And that's where Dan Fouts was in business.

Before the changes took place, I went to bat again for Harris in response to criticisms by broadcasters:

Last year, it was Frank Gifford and Alex Karris (on ABC) second-guessing the Rams quarterback about his play selection throughout a game with the Cowboys at Dallas, completely missing the obvious fact—one every other viewer was able to see—that the plays were being sent in to him by the Los Angeles coaches.

The other Sunday, it was Pat Summerall and Tom Brookshier (in the CBS booth) knocking Harris's passing technique at the same time James was throwing for a record 436 yards against the Dolphins in Miami—with a sprained thumb, no less. The Rams won that one, too, for the ex-Grambling star as they had won the earlier one from the Cowboys.

As 1977 was fading, Doug Williams, the sensational Grambling quarterback, was named to AP's All-America team at his position, a first. UPI named him to its second team, behind Guy Benjamin, AP's second team choice. The following year, he would be taken by Tampa Bay to begin a career that would be highlighted by a scintillating Super Bowl victory in the first appearance in that extravaganza by a black starting quarterback. But it wouldn't be for Tampa Bay.

Because the NFL was still using the old dodge about tan quarterback prospects not being tall enough or smart enough, I reminded the drafters in early 1978 that Warren Moon, who had guided Washington State to an upset Rose Bowl victory over Michigan, was 6 feet, 4 inches tall and an honor roll student. No use. He was ignored and went with the Edmonton Eskimos in Canada, where he led the team to five Grey Cup victories in six years. By the time he moved to Seattle as a backup quarterback for the 1997 season, he was pushing forty-one years of age and had racked up an astounding NFL and CFL (Canadian Football League) record of 65,015 combined yards and 398 TD passes, 43,787 of the yards and 254 of the TDs in the NFL (Houston). He was picked to start for Seattle in 1998. J. C.

Watts, the effective Oklahoma quarterback who later became a Republican congressman from his state, also escaped to Canada when the Jets wanted to switch him to another position.

James Harris and Doug Williams both played for the legendary coach Eddie Robinson of Grambling State University, who in 1996, with 405 victories, had won more games than any other college coach in the history of the game. Robinson, seventy-seven, had one more season before retirement to work out of his office on Robinson Street and coach home games in Robinson Stadium. He retired in 1997 with 408 wins, and former student Doug Williams, then a one-year coach at Morehouse College, succeeded him. Robinson entered the College Football Hall of Fame in 1998 after the three-year waiting period was waived for the first time.

When Doug Williams arrived in Tampa Bay to hook up with Coach McKay, the team had won exactly two games in two years. Despite brutal treatment from Tampa fans, Williams was made first string and held it during his five years with the Buccaneers. The fans called Williams all kind of names, sent him rotten watermelon, and stuck sewing needles in their Doug Williams voodoo dolls—but if they were seeking to put some sort of a hex on him, it backfired horribly on the fans and the Bucs. Doug took the team to three playoffs during his five years (1978–1982), but as of the end of 1996, the Bucs had not returned to the playoffs a single time in fourteen years.

McKay, who had stuck with Doug during periods when he did not play up to expectations as well as when he went through the razzing, would not support his quarterback's request for a salary of $600,000. The team figured $400,000 was all it was willing to spend on him—but went out and paid more to white successors who never matched what Williams did.

I expressed the belief that it was quite possible the Tampa Bucs never realized, maybe never cared, how their treatment of Doug Williams affected millions of blacks across the country. He was a young man in a tough situation, often taking unmerciful beatings to do what black quarterbacks weren't supposed to be capable of doing. He had built up an incredible amount of goodwill for the Tampa Bay Bucs, even among many blacks who were not football fans. They often wondered what he could do with a good team backing him. One day, they would find out.

Meantime, Moon was enjoying himself in Canada where he became the first quarterback in history—anywhere—to rack up 5,000 yards in a year, and Vince Evans was trying to stay alive playing for an inept Chicago Bears squad. So while notable progress had been made, college quarterback stars such as Phil Bradley, who set a Big Eight Conference career total offense record, didn't get a nibble from the NFL in 1981 and went on to play baseball with the Seattle Mariners.

Only two black quarterbacks were playing in the NFL in 1981, Doug Williams with the Tampa Bay Bucs and Vince Evans with the Chicago Bears. In November 1983, there was not a one—Williams was with the Oklahoma Outlaws of the United States Football League, and Evans had just joined the USFL's Chicago Blitz.

The USFL didn't last too long, but in 1984 it had five black quarterbacks: besides Williams and Evans, Reggie Collier was with the Birmingham Stallions; John Walton, a former backup in Philadelphia, was with the New Orleans Breakers; and Walter Lewis was with the Memphis Showboats.

Warren Moon, once snubbed by the NFL, was looking for an NFL team willing to make him the highest paid quarterback in the states, and the New York Giants, Tampa Bay Buccaneers, Philadelphia Eagles, New Orleans Saints, Los Angeles Raiders, Seattle Seahawks, and Houston Oilers (where he eventually landed) expressed interest.

In 1985, Philadelphia Eagles coach Marion Campbell made scrambler Randall Cunningham the number one quarterback for a team mired in the NFL East basement. He and Moon gave the NFL two black starting quarterbacks. Later in the year, the Dallas Cowboys would get Reggie Collier from the USFL as a backup.

At this time, there still wasn't a single black coach in the NFL. I began to feel that times were changing, though, because back on the college front in 1986, there were nine black quarterbacks playing in bowl games.

To finish the Doug Williams story, after the USFL folded, the only call he received came from Washington Redskins coach Joe Gibbs, who wanted a capable backup for starter Jay Schroeder. Williams pretty much rode the bench in 1986. In the off-season, only the L.A. Raiders expressed an interest in him.

During the strike-shortened 1987 season, Doug came off the bench three times to bring the Redskins from behind. When Schroeder got hurt, Doug carried on. Doug later went down and Schroeder was back. Then they turned it over to Williams. The Redskins made it through the playoffs. They were on their way to the Super Bowl to face the Denver Broncos and big-name quarterback John Elway. All week the most-asked question was how did Doug feel about being the first black quarterback to start in the Super Bowl.

Near the end of a first quarter that saw the Redskins fall behind 10 to 0, Doug went down. He got up but slumped to the ground again. When he came back for the second quarter, he was limping. It wasn't looking good. A lot of fans were holding their breath. But they need not have worried. During the most fantastic quarter in Super Bowl history, Williams engineered five touchdowns in nineteen plays, four of them touchdown passes, and racked up 228 of the total 340 yards he'd pass for that sunny day in San Diego. The Redskins won it 42 to 10.

A black quarterback in the December of his career, working on creaky knees, hopefully had put to rest any lingering doubts owners and coaches may have harbored about the capabilities of black quarterbacks—if indeed, they still needed any assurances. And that pleased me no end.

In January 1997, Williams—who had coached high school football, served as an assistant football coach at the U.S. Naval Academy and, at the time, was a scout for the NFL Jacksonville Jaguars—signed a five-year deal as head coach of football at Morehouse College, a Division 2 college in Atlanta.

Meanwhile, I was impressed by the progress in another sports sphere in which blacks had the opportunity to show leadership to the benefit of all players. In a September 1982 column I wrote, "It was Oscar Robertson (Cincinnati Royals) who spearheaded the fight in 1973 that resulted in the removal of restraints on National Basketball Association players . . . Actually 'spearheaded' is not adequate . . . Robertson WAS the fight."

With some behind-the-scenes promises of support, Oscar took the NBA to court and succeeded in having struck down the standard basketball contract that prevented athletes from shopping their services elsewhere once their original team commitments had been fulfilled. Truthfully, his success opened a financial flow that now has basketball salaries reaching staggering heights.

I felt that Robertson may have been inspired by Curt Flood, who three years earlier in 1970 challenged baseball's reserve clause, the infamous bit of contract lingo that kept all players confined to the team that signed them originally. It was something Curt and I had discussed in detail over breakfast at the rooming house where he and I lived during spring training in 1956 when he was with the Cardinals.

"He lost his suit in the U.S. Supreme Court because the majority (5-4) opinion stated that Congress had left a loophole in its antitrust act which gave baseball exemption . . . However, Flood succeeded in awakening the players' association to the likelihood that future challenges could be won . . . Because of Curt Flood—who is unknown to hundreds of today's ballplayers now reaping the rewards of his sacrificial act—there is unlimited freedom of movement among major leaguers," I wrote.

I again talked to Flood in the late 1970s at a bar he had bought down in Majorca in the Mediterranean after baseball shut him out. Flood, a center fielder who won seven Golden Gloves and was selected to three All-Star squads, died of throat cancer January 20, 1997, at the age of fifty-nine.

After the NFL's first in-season strike, I wrote:

> It could be that the average reader is not aware that the last three presidents of the NFL Players Association have been black—John Mackey, Kermit Alexander and Gene Upshaw.
>
> It also is likely that few realize that 10 of the player representatives are black—James Lofton, Green Bay; Robert Newhouse, Dallas; Elvin Bethea, Houston; Mike Davis, L.A. Raiders; Beasley Reese, N.Y. Giants; Marvin Powell, Wesley Walker, N.Y. Jets; Doug Wilkerson, San Diego; Lee Roy Selmon, Tampa Bay; and Sam McCullum (recently cut) of Seattle.

Although he had tough sledding along the way, Gene Upshaw, executive director of the NFL Players Association for a decade and a half, was recognized widely in 1998 as one of the most successful in all of sports.

Sam Lacy and his first wife, Alberta, with his sisters, Evelyn Hunton, *left*, and Rosina Howe, *right*.

Lacy, *left*, and team president and general manager Charles Hughes, *right*, with the Community Yellow Jackets cagers Lacy coached to D.C. title in early 1930s.

Sam Lacy and his late wife, Barbara, together for twenty-seven years.

Lacy as a pitcher for the LeDroit Tigers in 1922.

Lacy's daughter, Michaelyn Harris, a dance teacher in New York in 1998.

Lacy on the baseball beat in Mexico in 1943.

Lacy's son Tim, Larry Doby, and Tim's friend Donnie Bossard in Tucson during 1940s spring training. (Photo by Keystone Pictures)

Top: Jackie Robinson, *center,* with Lacy, *left,* and Dr. Carl Murphy, *right,* famed publisher of the *Afro-American,* in 1947.

Left to right: Sam Lacy, Dan Bankhead, and Wendell Smith of the *Pittsburgh Courier* boarding a flight to Santo Domingo for Dodgers training camp in 1948.

Boxer Joe Louis, *left,* and Jackie Robinson, *right,* together in a rare photo, with Lacy in Vero Beach, Florida, in 1948.

Lacy flanked by Roscoe McGowen, *left,* of the *New York Times,* and Rud Rennie, *right,* of the *New York Herald-Tribune,* in 1948 at Vero Beach, Florida.

Lacy introducing Olympic star Wilma Rudolph at Morgan State University in 1959.

Players from the New York Giants and the Cleveland Indians in Arizona for spring training in the 1950s. *Seated, left to right:* Hank Thompson, Giants; Dave Hopkins, Indians; Larry Doby and Al Smith, Indians; Willie Mays and Reuben Gomez, Giants; and Jose Santiago, Indians. *Standing:* Sam Lacy and Monte Irvin, Giants.

Lacy and former light heavyweight champ Archie Moore in a workout prior to the Moore vs. Jimmy Bivens fight in 1967. (Photo by I. Henry Phillips)

In Cooperstown, New York, at the 1971 induction of Satchel Paige into the Hall of Fame. *Standing, left to right:* Wendell Smith, Judy Johnson, Satchel Paige, Sam Lacy, and Monte Irvin; *seated, left to right:* Joe Reichler (assistant to Commissioner Bowie Kuhn), Frank Forbes and Eddie Gottlieb (booking agents), and Roy Campanella. (Photo by Andy Paranta)

Lacy inducted into the International Boxing Hall of Fame in 1978. (Photo by I. Henry Phillips)

Moses J. Newson and Sam Lacy at 1975 *Afro-American* newspaper awards ceremony.

Lacy, *right,* at 1979 testimonial dinner with Ryder Cup golfer Lee Elder.

"Sam Lacy Day" in Baltimore in 1980. *Left to right:* daughter-in-law Vernice Lacy, Lacy, then-Mayor William Donald Schaefer, and son Tim.

Honored in Miller Gallery of Greats "Black Journalists Then and Now" in 1987. *Left to right:* Sam Lacy, Mal Goode, Clarice Tinsley, Ethel Payne, and William Raspberry.

CIAA Hall of Fame event in 1986. *Left to right:* Skip McCain, Maryland State athletic director and football coach; Lacy; Sylvia Smith, granddaughter of Sid Smith, cofounder (with Charles Williams) of the CIAA; and Al Attles, coach/general manager of the NBA Seattle SuperSonics.

Negro Leagues reunion in Baltimore in 1993, *left to right:* Pam Fields, her father Monte Irvin, Lacy, and Leon Day.

In 1990, Lacy, *left,* and Frank Robinson, first black manager in major league baseball.

Top: Lacy, *center,* and two former Brooklyn Dodgers players, catcher Bobby Bragan, *left,* and pitcher Clyde King, *right,* speakers at a Jackie Robinson Day program at Frostburg State in 1996.

Center: Lacy accepting the 1998 Frederick Douglass Award from board chairman Lance W. Billingsley of the University System of Maryland Board of Regents. (Photo by John H. Murphy III)

Baltimore Mayor Kurt L. Schmoke congratulating Lacy. (Photo by John H. Murphy III)

Launching the Sam Lacy Scholarship at the 1998 United Negro College Fund (UNCF) event. *Left to right:* JaiElyn C. Obey, Maryland UNCF campaign; John J. Oliver Jr., board chairman/publisher, *Baltimore Afro-American;* Lacy; and Larry Doby. (Photo by John H. Murphy III)

In 1998, Lacy and Mamie Johnson, last survivor of three women who played with the Indianapolis Clowns of the old Negro Leagues. (Photo by Irving H. Phillips III)

Lacy receiving the 1998 special journalism award of the National Association of Black Journalists in Washington, D.C., from Mike Terry, *Los Angeles Times.*

Lacy and two members of his *Afro-American* support team, Elinor Washington, *left,* and Gainor Hackney, *right,* in 1998.

The Red Smith award, the highest honor given by the Associated Press Sports Editors, presented to Lacy on June 26, 1998, at the APSE's meeting in Richmond by George Solomon, sports editor of the *Washington Post*. Lacy is the first African-American recipient of the award. (Photo by Regina H. Boone/*Richmond Free Press*)

At ASPE meeting, Lacy and his son Tim with two of the organization's members. (Photo by Regina H. Boone/*Richmond Free Press*)

Top left: Hall of Fame–bound Lacy takes a bow at Orioles home season opening game in April 1998. (Photo by Tony White)

Top right: Sam Lacy in his office at the *Baltimore Afro-American* in 1998. (Photo by Irving H. Phillips Jr.)

Lacy addressing the Cooperstown crowd during Baseball Hall of Fame induction on July 26, 1998.

CHAPTER 9

THE FAIRWAYS, AIRWAYS

We Americans have made golfing one of the nation's most popular participation sports. It's one of the sports, along with tennis, that I place in the "elitist" category. Their historical link to country clubs has made them more difficult to master for those blacks who want to make a living in either.

Back in 1959, my column noted how some racial die-hards who were *not* members of the West Side Tennis Club (Forest Hills) appeared to be taking it harder than members when the club, after considerable hassle, agreed to accept Dr. Ralph Bunche, the United Nations official.

That same column reminded readers that the Pine Ridge Country Club at Pine Ridge on the New York–Connecticut border had rebuffed Jackie Robinson, who had been sponsored by two white friends he had golfed with there, John Hammond and Carl Rosen. It seems the wives of 8 of the 125 members objected to Jackie.

Even earlier, in 1955, I was complaining on behalf of golfers Charlie Sifford, Ted Rhodes, Bill Spiller, and others that they were severely handicapped in competition by not having the sponsorship support whites enjoyed through country clubs and major sporting goods firms.

> Each of the white pros on the tournament circuit is employed by a country club, which he represents. He has his expenses paid to the various tournament sites and he has no worries over the cost of his equipment—clothes, shoes, bags, clubs, balls, etc. These are all cared for by one or another of the several major sporting goods firms—McGregor, Wilson, Spalding and their like . . . result is they can bang away with only the usual pressure of the game.
>
> For the Siffords and Rhodeses and Spillers, it is a different story. They fit their tournaments in between working hours and, as often as not, are faced with the question of how they're going to pay their way back home. For them it's a constant realization that they've GOT TO WIN some of the prize money . . . or they may not eat.
>
> "A to Z" has pointed out to at least one of these big sporting goods companies the fact that, in view of the thousands of colored persons now playing golf, it would seem good business (no sentiment involved) to make some small gesture toward sponsoring one of the leading players of the race.

I felt obliged to say that the company apparently was still "giving it thought" even though the tournament schedule was already six weeks old.

Sifford saw the column and indicated to me just how tough it was on the circuit, saying he made as many tournaments as possible with the help of singer Billy Eckstine, whom he was helping with his game. Sifford told me:

> There are some tournaments that bar me. Strangely enough, the one at Pebble Beach which is run in Bing Crosby's name, won't let me play. Incidentally, I qualified for that one this year too . . . Consequently you can see how difficult it is for me to hold my top game. I'm either knocked out of tournament play by lack of money, or because I'm not wanted . . . One company gives me a bag and clubs, that's all . . . no balls, no entry fees, no travel expenses, no nothing . . . Grateful for that? I have to be."

When Willie Adams, prominent Baltimore businessman-sportsman learned that Burke Company in Newark, Ohio, was the only one sponsoring a black player, he went out and bought a new set of the Sifford model golf clubs, giving his other clubs to Gordon Chavis, a national junior champ from Douglass High School in Baltimore. Adams, along with D. Arnett Murphy (an executive of the *Afro-American*) and businessman Bill Dixon, brought the suit that resulted in Baltimore's municipal golf courses being desegregated.

By 1958, I was calling on black golfers to write to sporting goods firms asking them to endorse Sifford or another colored player. One friend told me that when McGregor Company was asked about putting Sifford on the payroll "they said through their representative (Tony Pena) they don't think golf is ready for sponsorship of a colored pro. You don't play enough tournaments . . . all the fellows on pay with us make the 25 tournaments and you and Rhodes make only 10 . . . It wouldn't be fair to them.

"Can you imagine such crust? The only reason Sifford and Rhodes play only 10 tournaments is that they can't play in any more. It isn't their fault if Texas and Florida and Louisiana, etc., won't let them in. What's fair about penalizing them for that?"

I did a piece in August 1958 saying "The Professional Golf Association—commonly known as the PGA—has steadfastly declined to remove its 'whites only' clause from membership qualification . . . Article 3, Section 1 of the PGA constitution reads: 'Professional golfers of the Caucasian race, over 18 years, residing in North or South America who can qualify under the terms and conditions hereinafter specified, shall be eligible for membership . . .'"

For a short time Sifford gained support of the Kroydon Corporation Golf Club Division in Illinois, which manufactured golf clubs with the Sifford signature.

You could bump into stories like this one. I was out covering the Eastern Open at the Pine Ridge course in Baltimore, when I ran into Alex Sutton, a twenty-three-year-old white youth from San Mateo, California, who caddied for Sifford and became friendly with him. He told me, "During the next two years he and I were together two or three times a week . . . he made a golfer of me. Last year two San Mateo businessmen hired me to play with them on a standing salary, with provisions in the contract that permit me to make all the tournaments at their expense . . . Charlie is still looking for a steady job."

My March 1, 1960, column reported that letters had gone out to key people responsible for the two televised weekly golf shows suggesting they might do worse than invite Charlie Sifford to participate on one or both of them. The programs were *World Championship Golf* and *All-Star Golf*. An effort was also made to get Sifford on the weekly *Challenge Golf* program.

I had an exchange in early 1963 with Henry G. Saperstein, president of Glen Films in Burbank, concerning Sifford's being invited to play on *All-Star Golf*. Saperstein wrote, "The only reason Charlie has not played up until now is that in spite of the fact he shoots as well as most of the topflight players, he has not recently won any major tournament."

I responded, pointing out that of four players being featured on the Saturday he was writing his letter, the last "recent" major win for three of them was in 1961 and for the fourth, in 1957. Also, I pointed out that Sifford was limited to challenging in only nine of the twenty-eight tourneys open to the others.

Sifford got his PGA membership in March of 1963, coming off the provisional listing. One of the letters I received during the campaign on behalf of golfers came from Joe Louis, who said Sifford had won about $35,000 in two of the last years and asked, "What does he need with a sponsor?"

Pete Brown became the first black golfer to win a PGA-sponsored tournament when he took the $20,000 Waco Turner Open in 1964.

I finally saw some returns on the campaign to get blacks featured on golf programs when the same Pete Brown, a long ball hitter from Detroit, was scheduled to be featured in May 1965 during the $165,000 *CBS Golf Classic*. He would pair with Ray Floyd against Tommy Bolt and Bob Wininger. It also was disclosed that Sifford would appear on *Shell's Wonderful World of Golf* when the series resumed the following fall.

Despite the progress on the television front, at the same time that due praise went to CBS for including at least two tan golfers among the thirty-two who would appear in the 1965 $165,000 *CBS Golf Classic*, I chastised the station for not including black announcers among the thirty-two broadcasters who would be handling announcing and color for its football games that fall. I had submitted a list of names of people who would be able to handle the job. On that subject, in an August 1964 column I'd wondered, "Couldn't CBS have found JUST ONE colored guy worthy of at least an audition? Emlen Tunnell? Buddy Young? Monte Irvin? George Taliaferro? Jack McClaren? Lowell Perry? Any of whom would be found articulate, knowledgeable and interesting. Or does CBS, like television in general, have to be prodded about everything?"

More good news came from CBS in April 1966. I had been tipped that Lowell Perry, a former halfback for the Rams and Steelers, would be among the announcers for Steelers games during the upcoming season. Perry's name was one of those I had submitted in writing to CBS.

Wimbledon winner Althea Gibson, on the golf circuit after scoring big in tennis, complained in a wire service story about discrimination because she hadn't been able to get a sponsor in two years and she couldn't play in some tournaments in Mississippi, Georgia, Louisiana, and Florida.

"A to Z" commented: "That's Miss Gibson today . . . through the years of the civil rights struggle (she) has maintained a hands-off, I don't need it attitude." Passages were quoted from her book, *I Always Wanted To Be Somebody*, in which Gibson said she got along okay with the regular American newspapers and magazines but got her brains beat out by the colored press because she wouldn't turn her tennis achievements into a rousing crusade for racial equality.

Miss Gibson's achievements in the sports world were always played up in the *Afro-American*. When she won at Wimbledon, I kicked off my July 9, 1957, column: "A Wimbledon championship has just been won by Althea Gibson . . . To my way of thinking, this is the greatest triumph a colored athlete has accomplished in my time . . ."

I observed how it is usually members of the monied class who have access to the best facilities and teachers and are able to hone their game by playing among the best, who get to Wimbledon. To put the proper perspective on her triumph, I added:

In our time we've watched the Talley Holmeses and Edgar Browns, the Sylvester Smiths and Eyre Saitches, the Lucy Slowes and Ora Washingtons, but great as they were in their day in the colored American Tennis Association, none had the audacity to speak of Wimbledon—or even Forest Hills—above a whisper . . .

This gal did it alone, a solitary brown American surrounded by strange faces, some friendly, some hostile. It was a long struggle for her, but she finally attained the top rung . . . Althea on Saturday parlayed her wooden-paddle beginnings in a Harlem side street into the most coveted crown yet won by a tan athlete.

One of my earliest stories on Gibson came when she was just gaining fame and was still a college student. I was observing her signing autographs. She was going through the entire bit of signing her name, her school (Florida A&M), etc., and I thought, "She'll learn."

The year Gibson won Wimbledon, she was received by the queen in England, she received a ticker tape parade on her return from Europe, and she took the United States Lawn Tennis Association tournament, tantamount to the national crown. I thought President Eisenhower should invite her to the White House to extend congratulations and contacted the White House. I was told the *Afro-American* was "a little late" because Miss Gibson had already received her bid to the White House and would be received by the president the next time she found it convenient to be in Washington.

The next time I interviewed Gibson, in Montreal, Canada, for my November 26, 1957, column, she told me : "I have never received an invitation to the White House. I remember a wire from "A to Z" in which some mention was made of such a bid. But aside from that, there has been no indication that my presence at the White House was desired."

A few years later, I mentioned another tennis-related example "of the little subtleties employed to minimize and manacle the progress of tan athletes in certain areas," this one involving Arthur Ashe, also a Wimbledon winner. I labeled it overkill as "it is a foregone conclusion that colored players cannot hope to threaten a takeover of the country club sports like tennis and golf."

What was happening to Ashe, I said, was "the use of the seed as a handicap . . . In every tournament he has played this summer, Ashe has borne an odd-number seeding (third, fifth or seventh) despite the fact that on numerous occasions the committee had to ignore his previous victories over players they sandwiched into slots above him.

"Now, all of this is to say that Arthur Ashe invariably finds himself in the same bracket with the No. 1 player among the entries, a sort of built-in guarantee that he'll have to contend with the adjudged best player on the scene sometime before he can expect to reach the finals. One doesn't have to be even as suspicious as 'A to Z' to regard this as a strange coincidence."

Regarding Miss Gibson, her career highlights in the 1950s included two U.S. Open triumphs and a French Open crown to go along with her two Wimbledon titles. In late 1996, at age sixty-nine, the tennis legend was in poor health and financial condition. "Friends of Althea Gibson," founded by Pam Hoffman, held a benefit for her.

Golfer Sifford and I were at odds for a time in 1966 after I expressed disappointment that he had not given credit to the man who defeated him during his appearance on the *Wonderful World of Golf.* Before long I had a letter from Sifford, complaining he had heard about my comments: "I can remember when you tried to help me, Sam, so I didn't think you would do this to me." I put a piece in the column to make it clear I had not been embarrassed because Sifford lost his match; that my reaction was about his failure in postgame remarks to pay tribute to the other fellow's success.

During this time, I had been trying to goad one or more of the black golfers in the Delaware, Maryland, and Virginia district to seek membership in the Middle Atlantic Association, which had "used every dodge in the proverbial book and has invented some new ones not previously employed to keep its ranks lily white."

Among black golfers, I was hearing that Lee Elder of Washington, D.C., had risen to the top. By 1968, black golfers were able to enter thirty tournaments. Five years before, only about fourteen were open to them.

A golf meet in 1968 caused considerable friction among members of the Cleveland Browns. Ross Fichter, a white player, and John Wooten exchanged words after colored athletes were barred from a celebrity tournament sponsored by Fichter. After they were called into owner Art Modell's office, halfback Fichter said, "Both my career and John's are in jeopardy. If all the colored boys on the team feel the way John does about this thing, then I don't see how I can continue playing here."

The tournament in question was held at the Ashland Country Club. Black players had been invited previously, but not this time. Fichter claimed it was because "they went off by themselves last year and refused to socialize." Wooten said it was purely racial. Most players said the incident wouldn't affect their play.

Two wires and three telephone calls from me in 1967 and 1969 had failed to bring any response from the Masters Golf tourney board chairman Clifford Roberts, so I was pleased to hear him say in April 1971 that the sooner a black golfer played in the Masters "the happier I will be."

However, when I examined the ten key criteria for invitations to play in the Masters, it was obvious that for colored Americans, seven of them pretty much represented barriers.

Never pleased with the way that South African golfer Gary Player spoke out in support of his country, I sought to discourage Lee Elder from taking Player up on an invitation in 1971 to visit South Africa. I accused Player of mocking the credo of the politician: "Say what they want to hear where you are."

Upon learning that Elder had accepted, I wrote:

Maybe he missed the ostrich lesson. Certainly, he has chosen to shut out the vision of what is happening all around him. Certainly he has elected to ignore the fact that he is nothing more than a tool for Gary Player and the South African attitudes which Gary fosters.

For if Player's motives are genuine, and he is truly interested in correcting a bad situation in his homeland, why has he never invited Papwa Sewgolum to "play together with whites" in Johannesburg? . . . Sewgolum is a black man who was born and raised in South Africa, and who just may be a better golfer than both Lee and Gary.

The influence of country clubs on the participation of blacks in golfing touched almost all levels. In May 1972, I had a story about a situation at Southern Methodist in which the school newspaper said the university recruited black football and basketball players but not golfers. Lee Carter Jr., an outstanding high school golfer anxious to attend the university, reportedly was being discouraged by golf coach Billy Martindale. The problem, the paper indicated, was that blacks were excluded by the Royal Oaks Country Club, which served as SMU's home course. However, Royal Oaks president Adrian Alter declared the club gave Martindale (and SMU) permission to use the facilities two years prior. "And that included anyone SMU signs up." Such "misunderstandings" often ended with no resolution.

In April 1974, Lee Elder won the Monsanto Open to qualify for the next year's Masters. He would be the first of his race to play in the prestigious event. I saw some irony in the fact he won it in the same tourney and at the same club where, eight years earlier, Charlie Sifford had been barred from the locker room until several white pros took out memberships so that he might enter as their guest.

What I knew about Lee Trevino left me wondering if he planned to accept a Masters invitation the next year. Trevino, a friend of Elder's who rode the same hustling rail on Texas golf courses to the tour as did Lee, had declined four of the seven invitations extended him since the Masters came under fire for alleged racism. Although he never had been vocal about the Augusta National policy, Lee never had used the clubhouse. On the three occasions when he did show up for the event, he dressed in his car.

In July 1982, there was concern when ABC-TV overlooked Calvin Peete during its telecast of the U.S. Open even though he was paired with Jack Nicklaus, on whom the camera kept a constant, 18-hole watch. I got a caustic telephone reaction at ABC in New York. Spokesperson Barbara Donoghue said, "I don't want to be quoted in your paper," and insisted the show was the highest rated ABC-TV ever had.

Calvin Peete was the first black golfer to win the Vardon Trophy, symbolic of the game's best scorer. He did it in 1984.

ABC-TV was at it again in June 1987, this time omitting Jim Thorpe in the U.S. Open in San Francisco. Again, Thorpe had a partner, Bernhardt Langer, who got his share of attention. I recalled how ABC had ignored Calvin Peete three years earlier while focusing on Jack Nicklaus. They actually showed Jack watching Calvin putt, but kept Peete out of the frame.

I accused ABC of displaying a blatant lack of sensitivity. To me it was clear evidence that despite its hiring of people like O. J. Simpson, Reggie Jackson, and Lynn Swann, some of its pronouncements on race relations were pure lip service. Moreover, "While Thorpe with a final score of 284, received no attention whatever on the final day, the ABC camera kept visible Mac O'Grady (284), Larry Mize (283), Lennie Clements (284), Ben Crenshaw (283), Seve Ballesteros (282) and even Keith Clearwater with his 288."

As might be expected, there were observers who assumed the networks were in cahoots with the country clubs in striving to downplay the participation of black golfers, or else they were bowing to concerns regarding the possible views of their advertisers.

Then there was the case in Ocala, Florida, in 1989. At the Golden Hills Country Club, a postwedding golfing party was ruined when the club refused to let the black member of the group play. It turned out that when it was realized he was Charlie Vinson, Emmy Award winning director of the Cosby Show and producer of numerous other television productions, the club would have let him play, but Vinson then refused, saying, "I'd feel very uncomfortable playing here now."

Among other publicized cases was the one in which the Cherokee Country Club in Knoxville was expected to turn down Wade Houston, the new basketball coach at the University of Tennessee, Knoxville. Memberships for top athletic department officials were paid for by the university. President Lamar Alexander adamantly declared the school "can't be part of any arrangement that even raises the possibility that a white coach might be treated one way and a black coach another." The university's athletic director and football coach resigned from the club. Houston's application was accepted, but he did not join the club.

Major changes were on the horizon in 1990 when PGA of America president Patrick Reilly announced that "exclusionary membership practices of a host site are a factor which must be considered" in the selection of a host for the PGA championship. The action grew out of the Shoal Creek Golf Club's unwritten policy that barred blacks. It was the host site for the championship. Reilly said that as a leader in golf, "The PGA also recognizes its obligations to foster and promote equal opportunity in the game."

It seemed to me that to a considerable degree, both television and country clubs were maintaining some of their old practices. In June 1991, CBS managed to ignore Calvin Peete. On the first day, he was at three under par, three strokes off the lead, "Yet, there was neither sight nor mention of him to TV viewers."

The big blow to country clubs interested in hosting golf tournaments came when major businesses announced that sponsorship money could dry up if changes were not made. Defiant Hall Thompson of the all-white Shoal Creek Country Club had declared the club would not be pressured into accepting black members. "The country club is our home and we pick and choose who we want," he said.

I reasoned that those private clubs interested in big tournaments with television coverage would come around. But I also figured that, partly because of economics, there probably would be no gold rush of blacks to enter the expensive country clubs.

On a related subject, the NAACP's Legal Defense Fund did a survey of the use of black athletes in commercials in the New York City area; it found just seven during a six-week period and I wrote:

> For some reason or other, Madison Avenue—where the bulk of TV commercials have life breathed into them appears determined to drag its feet. From all indications, Madison Avenue and the countless hundreds of sponsors represented there are firm in the belief that such New York pros as Walt Bellamy, Willis Reed, Matt Snell, Elston Howard, Al Downing, et al., neither shave, clean their teeth, groom their hair, eat cereal, smoke cigarettes or drive cars.

Columnist Hal Humphrey drew a comment from me regarding his piece on TV commercials, the gist of which was that the NAACP's Legal Defense Fund might find better use for the time it was spending urging the Federal Communications Commission to investigate the "possibility of racial bias in television commercials." Humphrey went on to wonder why blacks would want to play silly roles like the stupid teacher, the salesman with bad breath, or the guy with the headache "like two bull goats pounding." He suggested the ad agencies might be looking out for the image of blacks in not wanting to use them in such silly spots. "The people chosen for these roles generally are unappealing and common looking, and aren't creating the kind of image colored people need about now," Humphrey claimed.

Part of my rejoinder was to wonder where Humphrey was during the last hundred years, when whites were trying to make blacks look ridiculous and the ad agencies Humphrey suggested may be "trying to protect us" were creating the "Little Black Sambo" and grinning "Aunt Jemima"? I wondered why white athletes wouldn't seem to be lowering their dignity by going on screen to sell a product but a black would.

On November 2, 1971, there was another of those tongue-in-cheek letters in the column to "Dear Mr. Businessman." It started: "I had a real, down-to-earth belly laugh the other day. Someone suggested that you, or your competitor up the block, and possibly both of you, are prejudiced. Can you imagine anyone having the audacity to make such a statement . . . It was so ridiculous that I laughed so hard that tears came to my eyes."

I then eased into some of the reasons Baltimore Bullets star Earl Monroe was asking to be traded, noting that many of the white players in the area hang around in the off-season, having a stake in the city, but guys like Monroe, Frank Robinson, John Mackey, Don Buford, and Gus Johnson pulled out of Baltimore as soon as their seasons ended.

Going on with the letter, the skeptics were pressing: Ever hear Frank do a commercial? Don't his children drink milk as do Brooks Robinson's? Wouldn't Frank's clipped way of talking be as intriguing as Brooks's Arkansas drawl? Have you ever heard or seen an athlete more articulate and knowledgeable, and who makes a better appearance than Gus Johnson or John Mackey?

Taking over from my skeptic stand-in, I reminded the businessmen how entranced they appeared to be at the past winter's Scholar-Athlete Awards dinner as Earl Monroe delivered one of the most electrifying extemporaneous speeches this town had ever heard—it was obvious the man could talk. So maybe Monroe was way ahead of me. Maybe he was right to take his chances in another more promising town, where his future wouldn't end when his knees broke down.

With Hank Aaron of the Braves two homers away from shattering Babe Ruth's home run record, Magnavox announced it had signed Aaron to a five-year million dollar deal to hawk its products on TV. I did a positive column on it but also suggested major media columnists might be overstating the progress represented when they concluded that black athletes could no longer complain about being bypassed in favor of white players with inferior records when lush contracts were handed around for endorsements, commercials, and personal appearances. "A to Z" reeled off some names not yet in the big commercial money—Jim Brown, Arthur Ashe, Althea Gibson, and Wilt Chamberlain—noting that O. J. Simpson was beginning to win "some recognition that he can spend."

"A to Z" was back on the broadcasters' and commercial agencies' beat in December 1976. The column opened by observing that of the eighty-two men handling television and radio broadcasts for the American and National League games, only two, Bill White with the Yankees air team, and Jim "Mudcat" Grant with the Cleveland foursome, were black. It closed:

Finally, one example of the way black athletes are treated by advertising agencies and their clients in business may be found in the case of the Washington Bullets Mitch Kupchak. Before he had played his second game with the club, the former North Carolina center was on TV spieling for an area Ford dealership.

It took Wes Unseld and Phil Chenier six years and five, respectively, to get exposure on the air, and these appearances were in promos for the team. And if you've heard the cornbread-and-grits effort by Mitch, you have to believe the bypass of black Bullets was not due to faulty diction.

One day I would witness black athletes holding six of the ten top spots for endorsement income. In 1998, those athletes were Michael Jordan, Tiger Woods, Shaquille O'Neal, Grant Hill, Ken Griffey Jr., and Deion Sanders.

If a TV show had something about sports in it, I had no qualms about going after it, as was the case in this January 1969 piece:

Were it not for the fact that it is supposed to relate to basketball, an "A to Z" reaction to television's *The White Shadow* wouldn't reach print.

But the weekly CBS 60-minute stint, nauseating from its beginning, has become more objectionable with each showing.

The story line features a white basketball coach at a virtually all-black high school. It has yet to offer an episode in which the coach wasn't saving a black player from a scrape of one form or another—from shoplifting to narcotics to homicide—at the same time educating the school's black principal and vice principal.

The White Shadow, it seems, translates into CBS-TV's version of "The Great White Father."

Taking off on a case of mistaken identity when a reporter called Mike Davis "Mr. Norris" to start an interview after Oakland Athletics ace pitcher

Mike Norris opened the American League West division playoffs with a
four-hit shutout, "A to Z" said in October 1981:

> One who isn't likely to be mistaken is the fellow who hosts NBC's tele-
> casts of major league baseball, Bryant Gumbel. He won't ever be con-
> fused with ABC's Jim McKay or CBS's star Brent Musburger . . . he's
> better than both.

CHAPTER 10

SPORTS JEOPARDY

One didn't have to be a sportswriter to realize that athletes suffered a lot of self-induced tragedies. Sometimes other players took it upon themselves to purposefully endanger opposing competitors. Sometimes the jeopardy evolved out of doing what other Americans did with impunity. Pleasant or not, no matter how news came down the pike, I had to deal with it.

There was that late 1970s story out of the University of Arkansas involving three football players who were suspended a week before the Orange Bowl when an unclothed white girl was found in the room of another black team member after 2 A.M. My story asked some questions.

After coach Lou Holtz suspended the trio and they sued for reinstatement, why was the court hearing abruptly halted and the suit withdrawn after one of the accused disclosed there were approximately ten other persons (some white) in the room? Was the deal then that the three would be able to remain in school on scholarship if they dropped their suit, as they did?

Likewise, I wasn't at all clear what the young woman's pastor in Arkansas meant when he said, "She is a sinner like the rest of us but her only error in the current incident is overestimating her strength as a new disciple . . . She feels no animosity and feels it is best to let the issue die and not look back." It sounded to me as if he was trying to tell us something.

Probably the most frustrating part of this running story came for me the following December. Two of the same young men were in trouble again when a second twenty-one-year-old white girl, after leaving the athletes dorm around 5 A.M., said that she had been raped. I declared:

This latest incident points up two distressing facts. (1) That some people have a way of courting grief and (2) that there is no win for a black athlete in the social arena of the deep South . . . Common sense—and the experience of a year ago—should dictate better judgment than to allow themselves to be so enmeshed again . . . (They) evidently never heard of the admonition that "a burnt child dreads the fire."

Be that as it may, last week's major media play-up of the coed's charge . . . serves to emphasize the warnings issued here last summer. Athletes and the parents of athletes who are contemplating entering college in the deep South should carefully consider all aspects of their decision.

One which cries for attention is the question: What kind of social life can a virile young black man expect in such social hinterlands as Fayetteville, Arkansas, Auburn, Alabama, or Athens, Georgia, to name a few?

. . . Colleges leap at the chance of grabbing a top black prospect, and . . . do all within their power to keep him—until his eligibility expires. When that happens, of course, they have no further use for him as a person . . . The other cause of interest is the athlete's penchant for "forbidden fruit" . . .

There is no such thing as "consent" in the eyes of Dixie law when the complainant is a white woman and the defendant is a black man . . . whether she be 12 or 21.

Back on the subject in the spring of 1982, I listed some other problem cases that had occurred and tried to get through what seemed to be pretty thick skulls with this:

The athlete is equally to blame when this sort of thing occurs. More often than not, a topline basketball or football player becomes obsessed with the idea that he is BMOC ("big-man-on-campus") and as such he is entitled to behave in any way he chooses. Established in his own mind is the conviction that this requires him to prove he also is MSOC or "Macho-stud-on-campus" . . .

No matter how these upcoming cases turn out, there is a lesson here for all these athletes—and for every single one who follows. Sooner or later they'll learn that all humans are destined to face moments of critical decisions, but, more importantly, they'll come to realize that all women are built the same."

In November 1983, I tried to focus on another demon that helped keep afloat the unfair image of racial belittlement faced by blacks:

. . . It disturbs me greatly that a new form of typecasting seems on the verge of threatening the black person in general, the black athlete in particular.

I have to admit being confused by the overwhelming number of black athletes being caught up in the web of dope trafficking in one form or another.

Reeling off a list of twenty names from the top of my head, I pointed out that all but two were black. It came straight from the heart when I declared:

(We) have strived for so long to put the lie to the stereotype that the Stepin Fetchits and Pigmeat Markhams imbedded in the mind some years back . . . That of the shiftless, shuffling, good-for-nothing black person which, actually, represented an infinitesimal percentage of our culture.

And which, of course, was matched by a similar situation among other races. The only difference lay in the matter of public notice given to ours as opposed to the little attention paid to theirs.

. . . But, may God forbid that this relatively small group of athletes which soils my beloved world, will be permitted to introduce heroin and cocaine as replacements for the watermelons and pork chops of yesterday.

In May 1984, I thought high school graduation would be an appropriate time to repeat my "word of caution" to parents and graduates—particularly athletes—concerning the need to take great care in selecting a college:

> If the chosen school is one of those in the old South hinterlands which have been active in pursuing black prospects with such fervor, the social choices are more greatly reduced.
>
> Stay on campus and compete for the attentions of one of the half-dozen or so black females available in a predominately white clientele . . . or risk romantic entanglements that can be embarrassing and/or dangerous."

In June 1985, I denied being ready to wave the white flag of surrender on the drug issue, but had to recognize how troubling an issue drugs had become on the sports beat:

> Although it is something we hate to write about, it cannot be denied that drug abuse is the scourge of our time. It is with us, and the growing evidence is that it will be with us for a long time, if not forever—or until it comes to pass that the term "abuse" is erased by legalization.

With that introduction, I went on to praise new baseball commissioner Peter Ueberroth for coming up with a program to cope with the problem that had already resulted in twenty-five baseball players landing in drug-related trouble.

Not all the stories involving white women and black men in sports resulted in charges against the men—some were told merely for the titillation factor, apparently, or maybe as a gentle reminder.

No charges were brought against Duke Fergerson, but Jodi Zimbelman did file charges against the Seattle Seahawks in 1980, claiming she was fired because she dated the wide receiver. Fergerson was released two days after the woman was dismissed, and he went to the Buffalo Bills.

Seahawks general manager John Thompson said the woman was fired because she broke the club rule against dating other employees, not because she dated a black man. Zimbelman responded, saying she was the only person terminated for a violation of the "no fraternization" rule and alleged that she earlier had dated a white coworker with the knowledge of two members of management and without any problem. I didn't know the validity of her story, but I'd seen enough of that kind of thing to consider it plausible.

Pitcher Vida Blue was a popular man with the Oakland Athletics, winning more than his share of games at age twenty-two, but suddenly, he cut back drastically on interviews and was being slammed pretty good in the media when I dropped in to see him for an October 1971 column. Vida was talking to me about stress, the Cy Young Award, his appearance in the All-Star game, and his loss of a big game in the playoffs with the Orioles. He complained that all media people were asking the same question, and he was not a politician who could answer the same question five or six different ways. Then I cut to it: "Fine, Vida, but what about the report that you didn't clam up until a newsman asked whether your girlfriend is colored or white?"

Blue said it was true he had become reluctant to talk with the new reporters in for the playoffs but that he was still talking to local reporters he knew. He said the reluctance was "because they think they smell something" and they want to rout it out. He explained:

I'll tell you what it's all about, though. It started when a fellow I didn't know asked me whether one of the girls I had been seen with was white or black. She was white and I told him so, but it was his assumption that she was my girlfriend. And so he fed it back to Walter Scott, who edits a rotogravure gossip column called "Personality Parade."

The truth is that I meet a lot of girls in every city we visit during the season—white, black, Oriental . . . there are even a couple of Hawaiians and in one town a full-blooded Indian. When you're a ballplayer, and a popular ballplayer, you don't have to go looking for them. Every town you go into, they're at the hotel before you are. I'm single and I have a lot of friends, male and female. Some of the girls are white, most of them are colored. It's the same way with the men, too, but nobody seems to pay that any mind."

Even before the Blue case, there was a situation involving one of the big names with the Dodgers and a Hollywood glamour girl. According to the rumors, Dodgers shortstop Maury Wills, who also had a small combo that played gigs around the area, was romantically linked to actress-singer Doris Day.

At the time, Wills was the big league's base-stealing champ. Before clamming up about the rumors, Wills had denied the mentions hinted at by Walter Winchell, Dorothy Kilgallen, John Miller, and others. Having personally witnessed how the Dodgers hushed up this kind of hot topic in the past, I figured Wills was under wraps. But Wills was a Washington-born friend, so I gave it a try—several times, without luck.

On one of my calls, Mrs. Gertrude Wills answered. The temperature was sixteen degrees out in Veradale, Washington, at 7:30 A.M. But she was up getting the children ready for school and was glad to hear a voice from her Washington, D.C., hometown. Of course, she knew why I was calling from across the country. She wasn't able, or willing, to put me in touch with Maury, but she volunteered a comment of her own:

"Perhaps he hasn't received your messages and knows nothing about your effort to contact him. I do know that he has been harassed something awful since this thing started.

"Maury did make one statement that I saw. In that one, he described the story as 'ridiculous' . . . If my husband says that, it is good enough for me."

In the area of drugs, I always recalled the story Jackie Robinson shared with me in July 1970 about Jackie Jr., who had a problem for a while before getting his life together. The thing about Jackie's son was that he was never a demonstrative youngster; he and his father would usually shake hands, or pat one another on the back, but there were no hugs or that kind of thing. This is the touching story Jackie shared with me:

> Throughout his troubles with the dope business, it remained (for him) a man-and-man relationship. Of course, it appalled me, but Rachel and I had raised him to be his own man, to make his own decisions, so I had no choice but to accept his behavior.
>
> On the 31st of May, Rachel and I had sort of a picnic outing and invited about 20 of the youngsters who were being held along with Jack at

a rehabilitation center. They came and everyone had a truly enjoyable time. After it was over, each of the boys took his turn and came up to Rachel and me to express gratitude and to say what great pleasure he had derived from the affair.

Just before the group headed back to the bus for the return trip, Jack came to me to say goodbye. I smiled and held out my hand. He pushed it aside and threw his arms around me.

Everything else in a full life went by the boards. This, Sam, was my greatest thrill.

Unfortunately, Jackie Jr. died in a car accident when he was twenty-five years old.

Baseball's "beanball" was an often practiced part of the game that I despised. I didn't think any batter should have his life threatened by pitchers hurling a hard ball at ninety-odd miles per hour. I especially disliked the fact that, on average, black batters were hit much more often than were others.

Although the terms are used loosely, I made a technical difference between the "beanball" and the "brushback" or "knockdown." The latter two are thrown between the knees and shoulders; the more deadly beanball is a headhunter.

In an April 1963 column, I reported that San Francisco Giants manager Alvin Dark, in an effort to slow the opposition pitchers' assault on his star outfielder Willie Mays, declared that every hurler who threw at Mays would face a knockdown pitch when next he came up to bat.

Not sure the standing order would serve its intended purpose, I nevertheless said it was to Dark's credit that he assumed full responsibility while other managers "have taken the pious oath that they 'wouldn't think of' ordering their moundsmen to throw at rival batters, all the time maintaining a clubhouse dictum of stick it in their ear" in given situations. Dark added:

Here is the greatest player (Mays) in baseball being thrown at. And Willie McCovey and Orlando Cepeda and Felipe Alou, too. It isn't that Willie should be placed on a pedestal just because he is so great.

But if they ever threw at Ted Williams and Stan Musial like they do Willie, the world would become outraged and fines would be thrown all over the place. Knock Mays down, though, and what do you see? The umpire behind the plate laughing.

Frank Robinson of the Cincinnati Reds had something of a reputation around the National League for being quick on the temper with rival players, especially pitchers, and I thought there might be some justification for that attitude:

> The other day Robinson was hit by a pitched ball for the fifth time in 17 games. While this is entirely too often for a player to be struck by "accident," it still is low in average to what Robinson has become accustomed.
>
> Frank has been hit by enemy pitchers 100 times or more in each of the nine years he's been in the NL. He led the league (in getting hit) five of those nine years, was second twice and was fourth twice. He deserves a low boiling point, I'd say.

Larry Doby of the Cleveland Indians and Chicago White Sox was convinced it was more than coincidence blacks were hit more frequently than whites. "And don't tell me it's a matter of reflexes," he'd say. "Who has better reflexes than Sam Jethroe (former base-stealing champ of the Braves) and Minnie Minoso?"

About those two, I confirmed that Jethroe led the National League in "hit by pitcher" statistics for three years, and Minoso was tops in this department in the American League in ten of the twelve years he played as a regular.

Catcher Tim McCarver, redheaded catcher of the St. Louis Cardinals, was ejected from a game, fined a hundred dollars, and suspended for two days in June 1965 for challenging what appeared to be unfair treatment of pitchers in a beaning flap.

The story was that Pittsburgh relief pitcher Frank Carpin hit the Cardinal outfielder, Lou Brock, in the head. Umpire Ed Vargo did not warn Carpin. In the next inning, Cards reliever Barney Schultz knocked down Donn McClendon. Vargo crossed the plate toward Schultz, fingers shaking. McCarver followed him and ranted at the umpire until he was ejected.

McCarver called it unfair: "Not a word when Brock was hit and then warn our pitcher about knocking down their batters."

Both the batters were black, prompting this reaction from me:

I defy any of my fellow writers to cite any "knockdown" duel between two teams in which the guys being shot at were not colored. Has Mickey Mantle ever gone down because a Yankee pitcher threw at Brooks Robinson? Do you ever recall Ted Williams being decked because a Red Sox hurler brushed back Al Kaline or Roger Maris?"

On the other hand, I said, when the Giants and Reds play, the targets would be Willie Mays and Frank Robinson; the Phillies pitchers throw at Hank Aaron, and Milwaukee retaliates by dropping Richie Allen.

After giving more thought to the matter I wrote, "The stronger is the belief that Sad Sam Jones had the right answer when he was a hard throwing pitcher with the San Francisco Giants."

One day when Jones was pitching against the Phillies, "All during the pregame practice, Sad Sam let go with a repeated warning which he spoke in a loud clear voice. 'Knock down Willie today and the fun starts. Every damn one of you guys in the batting order goes down as fast as you come up—top to bottom, you're going to be playing like yo-yos.'

"Peace was established when the two managers and the umpires met at home plate."

Talking with me in June 1967, Frank Robinson accused pitcher Jim Coates of the California Angels of deliberately trying to bean him:

There is no doubt in my mind. I know he was trying to hit me. He has a history that dates all the way back through his minor league career of not liking our (colored) people. After he knocked me down, I tied into him from the dugout steps; reminded him that I was aware of his reputation and also that he hit me—also purposely—in the 1961 World Series when he was relieving for the Yankees against me when I played for Cincinnati.

Orioles manager Hank Bauer told me, "I would say Jim purposely tried to hit Frank. He has that reputation."

I wouldn't try to assess Robinson's assertions concerning Coates's racial feelings, but in checking the *Afro-American* score book for the October 8 game of the 1961 series, I found the notation: "Hit by pitcher, Robinson (by Ford); Robinson (by Coates)." Many of the good hitters I talked about expected to face brushback pitches in close games. But when Coates hit Robinson, the Yankees were coasting along with a 7-0 lead.

Orioles manager Earl Weaver and Washington boss Ted Williams exchanged barbs after a game in Washington following a sequence in which the Senators Joe Coleman put Frank Robinson on the ground with a pitch at his head (Paul Blair had homered before him), and Coleman had to duck a delivery from the Orioles Tom Phoebus. Williams, the former great Red Sox hitter, spoke up to say, "I've been thrown at a few times myself."

I had to comment: "Ted knows a lot about hitting, but little or nothing about being hit. In 21 years as a player, Williams was hit by pitches 40 times; that doesn't average out to twice a year."

Focusing on the damages batters could suffer from being hit, I noted that Roy Campanella had three terms in the hospital as a result of being struck; Minnie Minoso twice suffered skull fractures; and Sam Jethroe lost a number of games. A white player, Red Sox outfielder Tony Conigliaro, though not one of the usual targets, had just returned after a year and a half of forced idleness due to a vicious beaning.

Being against all head-hunting, I was just as irate over a beaning in April 1971 which did not involve any colored players. Milwaukee Brewers catcher Phil Roof was sent to a hospital after being hit in the head by a pitch from Bert Blyleven of the Twins. Brewers general manager Frank Lane accused Twins manager Bill Rigney of ordering the beanball.

"The resentment I feel is based on human emotion and not on racial antipathy," I wrote. It was gratifying to hear Lane repeat my recommendation that in such cases pitchers should be suspended for ten days and managers for three.

It had always been my position that, except in usually obvious instances of wildness, by the time a pitcher reached the majors, his control should be such "that fellow isn't likely to hit a man in the head unless he wishes to do so."

I have always remembered a beaning story about the late pitcher Sam "Toothpick" Jones that was repeated on the occasion of the announcement that Sad Sam would be inducted into the West Virginia Sports Hall of Fame in May 1981. It happened one spring training season in Clearwater, Florida, when the fireballing right-hander and the Cardinals were to play the Phillies. Several of the Phillies hurlers were considered "headhunters."

Sam was never adverse to slinging a brushback or two. After the Phillies Russ Meyer had taken shots at Curt Flood and Milt Smith, the two blacks among the first four Cardinals hitters, Sad Sam walked out to the mound, his face sober and devoid of expression. He then proceeded to knock down Eddie Waitkus, Richie Ashburn, Del Innis, and Willie Jones before being taken out for "lack of control."

Afterward, when being kidded for using the "lack of control" explanation, Sam said: "It's true, I didn't have my control. I missed every damned one of them."

It may sound weird coming from a sportswriter, but I never thought much of boxing as a sport although I covered numerous bouts and devoted considerable attention to the troubles former heavyweight champion Muhammad Ali ran into when he refused to respond to a draft call to serve in the Vietnam war because of religious beliefs.

My oft-repeated view of boxing went like this: "Any competition in which one opponent is expected to knock the other senseless (which is as near to death as one can get without donning the shroud) can hardly be called a sport."

From time to time I would take swipes at personalities in the boxing field, starting at the top and working my way down. In a July 1965 column, I was thinking out loud about a congressional hearing in Washington that struck me as "one of the most ludicrous performances ever devised by political minds . . . And, for those of us who occasionally pay attention to our Congress, this is saying something."

I did not understand how the House Commerce Committee could be holding hearings aimed at the eventual drafting of a bill designed to eliminate the ills in professional boxing without having a single black witness when "approximately eight of every ten fighters in professional boxing today belong to the darker races. How come that lily-white opinion exchange in Washington?"

Looking at the list of witnesses called by the committee headed by Oren D. Harris of Arkansas—former heavyweight champs Jack Dempsey,

Gene Tunney, and Rocky Marciano, the chairman of the New York Athletic Commission, the Colorado State Boxing Commission chairman, Cus
D'Amato, and Nat Fleischer, editor of *Ring* magazine—I wrote, "Except
for Fleischer, there was not a legitimate witness among the lot."

Dempsey, I wrote, had been to only one heavyweight fight in the past
six years; Tunney hadn't been close to boxing in twenty-eight years; and
"nice, clean cut, well-meaning" Marciano quit boxing when he couldn't take
care of his own business. I called the two commissioners politicians and
suggested a search of the records would not show Colorado as the site of
any major fight. I remembered D'Amato as the original fight-nobody,
pick-your-own-duck manager of Floyd Patterson . . . a man who acted as
though he regarded everybody as schemer, crook, gangster, thief, or what-
have-you.

Ringside at the 1964 fight in Miami where Ali beat Sonny Liston to
win the heavyweight crown, I thought I detected a lack of courage in Ali
when confronted by someone he could not cow. "I was wrong," I later wrote.

In March 1966, I had decided, "The Cassius Clay business smells," referring to the way the boxer was being treated in the Vietnam matter. I
wrote:

> Ever since my first day in our jim-crowed kindergarten class, I have
> been hearing how fortunate it is that we are living in a democracy,
> where all men are created equal, where liberty and justice prevail, and
> where freedom of speech is a right which no man or government can
> abridge.
>
> Elsewhere, the continuing story goes, a person dare not express
> himself without prior approval from the state and if he does, punish-
> ment is a foregone conclusion.
>
> A few weeks back, Cassius Clay made the mistake of believing all
> this. He spoke out against the United States participation in the fight-
> ing in Vietnam . . . and it got him in a world of trouble . . .
>
> But what did Clay say? Every single day for the past nine weeks,
> Sunday included, Senator Morse of Oregon, Senator Fulbright of Ar-
> kansas, Senator Gruening of Alaska and Senator Gore of Tennessee,
> among others, are in the national eye as bitterly opposed to the Viet-
> nam involvement."

As a result of Ali's remarks, his scheduled title defense was kicked out of Illinois and other states. I said, "The confetti hit the fan" when Ali went before the Illinois Boxing Commission and refused to apologize as it was expected he would.

Ali's draft status was changed to 1-A although "on two previous occasions, when the heavyweight champion was under scrutiny for military service, he was turned down by the military because he was found to be mentally unfit." When Ali spoke to a group of sports figures interested in his plight, he wanted all to understand his firm position:

I was offered assurances one time that I could spend most of my time in the special services. This would mean nothing more than giving exhibitions and holding clinics.

But, while it gave me guarantees of personal safety, it still meant donning the uniform of an agency waging war.

My religion is opposed to war and violence in any form. And as a minister, I preach that religion."

As for myself, I paid tribute to the late broadcaster Howard Cosell:

"When Muhammad was having his troubles . . . when he was being castigated by some blacks and a solid front of whites, Howard Cosell was the only one of the latter to support him.

White reporters and telecasters denounce him (Cosell) because they envy him. They are full of snide remarks because they became lethargic and let Cosell beat them to the hottest sports item of the generation . . ."

It certainly didn't help my overall disposition regarding boxing when I attended the announcement of Sugar Ray Leonard's initial professional bout at the Baltimore Civic Center. Longtime Maryland Boxing Commission member Chester O'Sullivan was saying how satisfying it was to see so many knowledgeable reporters on hand. Here's how it developed:

"Men like Vince Bagli and Jack Dawson and Clem Florio know the sport and do a great job of reporting it," said O'Sullivan. "And so does the boy from the AFRO."

My first impulse was to walk out. Afterward, however, I did single out the commissioner and confided to him: "I'm over 60 years of age, my friend, and I've been in the sports writing field for nearly 35 years. I have been on the Baltimore scene longer than any media person in this room, and I have reason to believe that others respect me as much as they respect any of those men you mentioned.

"So, I'm curious to know when I'll become a man in your estimation."

In 1971, a special section of the Hall of Fame and Museum in Cooperstown, New York, was formed to honor the most accomplished black stars, who had been barred from major league baseball for decades. It wouldn't be accurate or fair to link the formation of this section to Murphy's Law, which decrees that anything that can, will go wrong. However, my association with that section would bring me some flak.

I was among the supporters of the section and was one of the original ten members named to make the selections. The committee included two former owners of Negro National League teams, two sportswriters who covered these teams (myself and Wendell Smith), four former NNL players, a former umpire and major league scout, and a proprietor of two ball parks where many of the NNL games took place. Eight votes were needed to elect a player.

Shortly after Commissioner Bowie Kuhn and Hall of Fame President Paul Kerr announced plans for the special section, there was an outpouring of criticism, much of it in the media.

I opened my February 13, 1971, column thusly:

Those of you who have followed me in this space over the years know that, in racial matters, I have never been a party to compromise. That is why they will understand when I write that I vigorously resent the suggestion that such is the case in my acceptance of a position on the committee . . .

It is the "special section" reference that has raised the question in the minds of many as to whether this is a compromise—a throwback to this distasteful "separate but equal" philosophy. A few daily columnists have implied as much in their written reactions to the historic move."

Pointedly, I wrote that most daily newspaper writers never supported formation of the section and were in the forefront of the critics. Also, that Joe Reichler, former Associated Press sportswriter, and Dick Young of the *New York Daily News,* deserved a major share of the credit "for prying open the Cooperstown door . . . Once they joined our long and at times frustrating crusade . . . the two of them worked tirelessly to help bring it about."

I said of the critics that even in "the course of their self-righteous 'protest' they inadvertently admit that the rules of admission" would have to be altered to admit the older black players.

Although race was not mentioned in the Hall of Fame requirements for admission, I observed there were playing-time rules that made it impossible for most Negro National League blacks to be admitted into the main body as was being suggested by the critics. Those rigid rules for selection required a candidate to have played ten years in the majors, with at least a portion of the ten within the last twenty years. A second requirement was that legitimate records of achievement must be available as an affidavit to a candidate's right to enter the Hall.

Those rules, I explained, had "victimized some highly competent white players . . . Lefty O'Doul had a lifetime batting average of .349, and Addie Joss was a pitcher who averaged 18 victories a season with mediocre teams during his career, but each fell short by one year for meeting the standards."

I did have questions about the merit of some of the white players who made the Hall, as well as thoughts about how some of them would have fared had they been in competition with Negro League players at their positions. I wrote:

One has to wonder what was it that made Eppa Rixey so great, a pitcher who won only 15 games more than he lost (266-251) during his career . . . or Rube Marquard about whom so much is still being heard despite his 201-177 record, which represents only a 24-game edge on .500 as a lifetime mark.

Even Lou Gehrig, the highly publicized Yankee, may not have attained superstar status if he had been required to compete with Oscar Charleston or Highpockets Hudspeth for the first baseman's job . . . Would Pie Traynor have earned such widespread attention at third base if it were not for the fact that Judy Johnson and Ray Dandridge were hidden under the barrel of complexion? . . . Or Joe Cronin if he were battling the likes of Bill Yancey, Dick Lundy or Devil Wells for short-stop stardom?

Frequently over the years, I would do a potpourri of sports-related tidbits in pulling together the column. This was one of those items: "Stan McKenzie, who probably would have been the Baltimore Bullets outstanding rookie had there not been an Earl Monroe to reckon with last year, is about to become a rookie in the domestic league. He's chafing at the bit in anticipation of his marriage Friday at St. James Episcopal Church . . . The bride is Vashti Smith, daughter of former Big Ten hurdles champion Ed Smith and granddaughter of the late AFRO publisher Carl Murphy."

Another of them: While holding a part-time on-air job at WBAL-TV and wrapping up an account of a visit to Cooperstown for the unveiling of the bust for pitcher Satchel Paige, I wanted "to tell of the pleasant reunion with the one-time Newark Eagles and New York Giants star, Monte Irvin, and his wife, Dee, proud as a lady peacock of their daughter, Pam Fields, producer of her own television show on Baltimore's WBAL."

But in the summer of 1973, I was writing that "by no stretch of the imagination could I agree that Monte Irvin should be enshrined (as a star of the all-black leagues)" ahead of a number of other players whose names I reeled off. Pam Fields stopped speaking to me.

Twice in two years my Hall of Fame proxy had been used in a manner I did not approve. The first two players chosen by the Old Timers Committee were Satchel Paige, the internationally famed pitcher, and Josh Gibson, the catcher some considered the game's top home run hitter.

After that came the two I felt were not deserving of third and fourth ranking: Buck Leonard, first baseman for the Homestead Grays in 1972; and Monte Irvin in 1973. I had to get it off my chest:

Buck Leonard was a very good ballplayer, so too was Monte Irvin, but the mere suggestion that they were the third and fourth best players I saw in the years between the mid-twenties and early fifties is preposterous.

In my judgment, Oscar Charleston, the old outfielder–first baseman; Martin Dihigo, the old all-rounder; Rube Foster, the old pitcher who contributed also as an organizer, owner and promoter; and Bingo

DeMoss, perhaps the most eye-catching second baseman of the second decade, pared out to equal status in the grouping behind Paige and Gibson.

A notch just beneath would be Cool Papa Bell, Ben Taylor, John Henry Lloyd, Oliver Marcelle, Judy Johnson, Ray Dandridge, Turkey Stearnes and Dick Lundy. And in the next grouping would be String-bean Williams, Bizz Mackey, Ouija Monroe, Alex "Doubleduty" Radcliffe, and pitchers Bullet Rogan, Red Ryan, Dock Sykes and Leon Day.

In support of this position I said of my list:

Every man among them had his name appear at least once on the ballots leading up to the election of Gibson in the second year of the committee's existence. The same cannot be said of either Leonard or Irvin, although my colleagues in the assignment held both in high esteem.

After my proxy had been used to vote for a man whose name had not appeared on any preliminary ballot, I announced in February 1974, "I had no choice but to resign . . . I feel now as I have always felt: when you can't swim, get out of the water."

Having remained silent for a long time about the resignation (while receiving considerable criticism), this was added: "Inasmuch as the controversial elections were made at a time when I was a member of the committee, I felt it was an obligation for me to live with it, painful as it may be."

A number of the complaints I received referred to a column by a Washington, D.C., daily writer who accused me and other committee members of having set up a "Hall of Cronies" at Cooperstown.

I strongly believed, "The committee would not have been allowed to abandon its legitimacy had not two of its charter members died—sportswriter Wendell Smith and former player-scout Billy Yancey. Nor would it have deteriorated as it did, if some attention had been given the recommendations that Art Carter and Dick Powell replace the deceased pair."

When it was announced in 1977 that the committee would be disbanded, outspoken Mrs. Effa Manley, who with her late husband Abe, owned the Newark Eagles, told me she was furious. She declared:

It is enough that the committee was discontinued, but insult was added when it stated that the members felt they had completed their work.

To imply that just nine players qualify [Satchel Paige, Josh Gibson, Cool Papa Bell, Buck Leonard, Monte Irvin, Judy Johnson, Oscar Charleston, John Henry Lloyd, and Martin Dihigo] of the thousands who excelled in the Jim Crow era, is ridiculous.

Baseball's Hall of Fame Committee on Negro Leagues was at least supposed to partially atone for organized baseball's past sins of omission and commission.

How could anyone claiming to be just ignore Andrew "Rube" Foster, the greatest single force in the history of black baseball?

. . . That small-minded committee has done its worst, copped out and disbanded.

Because Paige was maybe the black leagues most popular player, in part for his many stories and quips, one of his true Hall of Fame stories fits here. It deals with pitcher Bob Feller, who once said he thought Jackie Robinson would be a good fielding, no-hitting player who would not make it. Feller ended up being inducted into the Hall of Fame at the same time as Robinson. Paige's induction was the occasion for the story, as I remember it:

After receiving his plaque from commissioner Bowie Kuhn, Paige, as is customary, reviewed a few of the personal experiences that are closest to his heart. "I remember," he said, "that I was playing with a team that barnstormed with Bob Feller and his All-Stars in 1947. A sportswriter in Kansas City went up to him after we had beaten him, 3-1, and asked him what he thought of Old Satch.

"The next morning the paper carried the story saying Bob had told the man if I was 20 years younger, I might be able to pitch in the majors. The next year I was on the team with him.

Then turning to the side of the rostrum where Feller sat with other members of the Hall of Fame, Satch laughed: "And here I am again, Bob."

CHAPTER 11

WOMEN, OLYMPICS, SOUTH AFRICA

A smorgasbord was my other term for the column's contents when it visited a number of sports interests under a single heading. The following in my 1960 "A to Z" could have been featured under a banner reading "Discrimination in Women's Sports, in the Olympics, in South African Sports (and Elsewhere)."

It may be interesting to note that the United States, as in past years, is devoting very little attention to the women athletes of its track and field contingent.

Swimmers, fencers and other distaff stars invariably get the full treatment from Uncle Sam's Olympic committee, and this year is no exception. As usual, the skirt brigade of runners and jumpers is virtually swept under a rug when international company is around.

"A to Z" charged eight years ago that the subordination of the country's women athletes in Olympic competition was probably caused by the traditional American practice of minimizing the importance of any venture in which colored contestants supplied the big effort. Through the years, the emphasis in men's track shifted from the sprints to the quarter mile to the high jump, etc., as tan athletes became threats in these various events . . . finally settling (for the present) at least on the mile and the pole vault. The same attitude seems to prevail now in women's track.

Eight years earlier for the Helsinki Games and four years later for the Melbourne Games, I'd wondered why this treatment existed when two tan participants had brought Uncle Sam the only gold medals captured in the past twenty-eight years by women.

The response was that there was a growing tendency throughout the world to ease up on women's sports. "A to Z" wanted to know, "But how come, then, that Russia and Australia and the Scandinavian countries hadn't heard about it. They were working just as hard in encouraging and developing their women into champions as ever before."

They shot me a line I wasn't prepared to dispute at the time: "Well, truthfully, it was pointed out, the U.S. is really more concerned about its womanhood than are the other nations. Girls who take part in competitive sports run the risk of destroying their femininity through pelvic disturbances, a prominent member of the committee told the AFRO. We've had expert judgment that athletic competition has a tendency to enlarge the pelvic muscles and crowd the birth canal."

Upon reviewing medical journal reports covering three studies on the subject, I concluded I'd been fed some "typical American hogwash." I further concluded my committee friends probably were aware of the reports and that was why they didn't try to explain Maureen Connolly, Alice Coachman, and Pauline Betz, all of whom were happily married and raising families after brilliant careers as champions in international sports competition.

From Rome, *Afro-American* correspondent Ollie Stewart was reporting there were more black coaches active in the 1960 Olympics than ever before but lamenting that only one, Ed Temple of Tennessee State University, held an assignment on the United States team. The truth was, I inserted, that Temple was not recognized as a member of the American coaching staff. Things weren't always what they seemed:

Sports fans in the United States know Temple as coach of the U.S. women's team, a job he has held for the last three Olympiads, but what they don't know is that actually he is not a member of the U.S. Olympic staff. It is lily-white, it has always been lily-white and indications are that it will be lily-white for some time to come. This is the great anachronism of modern sports.

I explained that the job held by Temple went to the coach of the school that produced the largest number of athletes for the squad and was not assigned by the U.S. Olympic Committee. The committee, I said, selects all the other coaches but "has nothing to do with women's track because it is the only sport not supervised by the National Collegiate Athletic Association (NCAA). Hence Ed's girls get him on the Olympic scene, the committee and its wishes notwithstanding."

Another question was why successful coaches like Morgan State's Eddie Hurt and Joe Yancey of the New York Pioneer Club were always passed over for the Olympics.

At the time, the Olympic committee listed the top coaches and they were chosen in turn for international coaching opportunities. Once a coach got an honorary post, his name was dropped to the bottom of the list, and he started climbing again. "This would be all right," I agreed, "were it not for the fact that Hurt's name (at the committee's convenience, possibly) reached the top just in time for the Pan-American Games last summer and just in time to hit the bottom as the Olympics came off . . . He might be forgiven for being suspicious of the U.S. Olympic committee attitude."

As for Yancey, he was dismissed because he coached a club rather than a college. However, Yancey was in Rome for his fourth Olympic, as coach for a West Indies entry.

Also in Rome as coaches for entries from other countries were: Howard University's Tom Hart; North Carolina College's LeRoy Walker (who one day would head the U.S. Olympic Committee); former Ohio State Olympian Mal Whitfield; former Arizona University javelin ace Bill Miller; quarter miler Herb McKenley; and boxer Hogan "Kid" Bassey.

"The dictionary defines anachronism as 'anything incongruous in point of time with its surroundings,' in other words, anything that is out of step with the times. A broader interpretation, particularly here, could make anachronism synonymous with Jim Crowism," I suggested.

In January 1961, I bylined a story that started with a quote by Pincus "Pinky" Sober, chairman of the American Athletic Union (AAU) track and field committee: "Who in his right mind would send colored athletes to a place where it would create controversy?"

That was Sober's way of explaining why the AAU had agreed to send an all-white team to South Africa for exhibition track meets that March. South Africa's invitation was for white athletes only. Sober went on: "You have never seen colored athletes in the Sugar Bowl. Should we keep all our boys out of there? We recognize such a situation exists and we abide by it."

It was a stunning statement and an in-your-face explanation. For my story, I interviewed some top black coaches who sharply disagreed with the decision by the AAU. Dr. LeRoy Walker, North Carolina College, said:

> I regret very much to learn of the AAU decision to send an all-white team to South Africa. Any athletic team which is to represent the United States should be selected on the basis of quality of performance. Whether the group is all white, all colored, or mixed, should not be a consideration.
>
> The AAU makes a serious error when it permits a foreign country, or an agency of this country, to make race a criteria of selection. It is a pity if the AAU compromises its position to the end of assisting South Africa perpetuate its attitude of racial bigotry.

Other coaches I quoted as taking similar stands were Eddie Hurt, Morgan State College; Joe Yancey, the New York Pioneer Club; Bert Piggott, A&T College; W. M. Bennett, Virginia State College; C.D. Paige, executive secretary, Virginia Interscholastic Association; Eugene Thomas, Southern University; Pete Griffin, Florida A&M; and Ted Chambers, Howard University. Beneath that three-column story I ran this comment:

> The AFRO wholeheartedly agrees with the stand taken by these men. Only a blind AAU official can fail to see what such compliance could lead to in the future. Other nations would be thoroughly justified in re-

questing all-colored or all-Jewish or all-Protestant teams. None of which would be truly all-American.

Someone should come to the rescue of Pinky Sober and Dan Ferris. It has been a long time since the heads of amateur athletes in the United States have been so in need of advice and guidance. It is time for SOS signals for the AAU.

Among others critical of sending an all-white team was *Sports Illustrated*, which concluded, "The solution is simple . . . The AAU should inform the South Africans that if they pick and choose among events and athletes in order to insure all-white competition, we will not send any team at all."

I took note of the indictment made against members of the U.S. women's track and field squad that lost a USA-USSR dual meet in Moscow in 1963. Coaches of the predominantly-tan distaff team complained that being "too fast" in hotel lobbies and "too insubordinate" on the cinder path cost the American women victory. "A to Z" commented:

Poor girls—victorious or not (which they've never been in these duels with Russia), they can't win. For one thing, the United States always insists that men's and women's scores be tabulated separately. So win, lose or draw, the importance of the girls' contribution is minimized . . . not minimized, just plain ignored.

Before they went away to compete, the American women speedsters already had tasted the total indifference of the American press and public toward those who bring honor to their country in international competition. A scant few weeks before they boarded the Moscow-bound plane, I recalled, the young women had been reading how speedster Wilma Rudolph had been snubbed in her hometown of Clarksville, Tennessee, when she tried to get a sandwich in a restaurant. "The 'key to the city' didn't fit any lock in town."

That was a reference to Wilma Rudolph's majestic return in 1960 from Rome, where she won three gold medals in the 100-meter and 200-meter events and as anchor for a world-record setting relay foursome. She was welcomed in queenly fashion and was the heroine of a ticker tape parade in

Clarksville. She was extolled by dignitaries at every level. But when Wilma elected to take her mother and a younger sister to dinner at a downtown restaurant, she was turned away. "All three of her gold medals couldn't buy a cup of coffee for Wilma at this downtown eating stop," I wrote.

Big trouble was brewing for the Olympics in 1963. The thirty-two newly independent nations of Africa were threatening to boycott the 1964 Olympics in Tokyo if South Africa and Portugal participated. Kenya, scheduled to hold an October planning meeting, said it would bar delegations from both countries.

"While it has not said so," I commented in August 1963, "there is evidence that the International Committee is finally awakening to the fact that patience with racism is rapidly running out . . . and that it plans to try to impress South Africa and Portugal of the gravity of the situation . . ."

To those who might wonder if I was okaying politics in sports, I wanted to make my position clear: "What my colleagues don't seem to understand is that colored people have never regarded morality and human dignity as being related to politics. They belong in the political arena, of course, but in the sense that they should be in the conscience of those practicing politics."

Near the end of the year, I noted "with pride and pleasure" the appointment of Eddie Hurt of Morgan State College to the coaching staff of the United States track and field team for the 1964 Olympic Games. Over the years, little Morgan College had knocked off the likes of Harvard, Yale, Princeton, Pennsylvania, Michigan, Illinois, Indiana, Maryland, and Duke on the cinder tracks.

As with golfer Lee Elder, once again I was headed for a public dispute with a black athlete I thought highly of over the South African issue. My last June 1964 column expressed the hope that tennis star Arthur Ashe "will do the right thing" if he were faced with playing South Africa's Abe Segal at Wimbledon. A nineteen-year-old Russian, Alexander Metrevelli, had forfeited his chance at fame by withdrawing rather than play against Segal. Two other Russians withdrew from warm-up matches with South Africans at Beckenham and Queens Club. Hungary's Estvan Gulsyas dissolved his partnership with Segal in protest against South African racism.

I flatly accused sportswriters of the American and British press of taking their lead from the Wimbledon brass. "The latter threw up its collective arms in horror. Politics in Wimbledon? Disgraceful!"

However, before the *Afro-American* went to press, a wire story quoted Ashe criticizing the Russian for balking at playing Segal and saying, "I would play Abe Segal any time." He was also quoted:

> I don't think you want political protests of this kind in sport—especially here in Wimbledon. If you want to be consistent, I wouldn't go out to play the Russians . . . I don't like what they're doing either . . . And I suppose I wouldn't play Pierre Darnon of France because De-Gaulle broke relations with Nationalist China.

I hammered out a boldface insert for the column, based on the wire story information:

> It is most unfortunate that Ashe couldn't have just gone on and played the role of juvenile as a 19-year-old tennis player. That he presumes to expert on international "politics" (he used the word, too), and suggests that he is as closely related, ethnically, to nationalist China, as he is to the oppressed South African, clearly demonstrates that he is educationally puerile or politically naïve.

As for Ashe's statement, "I would play Abe Segal any time," I put it to him the way it was: "Not if you were in Pretoria or Johannesburg or Cape Town, son."

Three years later, in his book, *Advantage Ashe,* Ashe said his statement made in Wimbledon "got me some praise from (colored) papers in Pittsburgh and Norfolk, and from the white *Richmond Times-Dispatch* but Sam Lacy of the *Afro-American*" was critical. He repeated what ran in my column. Ashe wrote:

> I don't care how Lacy feels. He has the right to his opinion. I never ask South African players their feelings about their government's racial policies . . . What could they do? . . . But I've kidded a lot with Segal and (Cliff) Drysdale, and with Rhodesian champion Roger Dowds as well . . . If I had the chance, I'd play in South Africa . . . But I'm not crazy enough to try to go."

I ran all of his retort along with the name of the book publisher and carried a column subhead saying, "should be read."

The late C. C. Jackson, a Baltimore recreation expert, was another of the successful track and field coaches. In 1965, he got his first crack at taking a women's team abroad, and for the first time, they were winners—in London and West Berlin. The team won plaudits from the press as "well ordered" and "as courageous and versatile as they are capable."

Valery Carter of New York won the hearts of the Germans for her bravery after she hurt herself. Jackson related the story to me:

> She was magnificent. She pulled a muscle shortly after the start and for some 70 or 80 yards, she ran while screaming at the top of her voice. Her punishment was brutal and there wasn't a person in the big stadium who didn't wonder why she insisted on continuing.
>
> It was such a courageous exhibition that the Germans brought special gifts to her at the international party they held afterward.

Out in California in November, Tommie Smith, then one of the nation's fastest colored athletes, and some of his associates announced plans to boycott the 1968 Olympics in Mexico to dramatize their resentment against continued racism in the United States. Despite the different position taken by Jesse Owens, Ralph Boston, Bob Hayes, and others, I said I could see nothing wrong with the boycott plans.

Although basketball All-American Lew Alcindor (later Kareem Abdul-Jabbar) and Tommie's San Jose College teammate Lee Evans were the biggest names mentioned, others who reportedly signed the resolution included Otis Burrell, high jump champ, and Mike Warren, crack UCLA basketball guard.

In deploring the plans, Owens, a one-man gang at the 1936 Olympics, said, "The Olympics help bridge the gap of misunderstanding between people in this country," but I commented that Owens did not say "what gap has been bridged since Jesse was a triple medal winner for the 'black auxiliary' (as Hitler termed them) 30 years ago."

I figured "just about no one gave more than passing thought to the threat" of a boycott at first. The picture began to change when Smith and

Evans described how, despite their heroics on the field, they were known by some of their professors as "the fastest n----rs on campus."

Elvin Hayes of Houston and Westley Unseld of Louisville, two more All-Americans, disqualified themselves as Olympic prospects and signed lucrative pro contracts. White All-Americans Neal Walk of Florida, Larry Miller of North Carolina, and Don May of Dayton, citing various reasons other than boycotting, pulled out. An unexpectedly large number declined to go.

Of course this was the year sprinters John Carlos and Tommie Smith, wearing black gloves, raised their hands high above their heads in a "black power" salute from the winners stand as the national anthem was being played. That protest against racism at home stirred bitter reaction in many quarters and resulted in the duo being banned from the Olympic site.

I was one of their critics. Although I had second thoughts about it later, their action provoked me at the time. My contention was if they wanted to protest, they should have stayed home. I felt, and I said in my piece, that I didn't think it was proper to bring their home country's ills into the international arena like that, where they had a captive audience. I was criticized severely for that. People felt that I was being a little too sensitive, or something. Afterward, I thought maybe I was a little hasty in my reaction; there's a strong possibility I could have handled it differently.

Of course, that incident was not the first, nor the last, that would have a black athlete expressing his unhappiness over racism by doing his own thing during the playing of the national anthem. One of the more publicized cases involved pitcher Jim "Mudcat" Grant of Cleveland in September 1960. This was my summation of it:

"Grant admittedly substituted his own words while singing the phrase 'land of the free and home of the brave,' in the Indians bullpen. On being cursed by coach Ted Wilks, who admitted using a racial epithet, Grant stormed from the park and was suspended by manager Jimmy Dykes for the remainder of the year."

Female jockeys were not popular in 1968 when I rallied to the support of white jockey Penny Ann Early, feeling an obligation "to condemn discrimination wherever it was encountered. To prejudge her ability solely on the basis of her sex is very similar to what has existed in the lives of 'A to Z's' writer and followers for countless years."

In talking to a race track acquaintance who planned to use jockey Barbara Jo Rubin the first chance he got, I quoted the friend as disclosing that the top male jockeys were not the ones raising all the protests against women riders. (Rubin rode that week and won on Brave Galaxy.)

The friend went on: "There's been a lot of talk about Webb's (trainer Bryan Webb) use of the girl on his horses. One of the things that's been said is that the whole thing is a publicity stunt . . . If you recall, they accused Branch Rickey of the same thing in 1947 when he installed Jackie Robinson at first base in Ebbets Field."

All the jockettes I backed at first were white: Rubin, Early, Kathy Kusner, Diane Crump, and Jennifer Rowland among them. Later, jockette Cheryl White came to Maryland from Ohio, only to be refused mounts at Laurel and Bowie. White had the double handicap of being both female and black.

Black colleges also had problems with the way women athletes were treated. I reported that Bonnie Logan of Durham, North Carolina, proved she could whip all the men tennis players in the Central Intercollegiate Athletic Association (CIAA), but was told she couldn't do it officially because "the conference considered women persona non grata in varsity athletics." As a result, I learned, her school, Morgan State, was faced with the alternative of setting up a two-woman tournament (with Ann Koger) "or telling Bonnie to stick to her studies."

In 1979, I was sorely vexed about a number of stories involving females and sports. The most exasperating was the one noting that Michigan State University was going to the Supreme Court "to try to avoid treating its women athletes the same as it treated its men's teams. To the Spartan authorities, Title IX means nothing." (Title IX, part of the Education Amendments enacted in 1972, prohibits discrimination on the basis of gender in schools, including athletic activities.) I mentioned Billie Jean King having to fight ten years to gain respect for women tennis players; Carol Mann facing constant criticism in golf; Renee Powell being compelled to go to Europe to find a coaching position; and said Ann Mahoney was railroaded off the Maryland Racing Commission. I conceded the situation for females in the colleges was a brighter picture, but that the Michigan State action showed maltreatment thoughts continued to fester in the hearts and minds of some men. The wrap: "For me at least, I find being a man embarrassing at times."

Less than a month later, there was this column headline: "Sorry, Ladies, I'll Have To Let You Down." It was the case of a bass fishing tournament in Phoenix, Arizona, in which "fisherpersons" remain in their boats with a randomly chosen partner for ten hours. I went along with the president of the Bass Anglers Sportsman Society of America in the view it would be difficult for ten hours out on the water to "maintain standards of decency and to insure sexual privacy."

Two women got the opportunity to try their basketball skills in competition with men. Neither made a career of it, but first, Lynette Woodard (a former Kansas University All-American), and then Jackie White (who played at Cal Poly Pomona and Long Beach State), enjoyed stints with the world famous Globetrotters. Their counterparts in baseball, in the declining years of the Negro leagues, were Toni Stone, Connie Morgan, and Mamie Johnson, who all had stints in the regular lineup for the Indianapolis Clowns. Stone, the first, played second base for the Clowns in 1953 and for the Kansas City Monarchs in 1954. Morgan replaced her at second with the Clowns in 1954. Johnson, a hard-throwing pitcher and utility player known as "Peanuts," also was with the Clowns in 1954.

The Olympic coaching makeup had improved when I reported in a July 1976 article that seven members of the black contingent in Montreal for the Olympics were coaches, two were team managers, and another a trainer. Four years earlier in Munich, there had been two head coaches, two assistant coaches, and a trainer.

For Montreal, LeRoy Walker was head coach of men's track and field; John Thompson was assistant men's basketball coach; and Brooks Johnson was assistant coach for women's track.

By July 1969, South Africa had still refused to budge on its apartheid policies. Back at Wimbledon, Arthur Ashe took a stand quite different from his previous posture, calling for the banning of that country's tennis players from some international meets.

In my column, I quoted from a speech made by Ashe before the newly formed International Players Association:

South Africa should not be allowed to play in the Davis Cup (competition) any more until they change their eligibility rules under which only whites can play . . . I think South Africa should also be excluded from the International Lawn Tennis Association because only whites in South Africa are represented by the South African Lawn Tennis Union.

The first two paragraphs of the next "A to Z" read:

I have the greatest respect for Arthur Ashe.

It takes a lot of courage to do what he did last week at Wimbledon . . . a lot more than the vast majority of observers may realize. The slender Virginian, who was under criticism two years ago for his indifference to the civil rights cause, asked for the disbarment of South Africa from world tennis.

I viewed Ashe's stand-up speech a tougher job than what the International Olympic Committee (IOC) had when it voted in Genoa in 1967 to bar South Africa from the Mexico Olympics. It was more courageous than the glove-fisted salute by Tommie Smith and John Carlos, though not as dramatic. I said the IOC action was backed by the African nations, Russia, Asia, and Scandinavia; that Smith and Carlos could gamble that they would have the sympathy of most of the nonwhite population on the field and in the stands. I said:

But at Wimbledon, Ashe was a lone battler. Further evidence of his courage is found in the revelation that Ashe didn't pick the stage for his fight. England is still Churchillian, a country where social reforms are even slower than in Arthur's American homeland . . . It was the British who held with Uncle Sam the longest in opposition to scratching South Africa from the Olympic picture.

My opposition to the sanctioning of U.S boxers going to fight in South Africa fell into the same antiapartheid vein.

"Top Rank, Inc., and the World Boxing Association [WBA], both of which have used the shoulders of black fighters as the vehicle for riding to worldwide power, have gravitated to a communion with South Africa, the one nation on earth that clings to a policy of rampant racism," was my position in 1979.

It was pointed out that the rival fight body, "The World Boxing Council has declined to do business with either (Gerrie) Coetzee or his (South African) countryman, Kallie Knoetze. The WBC rejection is in line with most world centers that will have no truck with representatives of the apartheid state."

Top Rank and promoter Bob Arum had signed South African Coetzee to fight American John Tate for at least half the world heavyweight title. Arum had promoted Knoetze in a fight in the United States the previous winter, with WBA's blessing, despite opposition from blacks and the State Department. Later, he staged another bout in South Africa that featured Knoetze and Tate.

My piece said, "Kallie (Knoetze)—whose brutality while a policeman controlling blacks in Pretoria, made him unpopular even in his homeland—was destroyed.

"By conniving with the WBA, which craves the power, and the South African government, which needs the recognition, Arum has backed Tate into a corner where he must take his title hopes to South Africa, whether he wants to or not."

In November of 1984, the WBA approved a bout for Sun City in South Africa, between its champ Coetzee and its sixth ranked fighter, Greg Page, whom I quoted as saying he "needs to make a living" so will fight anywhere.

"Whether it is because their conscience rejected the idea of giving pseudo endorsement to apartheid or because they had legitimate pressures cannot be ascertained but the top five WBA contenders were 'not available' when the call was made to them," my story said. The five who were not available for the bout in South Africa, all black, were identified as Larry Holmes, Mike Weaver, Michael Dokes, David Bey, and Trevor Berbick.

On a more positive note, I've always loved young people. Whether visiting schools, working with charitable organizations, or making myself available for interviews with them, I considered them a priority.

I also was a firm believer in the view that "the South's hostility toward integration is kept alive solely by adult leaders" and I pointed to some organized Little League activities to buttress that position. Within the span of a couple weeks time in the summer of 1955, there was decidedly different handling of Little League state tournaments, one in South Carolina, the other in Florida.

In Charleston, when the Cannon Street YMCA team sought to compete in its state tournament, red flags were hoisted. In South Carolina, the older heads pulled out the white teams when the colored kids were admitted. When they (the whites) discovered that they could not avoid playing the colored youngsters, they pulled out of the tourney. After it was pointed out that the admittance of the colored team was entirely legal, the South Carolinians decided they'd have none of that, so they broke up the league.

The black squad in Pensacola, Florida, the J.C. Little League team, also got off to a rocky start. The whites in the northwest section of the state, eleven white teams in districts one and two, balked at playing the tan youngsters.

"But the similarity ended there," I discovered. "Without any semblance of compromise (national) Little League officials immediately disqualified the 11 teams and declared Pensacola the area champion."

The J.C.'s from Pensacola, named after the Junior Chamber of Commerce that sponsored the team, went on to Orlando, where the team made history as the first black squad permitted to play in a Little League state tournament in the South. The Jaycees manager, Fred L. Hicks, said they were treated wonderfully and never heard a single racial slur while in Orlando. His team lost the game 5-0 and afterward the players from both teams "crowded around one another and it was the usual pat on the back, shaking hands, and 'hope to see you next year.'"

Hicks said Raymond Riddles, district manager in his area, tried to rule his team ineligible, but national president Peter J. McGovern told him any tourney without the Jaycees would itself be illegal. The district actually went on with a tourney without the Jaycees but the national headquarters in Williamsport, Pennsylvania, ordered the Florida state tournament supervisor to declare the Jaycees the winners. League president Clifford McQueen was requested to have the team report to the San Juan Hotel in Orlando.

"A to Z" reported:

Throughout both these Little League cases, the protests and withdrawals, etc., were the acts of parents or older leaders. The white boys wanted to play ball; against whom made no difference.

A good example is when the question was put to the Orlando kids, of whether or not they wanted to play the colored Pensacolans; the vote was unanimous in favor of going on with the game.

One of their managers resigned in protest against their decision, and the youngsters said: "Sorry about that but, well it was nice knowing you."

That was the kind of story I would follow up, so later in August, when the Little League World Series would be played in Williamsport, I was there talking to parents and their sons. Sure enough they differed widely in their views:

Robert Salter, a radio station manager in Auburn, Alabama, admitted before Thursday's semifinal game between Alabama and New Jersey that there would probably be no incident over the presence of three colored boys in the Jersey lineup. However, he added: "I'm just not ready to accept them . . . It's just one of those things that probably will take place when we're ready for it . . . We don't like the idea of being told we've got to do something, that's all . . . You know there are people in your race that you don't want to have anything to do with yourself . . . Well, we feel that way in the South."

Reminded that every race has its share of undesirables Salter replied, "You're right about that, but in the South we don't have many of that kind in our race and they predominate among colored people."

I had talked to Salter's twin sons, George and Frank, members of the Alabama team. Their team won the region five playoff in Rome, Georgia, the series from which the Cannon Street YMCA team of Charleston had been barred. Asked how they felt about playing against the colored boys, one said, "It didn't make any difference to me." The other one (I couldn't tell them apart) said: "To me either, as long as they know how to play ball and it wouldn't be a runaway, it was all right with me . . ."

Another father-son duo was included in the Alexandria, Louisiana, delegation. Sam Despino managed the Louisiana Little Leaguers and his son, Junior, was the star pitcher. Despino told me: "The colored kids played in our regionals. It was no choice of ours, but the Little League rules said we had to play them to qualify for the World Series, so we played against them. I can't say that we wanted to play with them or didn't want to play with them. It was the rules, that's all."

He didn't mind if I spoke to his son.

Young Sam spoke crisply, straight to the point, as is the custom of kids. "Colored kids played against us at Monroe. It wasn't any difference. I struck them out, too."

Carolyn King, proven to be as good as most of the Little League boys around Ypsilanti, Michigan, and backed by her parents, Mr. and Mrs. Gerald King, was the heroine responsible for taking Little League to court over its ban on females. I said that although age had resulted in Carolyn quitting the Little League Orioles and playing with the Swingers, she could "rejoice over the fact that her efforts have ended the frustrations of other little girls throughout the world."

With racial and sexual discrimination curbed in the Little Leagues, I stuck an "ugly American" face on the organization's decision to ban Orientals from the World Series:

. . . Majority America is never able to take a defeat kindly. It has this thing about getting whipped at anything. Last Monday, it embraced a new philosophy in which to find comfort . . . (it) kicked out the Orientals . . . It announced that henceforth the annual Little League World Series will be restricted to teams from the United States.

This action, needless to say, was designed to throw a third strike past the little fellow who has been repeatedly winning the championship . . . Teams from Japan and Taiwan have won seven of the last World Series . . .

The superiority of the youngsters from Asia has been so overwhelming that Little League officials started hinting two years ago that they suspected the team members were older than the 10 to 13-year-old age requirement (checks were made of teams in Kao Hsiung, Taiwan, and later in Tainan City without the finding of anything wrong) . . .

Being unable to pinpoint anything that would justify disqualification . . . Uncle Sam was faced with the choice of doing something about relieving the frustrations of his young nephews. He did something. He decided if you can't beat 'em, ban 'em.

Eventually, that ruling was lifted. But in 1997, having won seventeen titles since 1969, Taiwan announced it would not participate that year because of recently enforced rules by Little League Baseball that schools must create a league for every thousand students. Under that rule, 90 percent of Taiwan teams would have been ineligible because of the large size of many Taiwan schools. There also was the long-standing hassle over the use of paid coaches in Taiwan. Judging by reactions in the newspapers, among U.S. Little League leadership, no tears were shed over the loss of the winners of the 1996 title. In an unexpected turn of events, Mexico beat out the United States to win the 1997 Little League World Series.

Don't think for a minute that this kind of thing no longer is considered in American sports. Take long-distance running, where until recent years white male stars have dominated. Now that others, particularly stars from Kenya, are setting the long-distance pace in stateside contests, here's what we find: some races offer prize money to Americans only, some offer money to Americans who break U.S. records, some fix it so losers from America get more in prizes than winners from Kenya, and some limit participation by non-Americans. That's in 1998.

My habit of making myself available to young people has paid dividends. Some of the many students who interviewed me over the years did outstanding work. One, Peter M. Sheingold, a student at Hampshire College in Amherst, Massachusetts, used some interviews along with some research as the basis of his 1992 thesis for the bachelor of arts degree in American history. He titled it, "In Black and White: Sam Lacy's Campaign to Integrate Baseball." I considered it an excellent piece of work.

To keep up with the technology revolution, *Afro-American* newspapers publisher and board chairman John J. Oliver Jr. established a Web site for the *Afro-American* on the Internet; it often carried information about my work. Among the people who contacted me in 1996 because of the Web site were three teenagers from Burlington, Washington; they wanted an interview for a paper to enter in a history competition.

Sean Reehorn, Justin Holmes, and Josh Satterlee, students at the Burlington–Edison High School, focused on the AFRO's relations with Jackie Robinson and the role of the newspaper's sports department in supporting Brooklyn Dodgers president Branch Rickey in his crusade to desegregate modern professional baseball. The students' paper won first place in the city competition, second in the regional, first statewide, and third in the national finals held at the University of Maryland.

Baltimore's Project Survival, which assists students with financial aid to make college possible for them, has a scholarship in my name, and scores of young people have benefited. For years, my son Tim and I participated in a number of college-based golfing tourneys as a way of giving back to the community while thoroughly enjoying ourselves. The years have taken such a toll on my game that I play sparingly now, but Tim carries on the tradition.

As a firm believer in education, I had urged a rule to keep college freshmen out of varsity sports while they concentrated on their new surroundings and class challenges. Nevertheless, I also conceded the wisdom of some athletes leaving college early to sign big contracts with pro teams.

An old case which drew national attention was that of Moses Malone from Petersburg, Virginia, the nineteen-year-old son of a grocery store clerk, Mary Malone, and a high school basketball phenom. His situation, I thought then, was similar to that of thousands of other poor black kids in this country and elsewhere—except that his basketball talent made him a prize prospect for a college scholarship.

The calls poured in; recruiters found their way to the Malone home. Eventually, coach Lefty Driesell of the University of Maryland won the prize, got a letter of intent signed, and immediately predicted a national championship for his Terrapins. But it wasn't to be.

Two months later, the Utah Stars of the American Basketball Association came calling with a fabulous offer—$8 million over a period of years plus a paid-for home for his widowed mother. Malone wavered. Mrs. Malone threw up her hands in despair, leaving the decision to her son. He went for the bucks, straight out of high school to the pros. Yes, I applauded:

And so it is that "A to Z," as it has done repeatedly in the past, applauded the wisdom of Moses Malone. Whenever a black kid from a black ghetto finds himself offered a million dollars, he should grab it and run like hell.

This is not meant to downgrade the value of the college degree. Rather, it is designed to look at the situation from a realistic standpoint.

If the Moses Malones of today were to follow the advice of the self-serving Lefty Driesells, they might very well share the glory of a national championship. But what if they get hurt in any one of their four years of varsity competition? A shattered kneecap, a smashed ankle or a scrambled vertebra could leave their value to the pros at zero.

So, in the unlikely possibility that this might happen, they still would have their college degrees and virtual assurance of a job for later, you say.

Right, I say. But that job for a black man probably would be that of a teacher or coach. By paying his taxes on time, he might earn a million dollars in about 180 years.

It was always possible to further one's education during or after a professional career, I argued, knowing full well that a number of athletes and working people had done that.

Among the sports sponsorships that catered to young people, and some not so young, I had a favorite—the annual Penn Relays held in Philadelphia by the University of Pennsylvania. I wrote in April 1963:

> Long before Joe Louis broke through the white curtain of heavyweight boxing and Jackie Robinson opened the dams for major league baseball, many years before the Big Ten fielded anything but one-complexion basketball and the Atlantic Coast Conference learned there was a capable tennis player outside the country-club steps, the Penn Relays were providing a stage for "democracy in action."
>
> The track and field extravaganza which gets underway at Franklin Field in Philadelphia Friday, for nearly seventy years has fostered honest competition in contests of speed, endurance and strength. Taking part have been youngsters from elementary institutions to graduate school collegians, with absolutely no limitations based on the complexions they wear or the church they attend.
>
> They have cited and punished without regard to race, which is as it should be and has been for them for over half a century. It is not difficult, then, for one to offer an annual salute to the Penn Relays.

CHAPTER 12

1990s STATS SHOW PROGRESS MADE, NEEDED

By the mid-1990s, in sixty-plus years of sportswriting, I had witnessed dramatic positive changes. While seeing a need for further progress in some areas, institutionally, the fair play and equal opportunities I'd championed for minorities and women had significantly outpaced similar progress in most nonsports fields.

Oddly, less satisfactory in my view was the extent to which individual athletes remained susceptible to pitfalls in areas such as drugs, assaults of various types, and other sports-related shenanigans.

Over the years, more often than not I've supported athletes in their efforts to win better working conditions and higher pay, but frankly, I've found it difficult to justify in my mind some of the astronomical salaries now in vogue. That, of course, does not suggest that players should not run to the bank with the cash, deserved or not, as long as the team owners are forking it over.

After all the decades I've been part of the battle to eradicate barriers to full participation in sports to all eligible competitors, it is quite obvious that sports is a leader in the area of equal opportunity, although there still are some significant improvements that demand addressing.

I see no reason to quarrel with this conclusion reached in "The 1995 Racial Report Card" of Northeastern University's Center for the Study of Sport in Society: "There is no area of American society with greater opportunities for minorities than professional sports." However, the center's 1996 report concluded: "The intensity of the charge to change front office and on-field hiring practices in professional sports to include more people of color has clearly been disrupted over the past two years."

And in the 1997 report, it was observed that despite the merited integration among players, both professional and college sports continue to have lousy records for minorities and women as far as front offices and athletic departments are concerned.

The author of the center's annual report, Richard Lapchick, agreed in 1995 with the Rainbow Commission for Fairness in Athletics, which reported that the overwhelming majority of minorities performing on the field was grossly disproportionate to the lack of minority representation in team management. The Rev. Jesse Jackson, president of the Rainbow PUSH Action Network, founded the Rainbow Commission in 1992.

The affirmative action battles being waged in the larger community had not become a disruptive force in sports, and in 1996, baseball's National League was being run by its second black president, Len Coleman, who had followed Bill White. The National League also had Ricky Clemons as director of public relations. Still, none of the big-three leagues had teams with black or Latino majority ownership. Women owners had a baseball team in Cincinnati and a football team in St. Louis.

Although not in the big-three of sports, the most important and best known sports team owned by blacks is the Harlem Globetrotters, the world famous basketball magicians bought in 1993 by Mannie Jackson and Associates. Jackson is chairman and CEO of Harlem Globetrotters International Inc. These basketball jesters, who can play the game with some of the best when they are not into the clowning bit that has made them famous the world over, played game number 20,000 on January 12, 1998, in Remington, Indiana, a town of about thirteen hundred people.

By the mid-nineties, my major crusading done, I was content to sit by and observe the progress that had been made, some of which may have resulted, at least in part, from my early efforts.

In the 1994–1995 sports year, Felipe Alou (Montreal Expos) was Major League and National League Manager of the Year, and Lenny Wilkens (Atlanta Hawks) surpassed Red Auerbach as the winningest NBA coach of all time. And this followed 1993-1994, when blacks were Coach of the Year in college basketball (Nolan Richardson of the Arkansas Razorbacks), the NBA (Lenny Wilkens of the Atlanta Hawks), and the National League (Dusty Baker of the San Francisco Giants). Also, Cito Gaston, later dropped by Toronto, had become the first black manager to win consecutive World Series championships. Wilkens, enshrined as a player in 1989 and as coach in 1998, became the second two-time inductee into the Basketball Hall of Fame. John Wooden is the only other person to be inducted twice.

In 1996, Bob Watson, general manager of the New York Yankees, became the first of his race in that position to have a team make the World Series—and they won it. Watson, a .295 hitter during sixteen years with four major league teams, first served as a general manager for the Houston Astros in 1993. The Astros and the Yankees were among the teams for which he played. Watson announced his resignation in February 1998.

Black coaches listed in the NFL for 1996 were Ray Rhodes in Philadelphia, Dennis Green in Minnesota, and newcomer Tony Dungy in Tampa, all for National Football Conference teams. The American Football Conference listed none.

In basketball, an update showed as coaches Bernie Bickerstaff (Washington Wizards), Lenny Wilkens (Atlanta Hawks), and Daryl Walker (Toronto Raptors). Walker quit in February 1998 after team part-owner Isiah Thomas left in December for a broadcasting job, and the Raptors traded star guard Damon Stoudamire.

Minority baseball managers listed were Felipe Alou, Montreal; Don Baylor, Colorado; Dusty Baker, San Francisco; and Cito Gaston, Toronto. Half of them, Gaston and Baylor, were later fired.

After a number of shuffles, Wayne Embry of the Cleveland Cavaliers was the only black in any of the big-three sports serving as chairman, president, or chief executive officer. Elaine W. Stewart, assistant general manager and general counsel for the Boston Red Sox, was the only black woman in either of those positions with any major league team.

As the nation celebrated the fiftieth anniversary of the breaking of racial barriers in major league baseball by Jackie Robinson, I was pleased to see baseball issue a tough letter to all thirty teams, saying failure to improve minority hirings could result in penalties. It was signed by interim commissioner Bud Selig, National League president Len Coleman, and American League president Gene Budig. Jerry Reinsdorf, Chicago White Sox owner and chairman of the Equal Opportunity Committee for baseball, said Selig had approved his pushing the matter.

In May 1997, Selig hired Hall of Famer Frank Robinson, sixty-one, long interested in a general manager's position, as his consultant for special projects and director of the Arizona Fall League. In May 1998, Budig added Hall of Fame pitcher Bob Gibson to his staff as a special advisor. The former St. Louis Cardinal flame thrower became part of an American League staff that included 1998 Hall of Fame inductee Larry Doby. (In his book, *Stranger to the Game*, Gibson had complained about the lack of post-pitching opportunities in baseball.)

I devoted considerable attention in earlier years to the hiring of radio and television broadcasters. Thanks in large part to cable networks, a growing number of blacks are seen on television and heard on radio with sports broadcast teams. However, my interest in seeing blacks gain more leadership positions in pro football and baseball has not yet reflected the kind of progress that in 1997 could be rated spectacular.

I titled my August 31, 1996, column, "Question: Trend Or Odd Coincidence?" The piece was about the lack of a representative number of young black players in showcase baseball games. I came up with only one in the Little League championship game (with the Panama City team) in Williamsport, Pennsylvania. In the Babe Ruth (16-18) League championship game at Dare County on the North Carolina Outer Banks, New Jersey fielded just two black players when it faced Tennessee in the title game. In addition, I counted but one black player in the College World Series and one on the team representing the United States in the Olympic games in Atlanta. I called it "truly puzzling."

Rudy Washington, executive director of the Black Coaches Association, was one of the voices speaking out forcefully in 1996, when black coaches were virtually ignored as NCAA Division 1-A institutions went about the filling of a large number of head coaching vacancies.

I thought one encouraging hire in basketball in 1997 was that of Georgia coach Orlando Henry (Tubby) Smith as coach of the Wildcats at the University of Kentucky, to succeed Rick Pitino. Smith and a fellow black, Clem Haskins, the Minnesota basketball coach, were the last contenders for the job once held by Adolph Rupp, one of sports history's most rabid racists.

Rupp, who made no bones about not wanting black players at Kentucky, was shooting for his fifth NCAA basketball crown with all-white teams when he came into the final of the 1966 tourney in Cole Field House at the University of Maryland. His opposition was then called Texas Western, now known as Texas–El Paso. Rupp's wins had come against Baylor, Oklahoma State, Kansas State, and Seattle. There are still discussions about why Texas Western's coach, Don Haskins, decided to use only seven black players from his integrated team in the game against Kentucky. Haskins has said the seven just happened to be his best players. Texas Western took Kentucky 72-65 in an all-black versus all-white championship game. That hadn't happened before. It hasn't happened since.

To cap off his first season with the Wildcats, Smith coached them to the 1998 NCAA championship in one of the most unpredictable and exciting tournaments in the history of the March Madness basketball playoffs. Kentucky's basketball fans, some of whom initially had been skeptical, had themselves another sports hero: "Tub-by, Tub-by." Coincidentally, Clem Haskins's Minnesota team won the 1998 National Invitation Tournament.

Smith's victory made him the third black coach ever to lead teams to the NCAA crown. The others are John Thompson of Georgetown University in 1984 and Nolan Richardson of the University of Arkansas in 1994. Thompson's Hoyas lost in the finals on two other occasions, to North Carolina 63-62 in 1982 and to Villanova 66-64 in 1985.

Another remaining problem is that in addition to getting the short end of the administrative-type positions in college sports, the most recent reports suggest that black athletes still were not being graduated at the same rate as others from the colleges to which they contribute so much.

Yet, from where I surveyed events, by almost any measuring method, the year 1996 turned out to be a sports spectacular. It had its low points, but overall, topped off during the summer by the Olympic games in Atlanta, Georgia, and also by the astounding manner in which team owners were making multimillionaires of athletes, it truly was interesting.

Considering that the average value in 1995 of a big-three franchise was $174 million for the NFL, $127 million for the NBA, and $115 million for major league baseball, it was indeed eye-popping to witness contracts spanning several years topping the $100 million mark. Signing bonuses also were skyrocketing.

This is the truth. In 1997, one baseball player, Albert Belle of the Chicago White Sox, with a $10 million a year salary, was reported at one point to be making more than the entire Pittsburgh Pirates team, reportedly $9,071,667. And that's not all. As the 1998 season kicked off, Belle and Gary Sheffield of the Florida Marlins, each at $10 million, and Greg Maddux of the Atlanta Braves, at $9.6 million, were each making more than the $9,162,000 the Montreal Expos paid all its players.

Times do change, but I couldn't resist looking back to February of 1960 when I was pointing out how great black baseball players were doing salary-wise since Jackie Robinson integrated the game in 1947. These were the kind of figures I boasted about:

Within the next four months, they will be on the way to earning far in excess of a million-and-a-half dollars for 1960.

By June 1, organized baseball will be paying this amount in salaries alone to its contingent of tan stars, headed by Willie Mays, who now has become the highest salaried performer in the game. Three of these players—Mays, Ernie Banks and Hank Aaron—will gross $200,000 among them. Another trio—Frank Robinson, Minnie Minoso and Sam Jones—will gross another $100,000. By the time November 1 rolls around, salaries, World Series shares and other pickups (endorsements, personal appearances, bonuses, etc.) will run colored earnings close to 2 million dollars! In less than 14 years!

I often complained in those early years about the bonuses paid to black players. What set me off on the topic for a July 1962 column was a broadcaster saying the Chicago White Sox had been lucky to acquire Floyd Robinson for "a little more than $500." The broadcaster had been noting that outfielder Robinson was among the American League's top hitters.

It reminded me of a conversation I'd had with Leon Wagner before the first All-Star game to be played in Washington. Wagner, then leading the American League in homers and runs batted in and being tub-thumped by his Los Angeles Angels manager, Bill Rigney, as a strong MVP contender, was discussing his signing by the San Francisco Giants: "I was playing with a pretty good semipro team in Detroit when they approached me and I was aware that the scouts were buzzing about me and my prospects as a major league player. Just the same, the best I could get was the payment of a small mortgage on my grandmother's house and a promise to buy new uniforms and bats and balls for the Panthers, the team I was playing with at the time."

I went on to cite some other cases:

Wagner is only one of the many tan stars in baseball who had to sell their services for a song. Hank Aaron got $250 and a suit of clothes. Ernie Banks was given $20 and a plane ticket from his Texas home to Chicago. Jackie Robinson received $3,500, Roy Campanella got $1,000 and settlement in a divorce action. Frank Robinson's services were purchased for $500, and Willie Mays wound up with $500 upon arrival at the Giants farm base in Trenton, N.J.

Among the better bonuses was Earl Robinson's reported $50,000 from the Dodgers, which, I suggested, actually turned out to be much closer to $18,000.

To make my point about the differences in the way players were being treated, I cited some typical cases involving white players who fared much better in the bonus game "who couldn't and can't hold a candle to any one of their tan contemporaries."

I tell you, that situation has changed drastically. In 1996, when owners in the big-three sports suddenly decided to go all-out in annual pay and bonus payments to their key players, black stars no longer were at the bottom of the pile. Their status as top players was recognized as the dollars flowed.

Michael Jordan of the NBA champion Chicago Bulls, many experts' choice for best-ever in pro basketball, led the money parade with a one-year deal for more than $30 million—which was increased the next year.

Baseball players with high annual average salaries (counting bonuses) included Barry Bonds of the San Francisco Giants, $11.5 million; Albert Belle of the Chicago White Sox, $10 million; Cecil Fielder of the New York Yankees, $9.2 million; Ken Griffey Jr., Seattle Mariners, $7.5 million; and Frank Thomas, Chicago White Sox, $7.1 million. Similar kinds of salaries were being handed out in pro football.

I was assured by experts who know about such financial things that it's doubtful many of the athletes would actually collect all the millions not guaranteed in those publicly announced contracts. Some already were being cut in "cap" problems and rehired at lower salaries or picked up by other teams for less money. Still, agents who handled these athletes were among the big winners.

Only a handful of the successful agents were black. The first black firm to represent a "number 1" in the NFL draft was Professional Sports Planning of Farmington Hills, Michigan, run by brothers Kevin and Carl Poston. In 1997, they represented Orlando Pace, the Ohio State offensive tackle taken by the St. Louis Rams. The firm also represented the Orlando Magic's Anfernee "Penny" Hardaway, and others. Famous attorney Johnnie Cochran Jr. joined the ranks of agents certified by the NBA Players Association before the June 1997 draft.

In my lifetime, I'd never witnessed anything approaching this degree of wealth-spreading among athletes. There was no way to predict how it all would play out but I was certain of two things: There would be even more dramatic dollar spreads between what a relatively few players were hauling down and what lower-paid teammates collected, and the required hikes in ticket prices would be bad news for the average fan—especially the black fan.

I hope it's not true that the more some things change, the more they remain the same. I bring that up because while 1996 brought some exciting events and welcome signs of change, racially, the professional sports of golf and tennis—as far as numbers of black pros were concerned—remained discouragingly similar to what their images were in the past. In fact, the television networks covering some of these events at times would slip back into the old overlook-'em pattern of the past. On July 27, 1996, I ran this open letter addressed to broadcaster Jim McKay:

> Dear Jim: The network did it again.
>
> It had to be the network (ABC) . . . because I know personally that you have no complexion hang-ups.
>
> But, what happened in the weekend telecast of the British Open golf tournament must have been noticed by you.
>
> On Saturday, Vijay Singh, the Fijian star whom many African-Americans admire, played in a twosome with Ernie Els of South Africa. On Sunday, he was paired with American Mark Brooks.
>
> Yet in 36 holes of golf, the ABC cameras avoided showing a single stroke (or putt) made by this black man.
>
> On Sunday, the treatment was dastardly. Cameras isolated Brooks throughout the 18 holes as though he were playing alone.
>
> Just thought I'd call attention to this scurrilous behavior.

I had not seen dramatically significant change in the world of golfing, that is, scoring on the PGA tour courses and on the commercial-sponsorship front, until twenty-year-old Stanford University student Eldrick (Tiger) Woods turned professional in late August 1996, and soon afterward signed contracts estimated at $40 million with Nike and $20 million with Titleist. Woods garnered a $2.2 million advance from Warner Books to write two books, an autobiography and a golfing instruction book. In May 1997, he signed a deal for $13 million over five years with American Express. That overall package called for $30 million in advertising and promotions featuring Woods and included a $1 million contribution to the Tiger Woods Foundation. Rolex decided to name a watch for him. Wheaties brought him into its lineup of personalities. He also was collecting handsome appearance fees. And others were getting on board.

Woods had stirred excitement a few days before turning pro by becoming the first golfer ever to win three consecutive U.S. Amateur titles. In all my years around golf, I'd never seen anyone have the kind of impact this young multimillionaire phenom had in attracting huge crowds, boosting television audiences—and winning.

Still, to emphasize the puny participation of blacks in pro golfing, I was reminded that of all the active players, only Jim Thorpe was a regular on the PGA tour before Woods joined it. Charlie Sifford and Lee Elder, players I supported decades ago, were in the super senior ranks, over age seventy. Seniors in addition to Jim Dent were Calvin Peete, Walter Morgan, and Bobby Stroble. Gone were players the likes of Bill Spiller and Jim Black, the latter once invited by Sally Little of South Africa to be her doubles partner.

I'm quick to recognize that over the years, the handful of black golfers on the pro circuit, including Ted Rhodes, probably made more money at it than they would have in some other work. They also had the opportunity, despite the cruel limitations placed on them because of their race, to follow the career of their choosing. Moreover, some were making out rather handsomely on the senior circuit. As example, Jim Dent, fifty-nine, became the first player to repeat as champion of the Home Depot Invitational in Charlotte, bringing his year's winnings in May 1998 to $314,161.

I found Tiger's willingness as a big-money star to take a stand on the racial situation quite refreshing. To his credit, Woods realized that despite his good fortune, all the elitist hurdles in the world of golfing had not yet been erased. In a three-page "Hello World" advertising spread Nike ran on him in the August 29, 1996, *Wall Street Journal*, Woods included this statement along with information about his golfing accomplishments: "There are still courses in the United States that I am not allowed to play because of the color of my skin." Similar commercials ran on television. Nike chairman Phil Knight saw Woods as one of the few special athletes like Michael Jordan who transcend their sports. His firm was willing to work with Woods as an ambassador of change in encouraging more minorities to become golfers.

By the time Woods turned twenty-one on December 30, 1996, he had won the *Sports Illustrated* "Sportsman of the Year" award. The Associated Press made his story the third best of the year in sports behind track star Michael Johnson's record-setting victories in the 200- and 400-meter events during the Olympics in Atlanta, and the Olympic event itself.

My guess then was that the best of Tiger Woods was yet to come. Fittingly, his shining hour would play out on the hallowed Augusta National course in Augusta, Georgia, home of the world famous Masters. There, where blacks had not competed for a green jacket in a Masters until 1975 when veteran golfer Lee Elder broke through, and where there were no black members until Ron Townsend joined in 1991, Woods claimed the title by a record twelve strokes over a field of the best golfers in the world. His record-setting 18-under par triumph made him, at age twenty-one, the youngest winner ever. Elder was there to see his young friend win and to hear Tiger pay tribute to him, to Charlie Sifford, who at age thirty-eight became the first black PGA tour rookie in 1960, to Teddy Rhodes, and to other golfing pioneers.

After the Masters, the warm embrace Woods gave his father Earl, who had groomed Tiger to play since his toddler days, was an emotional moment for the millions who had tuned in by television in unprecedented numbers. There was renewed hope that Woods's brilliant start as a pro would inspire other young minorities to play golf. Toward that goal, the Tiger Woods Foundation already had scheduled youth golf clinics at Disney World and in Dallas, New York City, Chicago, Memphis, and Miami. Others would be added.

Woods set a string of records in winning one of the four major championships: youngest winner; low 72 holes at 270; widest victory margin, 12 strokes; low middle 36 holes, 131; low last 54 holes, 200; most under par on the back nine with 16 under; and most threes on a winner's card with 26. He also tied the low first holes record with 201 and tied the rounds better than the field with two.

For pure sports excitement, Woods's triumph reminded many of us of some other historic actions by great athletes: March 2, 1962, when Philadelphia Warriors center Wilt Chamberlain scored a hundred points in a win over the New York Knicks; the night of February 25, 1964, when Muhammad Ali (then Cassius Clay) upset Sonny Liston to claim the world heavyweight boxing title; and the May 16, 1980, game when Los Angeles Lakers rookie Earvin "Magic" Johnson replaced injured center Kareem Abdul Jabbar and racked up forty-two points, fifteen rebounds, and seven assists to lead his team to the NBA title.

I got the feeling Woods's handlers hadn't been on their jobs during this heady period when a national magazine ran a story on Woods, quoting some off-color remarks he had made of a racial and sexual nature. The young man said he had learned a lesson about making joking remarks around reporters. It's one of the things he should have been firmly warned against. Shortly after his Masters win, Woods learned that older golfers also run into jokester problems with the media when Fuzzy Zoeller referred to him as "that little boy" and suggested Woods not make the menu for the next Masters Champions dinner "fried chicken . . . or collard greens or whatever the hell they serve." Zoeller apologized and a "disappointed" Woods accepted. Zoeller went so far as to stop touring for more than a month until he and Tiger had lunch together on May 20.

I heard that strange word Tiger concocted to explain his racial mix—"Cablinasian," for Caucasian, black, Indian, and Asian. His mother, Kultida, was born in Thailand. But what I heard from him at the Masters when he paid tribute to Sifford, Elder, and Rhodes for paving the way for him in golf, suggested that Woods understands that in this country, most people are going to see him as African-American. That also was the message many got from his commercial featuring Sifford, Rhodes, and Elder, in which Tiger promised not to forget what they had done before him.

Phenomenon or not, golf takes the measure of every player, and after July 1997, Tiger did not win another PGA tour event until May 1998.

I saw little encouragement in 1996 on the tennis front, despite stellar play by some of the still relatively few black male and female high-level participants, and a handful of promising youngsters. Too few players were moving up into the top ranks.

Among the men, I noted Ron Shelton and MaliVai Washington. Washington had a great run at Wimbledon in 1996, becoming the first black man in the finals in the prestigious contest since the late Arthur Ashe, who won it in 1975. In 1997, Washington was ranked number 24 in the world.

Among the female tennis players, Chanda Rubin, Lori McNeil, Zina Garrison-Jackson, and Venus Williams were the most successful since Althea Gibson. During her career, Gibson won about every major women's crown. Venus Williams, seventeen, had scored some success as a young teenager, although she and her parents seemed more interested in her getting a good basic education before going all-out for the top in the pro ranks. Venus and her younger sister Serena, sixteen, were showing considerable potential. Playing in the new Arthur Ashe Stadium, Venus lost to world number 1–ranked Martina Hingis in the finals of the 1997 U.S. Open. The first black woman to make the finals of the U.S. Open since Althea Gibson,

Venus Williams started play ranked number 66 and came out at number 27. Serena also was making major advances in her game—and the two were playing well as doubles partners.

In the sisters' first face-off on the pro tour, Venus defeated Serena in the Australia Open in January 1998 before losing to Lindsay Davenport, who was quoted as saying she definitely did not want to lose to Venus. Venus teamed with Justin Gimelstob to win the mixed doubles in Australia. The Williams sisters scored big in the IGA Tennis Classic in Oklahoma City as Venus won her first pro title and the sisters teamed up to win the women's doubles crown. Venus, moving from number 14 to number 12 in the world with the victory, made it to the finals by defeating Lindsay Davenport after losses to Davenport in three previous meetings. The sisters had been invited by Billie Jean King to play for the USA Federation Cup team that April in South Carolina, but their father Richard Williams nixed that, saying "they're just too far behind in their homework."

By March of 1998, there was no longer any doubt but that the Williams sisters were for real. Venus won her second tourney in the Lipton Championships by defeating Anna Kournikova. The Russian teenager was ranked 16 but had knocked off four top-ten players to reach the final. Two days before, Venus had beat number 1 Martina Hingis and left the Key Biscayne, Florida, meet ranked number 10 in the world. In 1997, she had come into the Lipton ranked 110. Not only did Venus defeat Hingis in the semifinals, but in the quarterfinals, Hingis barely got past Serena by surviving two match points. In less than six months Serena's ranking had soared dramatically from 453 to 30. The Williams sisters definitely were among several teenage players tabbed for stardom on the women's tennis circuit.

Venus defeated Serena in their second tour meeting in the quarterfinals of the 1998 Italian Open in Rome. On October 4, 1998, then ranked number 5, Venus won the inaugural Grand Slam Cup in Munich, Germany, collecting $800,000.

On September 7, 1996, I wrote that no black woman tennis player had moved up as fast as Chanda Rubin since Althea Gibson dominated the women's game in 1957–1958. "But she and her parents—as well as thousands of supporting fans—were beginning early to wonder if nagging injuries will continue to plague her career." Wrist injuries led to her pulling out of some top meets, including the Olympics and Wimbledon, where she was ranked number 11. Rubin, after hand surgery, was back in action in November 1996, then ranked number 14 in the world. Zina Garrison-Jackson, in 1990, became the first woman of her race to reach the finals at Wimbledon since Althea Gibson in 1958.

In 1998, a record number of four black women competed at Wimbledon—Serena Williams, Venus Williams, Lori McNeil, and Chanda Rubin. All scored some victories, but the only finals winner was Serena Williams. She and partner Max Mirnyi of Belarus won the mixed doubles.

With their mixed doubles partners, the Williams sisters scored a 1998 tennis grand slam, never before accomplished by family members. Venus and Justin Gimelstob won the Australian and French Opens; Serena and Max Mirnyi won the U.S. Open as well as Wimbledon.

As far back as 1975, I had been speculating about greatly increased participation of black women in the professional tennis ranks. That was the year Margot Antoinette Tiff, twenty-two, of Shaker Heights, Ohio, became the first of her race to move onto the pro tennis circuit with the Cleveland Nets of World Team Tennis.

A truly welcome opportunity in sports for women developed in 1996. For years, young women basketball stars had to go abroad, largely to European countries, in order to play their game professionally. Suddenly, in mid-1996, two new stateside leagues for women were gearing up for action.

The American Basketball League (ABL), which had signed most members of the U.S. Olympics team that blew away all the competition in the Atlanta Games, began playing its forty-game schedule in October of 1996 with eight teams. It was a history-making event in sports opportunities for women. The teams were the Colorado Xplosion, New England Blizzard, Portland Power, San Jose Lasers, Columbus Quest, Seattle Reign, Atlanta Glory, and Richmond Rage (moved to Philadelphia for the second season). Long Beach, California, was added as the ninth team for the second season. The ABL had arranged to have games televised regionally on the SportsChannel and its Prime/Fox affiliates. By January 1997, it had added the Black Entertainment Television network. The ABL dropped Atlanta and added Chicago and Nashville for the 1998-99 season. A highlight of the ABL's second All-Star game's halftime program was the first-ever women's slam dunk contest. It was easily won in spectacular style by Sylvia Crawley, then with the Colorado Xplosion, who paced off ten steps, put on a blindfold, then jammed home the dunk. CBS agreed to carry two ABL playoff games in the next two seasons.

The second league, the Women's National Basketball Association (WNBA) launched its ten-week season with eight teams on June 21, 1997, starting with three television networks to carry some of its games. As the NBA owns this league, it was Commissioner David Stern who announced the league had lined up NBC, ESPN, and "Lifetime" and that healthy commercial backing had been secured. The teams were the Cleveland Rockers, New York Liberty, Utah Starzz, Los Angeles Sparks, Houston Comets, Charlotte Sting, Phoenix Mercury, and Sacramento Monarchs.

Initially, some women players feared the explosion in competition might lead to the failure of both leagues. Average pay in the ABL was reported to be about $80,000, with the Olympians making around $125,000 for a season that ended in March. The pay scale reportedly ran from $40,000 to $150,000. By the end of the regular season, the eight teams were averaging 3,536 fans. Columbus won the first league playoff championship 3-2 over Richmond.

The ABL lost money in its first season, as was expected. In signing top-flight players for its second season, ABL president Gary Cavalli was pleased that the league's catches included AP player of the year Kara Wolters of Connecticut and Kate Starbird of Stanford, rated by many the best of the year. Average attendance climbed to 4,333 for the second year, still far below what the WNBA was attracting.

Popular Olympians Sheryl Swoopes, Rebecca Lobo, and Ruthie Bolton-Holifield were among the early signees announced by the WNBA. With Lisa Leslie, they were heavily hyped in preseason promotions, but it was Cynthia Cooper of the Houston Comets who won the league's MVP award in a unanimous vote. The Comets won the league championship, defeating the early-season favorite New York Liberty. Swoopes, who was with the Comets, and husband Eric Jackson became parents four days after the season started. Swoopes got into action early in August. The WNBA pay scale reportedly was between $15,000 and $50,000, to be supplemented by advertising and promotion fees.

The well-marketed WNBA also lost money but averaged 9,699 fans for regular season games. League president Val Ackerman said plans were to add two teams, increase salaries and add games to the front-end of the schedule. The new teams were in Washington and Detroit. For the 1999 season, Orlando and Minnesota teams would join. The new, increased WNBA salary scale ran from $15,000 to $50,000 for new players, higher for others. Some WNBA players were beginning to talk about unionizing.

I initially agreed with those who thought the WNBA had the best shot at success because of the NBA ownership, superior television coverage, and marketing prospects. But I was extremely happy about new opportunities for women cagers in both leagues. I hoped both would prosper and eventually engage in a championship playoff, although that would be difficult as long as they display their talents during different seasons.

In the past, the TV networks virtually ignored women cagers except for their college championship games; some of the major colleges have slighted them by resisting Title IX, which has kept them from having the exposure they deserved. Many of these schools refused to field teams and give them the kind of financial support they gave men's teams. I think those practices have been very discriminatory. In 1997, the United States Supreme Court upheld the validity of Title IX during its twenty-fifth anniversary year, a major victory for women athletes.

Having covered a string of Olympics, I was a big booster of the games in Atlanta, but I refused to change my position of preferring that the United States be represented in basketball by college players rather than by NBA professionals. Never, though, did I entertain any idea that the controlling powers would change—and take a chance on not winning the gold in basketball.

I derived some comfort in knowing that Dr. LeRoy Walker, first black president of the U.S. Olympic Committee, was not pleased about having no college players at all on the U.S. team. Walker said, "I do not like the fact that no college players are representing the United States. The current system bothers me . . . Don't tell me we can't field a mixture of talent. But right now, a young kid simply doesn't have any hope of making the current team. We should have more young kids on this team."

Some of my concern was steeped in the view that young basketball players were frequently taken advantage of by their college teams and the NCAA, so at least they should reap the rewards of an opportunity to play in the Olympics.

The NCAA was a target of mine because of certain restrictions it placed on young athletes. The last available report showed that the NCAA's standards, based largely on tests many experts term racially and culturally biased, were knocking 26.9 percent of potential black college athletes out of freshman-year competition. Often, after they are accepted, NCAA schools will use these kids as long as their eligibility is in force; as soon as it is up, they are expendable, and then it's four years, or three years, for nothing—not even a good education in too many instances.

Meanwhile, these young kids could see that they were making millions of dollars for their conferences. The Atlantic Coast Conference (ACC) alone can take millions of dollars out of the 64-team NCAA elimination. Now if the kids want to make a telephone call home, they can't get the coach to give them a quarter under the rules. That's unfair. At least by the summer of 1998, the NCAA had agreed to allow college athletes to make up to $2,000 a year in part-time jobs. That unfairness in the rules was part of the reason I said, at least give *them* the opportunity to make the Olympics, instead of the NBA players.

Of course, that wasn't to be. But I did see something in the games in Atlanta that warmed my heart, something that had been increasingly obvious every four years: America's black athletes, including its once-unappreciated female track contingent, were promoted and accepted universally as first-class representatives whose exceptional talents were counted on to ensure that the hosting country stood tall in the centennial observance.

These athletes produced some of the biggest thrills of the spectacular event, particularly in the track and field contests. By my own count, the United States won 44 of the 271 gold medals awarded. Black competitors accounted for about 15 of these as individuals, as teams, and as members of integrated squads: men's basketball and women's basketball, women's gymnastics, and women's soccer. Women as a group accounted for 19 of the 44 gold medals. Women marked another first when a longtime champion of their participation in the Olympics, Anita DeFrantz, forty-four, a Los Angeles attorney, became the first woman elected vice president of the International Olympic Committee in September 1997.

For my main readership, these were some of the Atlanta games highlights: Michael Johnson became the first man ever to win the 200- and

400-meter races at the same Olympics. Carl Lewis, at thirty-five, won the long jump for his record-tying ninth gold medal and retired in 1997. Gail Devers became the fastest woman in the world by winning the 100-meter with one-time detractor Gwen Torrence taking the bronze and the victory lap with Devers. Injuries forced one of the all-time great women athletes, two-time heptathlon winner Jackie Joyner-Kersee, to settle for a bronze in the long jump. As the only black woman gymnast at the Olympics level, Dominique Dawes shared in an American women's first-ever gold medal, and also won an individual bronze to go along with the team bronze she shared in 1992. Among U.S. men gymnasts, Jair Lynch took an individual silver, the only medal the men's team garnered. It was left to light middle-weight David Reid to win the only gold for America in boxing. That puny showing probably played a part in California labor lawyer Chris Campbell's becoming the first black executive director of an American Olympics sport as head of the federation that runs amateur boxing.

Jackie Joyner-Kersee would wind down her brilliant fifteen-year career in the 1998 Goodwill Games in New York with a dramatic victory in her specialty, compiling a year's best 6,502 points in heptathlon, her twenty-fifth heptathlon win. All over-7,000 point victories belong to her. At thirty-six, her last hurrah was a long jump in the U.S. Open held about fifteen miles from her birthplace, East Saint Louis, Illinois.

Speaking of boxing, the years failed to improve my lack of appreciation for the sport. In a September 1996 column, I dubbed ex-heavyweight champ Joe Frazier as "a bitter man long after his presence in the sordid world of professional boxing was ended." I said this because Frazier made disparaging remarks after revered former heavyweight champion Muhammad Ali was honored by the U.S. Olympic Committee with the role of lighting the symbolic torch opening the games in Atlanta.

In that same issue, I had this to say about two other well-known fighters who at one time were favorite warriors: "Sugar Ray Leonard, who already has twice retired and un-retired, plans to fight Hector Camacho in late fall or early winter. But get this: Grandpa Larry Holmes, 48, is chasing grandpa George Foreman, 48, seeking what he promises for the fourth time will be his 'final farewell.'" Sugar Ray lost his comeback fight in a fifth-round TKO and promised, again, that he was retired for good. In a matter of hours he un-retired himself, again.

After referring to other boxing intrigue and skullduggery, I aimed an arrow at the scheduled heavyweight bout that pitted Mike Tyson against Bruce Seldon for promoter Don King. Conceding some readers would consider it a mean shot, I went on to describe the "heavyweight title" bout as one "in which an ex-convict is opposing an ex-convict in a match promoted by an ex-convict." In fairness, I added, "While that, in their own words, is factual, it should be made clear that each has paid the price to return to society."

See if you can follow me now on this heavyweight boxing picture. Tyson, who converted to the Muslim faith and insisted he was a new and better person, stopped Seldon in one minute and forty-nine seconds of the first round in the bout at the MGM Grand Garden in Las Vegas for his $15 million payday. The loser got $5 million. So, in the titles thicket of heavyweight boxing, Tyson had won the World Boxing Association title to go with his World Boxing Council crown. He and promoter Don King planned to unify the heavyweight division by also taking Michael Moorer's International Boxing Federation (IBF) title. Still out there in the heavyweight maze, though, would have been the World Boxing Organization and the World Boxing Union titles. The WBA and WBC have talked about unifying.

But first, the plan was to tune up with a multimillion dollar fight against former two-time champ Evander Holyfield. Pending that fight, in the heavyweight title jungle, it came about that Tyson's WBC crown went by the boards (reportedly in a contract deal) as a result of Tyson's fighting Seldon instead of Lennox Lewis, who, according to an announcement by his copromoters, was ready to take on challenger Oliver McCall. The next big announcement concerning the Lennox Lewis–Oliver McCall WBC title match was that Don King had won the right to promote that bout. Then, big-time upset in the Holyfield tune-up. The 10-1 underdog Holyfield stopped Tyson in eleven rounds. But not to worry; King announced he also had promotional rights to Holyfield's next outing. McCall refused to throw any punches in the fourth and fifth rounds of his fight and lost it. Promoter King was still in there when Holyfield took Michael Moorer's IBF crown and planned to be around when Holyfield took on Lennox Lewis for his WBC title.

Next boxing news, the same Julio Cesar Chavez who testified against King in an insurance fraud case that ended with a hung jury had an announcement: "Don King has great plans for me." The plans included Chavez's appearing on an upcoming boxing card for King. Meantime, prosecutors in the fraud case got another indictment against King, this time including a fraud charge against his Don King Productions Inc. However, the federal judge who granted the new trial reportedly suggested that the case seemed to be based almost entirely on inferences. Anyway, King won again with Baltimore attorney William H. "Billy" Murphy Jr. playing a key role. And, thus, the boxing game's band played on in tune.

In all of sports, Mike Tyson was judged by *Forbes* magazine to be the top money maker in 1996 with a one-year record income of $75 million. He had been involved in most of the biggest money-grossing bouts of all times.

Some of us doubted that Tyson, who was nearing his thirty-first birthday, had managed to overcome his troubled background and history; we were somewhat encouraged to learn as he trained for his rematch with Holyfield that he had married longtime fiancee Monica Turner and was talking about being a good father.

Maybe his intentions were good. But we were about to witness another zany side of Tyson on June 28, 1997, during his Holyfield rematch, reportedly the largest overall moneymaker in boxing history. In the third round, Tyson bit Holyfield on his right ear, and after being warned by referee Mills Lane, bit the champ on the left ear, resulting in his being disqualified—and roundly vilified.

My view was that Tyson's boxing career should have been finished, but it doesn't necessarily work that way in the pugilistic game. The Nevada State Athletic Commission heard Tyson's "I just snapped" apology and fined him nearly $3 million—the 10 percent limit of his purse it could take at the time—plus it revoked his license for at least a year. After a year he could reapply. My guess had to be that Tyson would be back, and that the new Nevada law allowing the commission to take all of a fighter's purse won't be used much.

Tyson's first appeal to get back into boxing was not in Nevada but in New Jersey, where many of his bouts had taken place. Before a ruling was handed down, Tyson decided to end the New Jersey appeal and make it in Nevada. Before the new law went into effect, we saw Lennox Lewis claim the WBC title when Oliver McCall turned crybaby and declined to fight back. After the new law was on the books, Lewis won again when Nigeria's

Henry Akinwande wouldn't stop holding him. The Nigerian collected all his million-dollar purse. So guess what? The next guy reported to be in line to fight Lewis was Andrew Golota. He's the boxer who was disqualified for repeated low blows in two consecutive fights with Riddick Bowe. It turned out that next up for Lewis was Shannon Briggs, who went down for good in the fifth round. Riddick Bowe won himself a lot of publicity when he decided to quit boxing and live out his dream of being a Marine. He lasted a matter of days.

The absolutely meanest reaction I heard regarding the Tyson disgrace, a reaction that didn't get nearly the media coverage it deserved, came from boxer Hector Camacho, in a vicious racial slur on CNN/SI. One of his stupid remarks about Tyson's problems was that, "He's got too many n-----s around him." Camacho included disparaging remarks about King.

As previously noted, I'm not a big King fan, but I can say on his behalf that his detractors and competitors had tried unsuccessfully for years to bring him down, attempts that included a series of court battles. The savvy promoter always seemed a step ahead of them. *Sports Illustrated* listed him as one of the forty most influential sports figures of the past forty years. He regularly had a string of top fighters in his stable. A popular draw for him was Christy Martin, women's top boxer.

In June 1997, King and Sugar Ray Leonard, who at various times held five world boxing titles in different weight classes, were inducted into the International Boxing Hall of Fame. King was cited that summer by the NAACP for his various charitable efforts. He also was honored during the summer as a "cherished American celebrity" by the New York City Council's Black and Hispanic Caucus. A movie based on a book about King, not one of his favorites, was made with Ving Rhames playing King. So, although Don King continued to face challenges to his reign, he was tremendously successful at promoting big-money bouts and outmaneuvering some of the nation's most powerful boxing/entertainment moguls and legal eagles. Last word from the Tyson-King camps was that Tyson had sued King for $100 million or so, claiming he'd been ripped off and Tyson, in turn, was being sued by a couple of women, who, Tyson's lawyer said, were trying to rip off the fighter. Also, Tyson was reportedly picking up a few million bucks acting as a special enforcer at some wrestling shows. To quote the boxing game's top promoter in 1996: "Only in America!"

No matter which way I turned, there was no escaping the headlines of 1996–1997 that told the sad stories of how athletes had been unable to escape many of the personal life habits that brought discredit to them and pain to others. They involved the collegians and the professionals, poor guys hoping to strike it rich and rich guys near the top of their professions.

The disturbing sports-related stories poured out on a regular basis. Assaults on young women, girlfriends, wives, and other relatives—sometimes with weapons. Drugs. Drunken driving. Tax evasion. Point shaving in games. Repeated public temper tantrums. Spitting incidents (football and baseball). Broadcast vulgarity. Kickings. Embarrassing showboating. Failure to pay debts. Even $25,000 and $50,000 fines. As well as assaulting a coach at a monster-bucks cost of $6.4 million in lost salary during a sixty-eight-day suspension. And, sadly enough, nowhere in sight could I detect any promise of improvement in this bad picture.

Apparently the images of athletes were at such a low level that women like Nina Shahravan in Texas felt emboldened enough to initiate false assault charges against two Dallas football players. These were publicized nationally without being adequately checked out either by police or the media. The two players split $2.2 million as a result of the settlement of a defamation suit against Fort Worth–based WXAS-TV and reporter Marty Griffin. The two also filed a civil rights legal action against Dallas police for naming them as suspects. No charges were filed against the players in this case.

I can attest to this: Thus far, women athletes were compiling totally different personal conduct records than men. Olympian Lisa Leslie of the WNBA league expressed the widely held view that male athletes were getting out of hand with some of their antics. It remained to be seen how the increased opportunities to compete at both the college and professional levels might narrow the gap between the conduct of women and some of the men.

Before the women of the new American Basketball League completed their first All-Star game, one of them had been accused of rough play, suspended for two games, and fined $1,500 by the league. Considering their more modest pay as compared to male stars, the ABL was demonstrating quite clearly that it would not tolerate such conduct. In its first month, one of the WNBA's stars was hit with a $500 fine for holding another player by her neck.

I accept the possibility that negative incidents involving athletes are no more prevalent than they are in the population as a whole, which is not terribly good, but because they are in the limelight, the publicity creates the impression that too often they simply don't stop to think of the consequences of their actions. Although most sports stars go out of their way to create mountains of goodwill, too many others seem to do just the opposite.

I sincerely believe that no matter the distractions, sports and athletic competition continue to hold a special place in the lives of Americans. The talented competitors and their often fantastic game-time achievements, individually and as team members, spread joy, lift the human spirit, and serve as a constant reminder that in everything, there are ups and downs.

In a nationally televised program with sports figures on racial progress and shortcomings in the area, President Bill Clinton said Americans, rightly or wrongly, often see games as a symbol of what we are as a people.

I could, but won't, rattle off numerous stars and events that helped make 1996 another heartwarming year in sports for me.

As soon as I heard that baseball would be honoring the fiftieth anniversary of Jackie Robinson's breaking the racial barrier in major league baseball throughout 1997, I surmised that a bit of media attention probably would come my way because of my connection to Jackie and my long crusade to integrate baseball. Over the years, the media often sought me out when doing something on these subjects and on the old Negro baseball leagues.

It started as a trickle. The first notable interview request for a program to be used during the 1997 celebration year came from a London-based television outfit late in 1996. Then it turned into a deluge. At my request, Gainor Hackney, my special assistant at the *Afro-American*, tried to hold back the tide, but I had known many of the people involved for years, so I wanted to cooperate with as many of them as possible.

Events were scheduled throughout the year. There were interviews for radio, television, newspapers, and magazines. I was honored with awards from sports and journalism associations, including the Red Smith award from the Associated Press Sports Editors, and induction into the writers wing of the National Baseball Hall of Fame. I was especially glad to learn that two scholarships had been established in my name, and that I was the winner of the Frederick Douglass Award from the University System of Maryland Board of Regents.

Celebrity is all right for some people. I don't like it. In all honesty, I can't claim to have done anything to justify all the attention, though I do appreciate it. In the case of baseball integration, I just happened to be in the right place at the right time. I think that anyone else situated as I was and possessing a bit of curiosity and concern about progresss would have done the same thing.

A COLLECTION OF LACY COLUMNS

Over the years, I must have written more than three-thousand of my regular columns, "Looking 'Em Over," "A to Z" and "Sam Lacy." This section includes a number of those columns, dealing with diverse matters. They run from the hard-nosed to the compassionate, from occasions of fun to expressions of the highest tribute to featured subjects.

This one was written in January 1965 when the American Football League's All-Star game had to be moved out of New Orleans because the twenty-one black players refused to play there after running into racial bigotry.

Only in Times of War and Taxes

The American Football League's All-Star game was played Saturday at Houston, Texas, and the West defeated the East as was expected . . . in four years of these annual meetings the West has never lost to the East . . . Also, as seemed a certainty, San Diego's mammoth Earl Faison, Ernie Ladd and Frank Buncom, and the Kansas City's Bobby Bell were tremendous on defense . . . and Buffalo's Elbert Dubenion and Boston's Larry Garron joined Keith Lincoln of the Chargers in the offense limelight.

The fact of the matter is that everything about this game went just about the way it was expected to go. Only the events leading up to the affair went against the script . . . Chief among these events was the wholesale bolting of the original site of the contest by 21 colored athletes.

When these young football players packed their gear and quit New Orleans in protest against local bigotry, the action was so totally unexpected that it rocked the entire sports world . . . and I, for one, just loved it.

Official New Orleans reaction to the colored walkout was at the same time typically unrealistic and tragically amusing.

"If these men," said Mayor Victor Schiro, "would play football only in cities where everybody loved them, they'd all be out of a job today . . . Their reaction will only aggravate the very condition they are seeking, in time, to eliminate . . . They," the mayor continued, "should have 'rolled with the punch' and played" . . . Dave Dixon, the promoter who was serving as the local custodian for the AFL game, said he "seriously questioned the wisdom of the peremptory action which they took to redress these alleged grievances" . . . and, declared Dixon, it was "made clear to these players that militant action such as they were contemplating (before the walkout), would not only damage this city, but would greatly retard efforts by men of goodwill to achieve harmony in the most difficult problem of our times."

Jewish tackle Ron Mix of the San Diego Chargers, told readers of a *Sports Illustrated* article last weekend that he tried in vain to convince the players they were wrong in their method of protest . . . There were other ways, he said he told the assembled group of tan stars, to focus national attention on what was going on . . . "News stories could pour out of the city every day," Mix asserted, "and that would give us some time to resolve" the problem.

Before going into an assessment of these arguments, suppose we take a look at some of the player complaints that multimillionaire Dixon rejects as "alleged grievances."

In the first place, the colored athletes had not even reached the city before being exposed to the pattern of treatment they were to anticipate in New Orleans . . . They had difficulty getting from the airport when taxi driver after taxi driver either ignored their bidding altogether or, in face-to-face confrontation, refused to take them.

Several of the stars were marooned at the terminal for more than three hours . . . In the city, it was much the same.

Ernie Warlick, a graduate of North Carolina College who acted as spokesman for the group, was berated for using a restaurant coat rack . . . Ernie Ladd of Grambling University, and Dick Westmoreland of A&T College, were told to "get the hell away from here" by a Bourbon Street club's doorman who made a gesture toward his hip pocket as though reaching for a pistol, when they sought to enter the place . . . Abner Haynes, who was the first colored graduate of the then otherwise white West Texas State College, thought he had it made when he was readily accepted by the cab driver stationed in front of the team hotel . . . Haynes gave the name of a club where he was to meet several of his teammates of both races . . . Instead of being taken there, however, the two-time AFL most valuable player was carried to the opposite end of the city to a hangout frequented by [undesirable characters].

Now . . . how about that Mayor Schiro? . . . Since when do you have to "love" a man to extend to him the same rights that you enjoy? . . . and being a politician, he should be able to answer this question: In how many cities could he sit as mayor if he waited for everybody to love him? . . . His job is no more important to Schiro than is Warlick's job to him, or Westmoreland's or Haynes's or Ladd's.

And Dixon . . . The promoter, who once was described to "A to Z" as a "money counter" when query was made concerning his occupation, makes reference to the "peremptory actions" of the players . . . This is a laugh . . . Notice had been served on AFL officials well in advance of the game that colored players would refuse to participate in any contest not covered by contract agreement, where they were likely to be confronted with prejudice and discrimination . . . The action these fellows took last week was only "peremptory" because Schiro, Dixon, etcetera, didn't believe them.

As for the promoter's purported warning that "such militant action would greatly retard efforts by men of goodwill" to eliminate the problem, that too, is imbecilic . . . Men of goodwill have been making such efforts for lo too many years . . . with their hats in their hands . . . Warlick and his contemporaries—like the sit-inners, the Freedom Riders and the Washington Marchers—are simply wearing their hats . . . They didn't stretch themselves in front of the cabs or knock down the doors of the jim-crow eating places . . . They just packed up and said: "Go on, have your football game; we'd rather not play."

Mix? . . . Now Ron should have known better . . . his argument was pathetic . . . "News stories," he said, "could pour out of the city every day" that would focus national attention on the situation . . . How naive can an educated white boy get? . . . News pictures and television reports on the police dogs of Alabama and Mississippi, and pulpit criticism of church bombings and campus riots didn't succeed in shaming the Dixiecrat elements . . . and if over a hundred years of waiting isn't "giving us more time to resolve the problem," just how much more is more time?

Ron pointed out that he is a Jew, and because of that fact he fully understands the feelings of the colored players . . . But he had no trouble getting into town from the airport and he enjoyed the hospitality of four Bourbon Street clubs the first evening he and his San Diego Chargers teammates were in New Orleans . . . so, apparently Mix means well, but what does he mean?

Finally, this business about "rolling with the punch" deserves some comment, brief though it may be . . . My grandfather and yours "rolled with the punch" and their grandfathers before them did the same . . . Today's grandfathers of the future are asking why it is that colored people are destined to be the only ones in this country showing the Christian attitude of turning the other cheek.

They're interested in knowing why it is that we must content ourselves with being first class citizens only when the bugle blows for war and at income tax time.

Boxing was on my beat. I often covered small and major boxing matches, and I interviewed personalities in the field, but this column represents my feeling about what takes place inside the four-cornered ring.

OK, Let's Face It Now: This Is a Sport?

Obviously, mine is a fieldmouse voice of protest in a meadow of screaming coyotes, but I cannot abandon my continuing and increasing abhorrence for professional boxing.

Perhaps, the regular readers of this column are thoroughly bored by my constant repetition of the theme . . . Just the same, I cringe at the realization that thousands accept as a "sport" an activity in which the prime objective is to beat an opponent into a state that is as close to death as it is possible to achieve without going over the line.

Playing "brinkmanship" with a person's life is not my idea of healthy competition . . . At this desk, trying one's best to knock a rival unconscious is not too far removed from Russian roulette.

What power does any man possess that enables him to stop just short of a point of no return in administering a beating to his foe in the other corner? . . . And what protection is offered by a referee when, in most cases, that referee is neither a doctor nor, even, a former boxer himself?

Zach Clayton, who is a longtime friend, has served as third man in the ring in scores of important fights . . . But Zach's preparation for such assignments? . . . He was an excellent basketball player and an average baseball first baseman.

Clayton is just one of a hundred or more untrained men working as the main officials in a "sport" in which other men's lives are at stake.

Make no mistake, I am fully aware that a rigid curtailment of professional boxing would take a lot of money out of a lot of pockets . . . A hefty chunk of that money would be lost to promoters and fight managers, none of whom receives the first blow in a bloodletting fight.

As for the fighters themselves, it would be an opportunity to pursue another career . . . Several have done just that, the latest being Leo Randolph, an Olympic gold medalist on the same U.S. team that produced Sugar Ray Leonard and the Spinks brothers, Leon and Michael.

A fighter who didn't walk away was Cleveland Denny, a young husband and father who died from a beating he absorbed on the undercard of the Leonard–Roberto Duran title bout two months ago . . . There have been eight ring deaths this year already, and 1980 still has four months to go.

This feeble cry from here follows all such unfortunate incidents as the one involving Denny and others before him . . . including the beating suffered by 24-year-old Derrick Holmes in Las Vegas on August 23.

Young Holmes, perhaps inspired by his suburban D.C. neighbor Sugar Ray Leonard, undertook to dethrone WBC super bantamweight champion Wilfredo Gomez . . . He didn't lose his life in the brutal beating, true, but he sustained a shattered jaw, among other things.

And Dr. Daniel Orr, the surgeon who treated Derrick, described what he found during the operation:

"I was amazed that he hung in there for as long as he did after suffering the break," Orr said. The fracture had come in the second round but the fight wasn't awarded to Gomez until the fifth.

"He had a displaced compound fracture. The bones were protruding into the mouth. His (upper left) wisdom tooth was split right in half. If you followed that line of fracture it matched the one in his jaw. The tooth was split by the same punch that broke the jaw.

"Every time Gomez hit him, it was making pieces of tooth and bone fall in his mouth. It must have been like sticking your finger in a light socket. Just bouncing around displaced the fracture."

Holmes was down eight times for counts, once without getting hit. He went down five times in the fourth round. His manager signaled referee Joey Curtis to stop the bout after Holmes went down for the second time, 2 minutes 39 seconds into the fifth round.

"The raw nerve ending was exposed," the doctor said. "The tooth was hanging out, then the jaw bone was displaced. There is a nerve going through the middle of the jaw bone that held the jaw together. The nerve itself wasn't injured."

I ask you, friends, does that sound like a sport? . . . It certainly doesn't to me . . . Forty-three states ban cockfighting, mind you.

The failure of many colleges and universities to insist that athletes get the kind of education they deserve regularly gained attention. Here was a case in which it was felt the school had used a student and then sought to take credit for dumping him when his services were no longer important to the university.

Yes, Virginia

If you happen to live anywhere close to the region exposed to Atlantic Coast Conference influence, you saw daily sports pages emblazoned last week with the news that Barry Word had been declared academically ineligible and would be unable to play football for the rest of the season at the University of Virginia.

At first look, that would make out the Cavalier program as a martyr to the principles of education . . . Virginia was sacrificing one of the seven leading rushers in the nation for the sake of maintaining its reputation as a school which caters to would-be scholars, not to students who aim to get by because they're athletes.

That, my friends, is hogwash, poppycock and genuine, A-one bee ess!! . . . at least in this case.

Barry Word gained a school record 1,224 yards this season—best in the ACC—and gained more than 100 yards in five straight games . . . His 5.9 yards per carry is third best in the country—right up there with Heisman hopefuls Bo Jackson of Auburn and Keith Byars of Ohio State . . . Nor does he lack for speed, as evidenced by the fact he made the Olympic trials as a hurdler.

For the Cavaliers to take such drastic action and set aside a potential All-American, they expected—and received—a lot of ink in the major press . . . surefire advertisement for the University of Virginia image . . . at first look.

But consider this . . . Barry Word is a senior . . . He has been a student (on football scholarship) for four years, yet only now has he run afoul of the classroom standards . . . Only now is it revealed that he was suspended from the football program "for his failure to meet a set of academic requirements," according to the brief announcement from the College of Arts and Sciences.

While neither the university nor head coach George Welsh has confirmed it, a Roanoke (Virginia) newspaper reported that Word had been placed on academic probation before the season started . . . Still the young athlete was permitted to play, obviously because it was felt no one would notice the classroom problems while he was compiling statistics that seemed to assure him ACC Player of the Year honors.

This is another of those cases assessed so often by the AFRO as pure and unadulterated exploitation of a young black who continues protected by a major college until his athletic eligibility is exhausted . . . After that, see ya!

On November 23, though he had not turned in a classroom paper which reportedly was long overdue, Word gained 170 yards rushing and led the Cavaliers to a 24-22 victory over archrival North Carolina . . . Two days later, his suspension from school and football was daily paper headlines.

The AFRO adamantly refuses to accept this as a well-intentioned move on the part of the Cavaliers, and for several reasons: (1) Word has four years of what we're led to believe was a good mix of academics and athletics behind him . . . (2) The Cavaliers have only one game left on their schedule, which will have no effect on their ACC standings . . . (3) They are not going to any postseason bowl game, so the loss of Word for one contest doesn't hurt them in the least.

The AFRO doesn't buy the posturing . . . But the major media do . . . Yes, Virginia, there is a Santa Claus.

Eddie Murray, one of the Baltimore Orioles best players ever, took a media/talk show/team owner beating in Baltimore before asking to be traded. He left in 1988.

Players have their own assessments of their teammates, based on professional and personal relationships. So, when Orioles all-star shortstop Cal Ripken broke Lou Gehrig's consecutive games played record with 2,131 on September 6, 1995, he mentioned by name four individuals for special thanks: his father, Cal Sr., mother Vi, wife Kelly—and Eddie Murray, then with the Cleveland Indians.

Ripken said, "When I got to the big leagues, there was a man, Eddie Murray, who showed me how to play the game day in and day out. I thank him for his example and for his leadership. I was lucky to have him for my teammate for the years we were together."

On July 21, 1996, Orioles owner Peter Angelos brought Murray back to Baltimore in a trade with Cleveland. He would later play with the Anaheim Angels and end his career again with the Los Angeles Dodgers. But in his first game back with the Orioles, Murray hit his 492nd career home run. His 500th on September 6 made him, Hank Aaron, and Willie Mays the only major leaguers with 500 homers and 3,000 hits. In 1997, the Orioles brought Murray back as a coach. He was moved to tears on June 7, 1998, when the team formally retired his number 33. Popular with most Baltimore fans, when Murray came to bat for the Orioles or even when he visited with teams like Cleveland, he often would be greeted with an "Ed-dee! Ed-dee!" chant. That was the one-word title for this column in 1986.

Ed-dee!!

Because of the continuing interest in Eddie Murray's flap with the Orioles, this column is a reprint from the weekend Baltimore edition.

It must be obvious to virtually everyone, whether sports fans or not, that it is "whipping time" for Eddie Murray on the Baltimore plantation.

The slovenly first baseman of the baseball team got uppity last week, and had the nerve to imply that he didn't like the way he was being treated. He had the gall to complain that overseer Hank Peters wanted him to answer questions—the majority of them stupid—posed by gentry from the surrounding area.

Also, this Murray fellow had become a boy who had the guts to be disturbed by unceasing criticism of his cotton-pickin' by the righteous folks who ran radio talk shows as a sounding board for their gripes.

Then when Massa Ed Williams came over from the Big House and tamped into him for leading astray plantation-mate Floyd Rayford, that smart-aleck boy asked for his freedom.

Of course, all the foregoing is written in a facetious vein. There is no inclination to liken the Oriole operation to the running of an early Dixie estate with its resident laborers.

In the light of recent developments the temptation is present but not the inclination.

The unrest between Murray, the Orioles and the Baltimore community came about when the player, seething under what he considered wholesale carping about his presence in the lineup, talk-show speculation on getting rid of him, etcetera, went to general manager Hank Peters and asked to be traded.

There was an ironic twist in statements attributed to Peters in the wake of the visit.

The general manager accused Murray of picking "a bad time" to ask to be traded.

"I like to think we're still in the race (for the division title). Nothing else—no individual player—is going to detract from that," declared Peters.

The general manager, however, did not touch on the equally poor timing of Edward Bennett Williams's attack on Eddie Murray's performance and dedication.

And it was the owner's tirade that triggered Murray's reaction.

Let's give EBW the benefit of the doubt, whether deserved or not.

In doing so, we can equate his "lecture" as being motivated by one of two things: (1) he was giving vent to frustration caused by the shortcomings of a team he spent millions of dollars to assemble, or (2) he was attacking his best employee to impress upon the rest of his crew that not one of them is sacred.

Overlooked, though, was the fact that Eddie Murray is an extremely sensitive human being. And the open reprimand by an employer who should be expected to understand this, was the proverbial "straw that broke the camel's back."

Proof of Eddie's sensitivity may be found in his act of purchasing and donating blocks of game tickets for daily use by hundreds of inner-city youth, his frequent unannounced visits to area hospitals, and finally last fall's establishment of a recreation center for the needy, bearing the name of his mother, Mrs. Carrie Murray.

Then there is the beef about Murray's reluctance—nay refusal—to submit to interviews by the media types.

While there is widespread criticism of him for this estrangement, there is both sympathy and understanding at this desk.

I have spent many hours in the midst of the typical mass interview, and I have witnessed the results.

Pitcher Steve Carlton of the Phillies held out for years against media attempts to quote—or misquote—him.

Unlike Reggie Jackson or the late Casey Stengel, whose eyes lit up like Christmas trees at the sight of a microphone or a note pad, Eddie is a private person.

He totally dislikes the thought that something he says in a gathering of reporters will emerge in a wide range of versions. Many of these are controversial opinions which he is asked to respond to the next day.

As for the talk shows, Murray and his admirers are stung by the tone which suggests that the potential of young newcomer Jim Traber makes him expendable.

But there is a disturbing lack of foresight here.

Traber is in the very early stages of what may be an outstanding career—or may not be. Opposing pitchers have yet to discover the idiosyncrasies that are part of every new hitter.

Moreover, there can be a distinct misconception with regard to the young man's figures, especially when his heroics at the plate are compared to Murray's performance.

Traber is hitting a lusty .320 and winning the adulation of local fans; Murray is batting a respectable .305, fifteen percentage points lower.

In case one isn't aware, 15 percentage points, however, can be erased in the course of two games.

What also should be recognized is the fact that batting averages have a tendency to soar when a few games (and at-bats) fall into the equation, plummet when more games are considered.

Eddie's .305 average represents his production through 99 games, Jim's .320 is for 35 contests. Murray (at this writing) has been to bat 350 times, nearly three times more often than Traber's 124.

It will be interesting to compare the numbers when Traber has made up the 64-game difference. That won't be this year, of course, because (at this writing) only 32 games remain in the season.

Another of the talk-show knocks against Eddie speaks of his defensive fall-off—mentioned by owner Williams in his public scolding of the first baseman.

Yet Eddie's 10 errors afield are exactly the same as have been committed by the fair-haired Cal Ripken Jr., at shortstop. And Ripken has not been plagued by injury as has Murray.

Finally, at the risk of appearing repetitious, I must point out that Murray has been the most productive offensive player in recent Baltimore history—in fact in all of baseball.

Since his arrival here in 1977, Eddie, through 1985, had driven in more runs than the likes of Jim Rice of the Red Sox, Dave Winfield of the Yankees, Mike Schmidt of the Phillies, Tony Armas of the Red Sox and Don Baylor, all recognized and highly paid sluggers, and all with greater longevity at the plate.

This piece looks at another aspect of television—how blacks were being covered in golfdom by the networks. It was an issue the writer paid considerable attention to, and too often didn't appreciate what he saw, as this 1987 offering illustrates.

Did ABC See?

The lines read: "Oh, say can you see . . ."

The answer for many of us is: no, we couldn't see . . . And that is because ABC wouldn't let us see . . . Certainly, it wasn't because ABC didn't see . . . Because, you see, Jim Thorpe is black.

And in the U.S. Open golf tournament last week, Jim Thorpe—being the only black player in an otherwise all-white field—had to be as conspicuous as a cicada in a bucket of milk.

But, obviously, ABC didn't care . . . And this wasn't the first time that ABC didn't care.

The network coverage was similarly cold-blooded a few years back . . . It was either in 1983 when Larry Nelson won at Oakmont or 1985 when Andy North was first at Oakland Hills, that ABC went black-blind.

That was the tournament in which Calvin Peete finished in 6th place . . . Remember when Peete and Jack Nicklaus were playing partners for the last round?

And when ABC-TV actually wrapped its electronic tentacles around Nicklaus from tee to green, to the complete dismissal of Peete?

And this at a time when Peete was shooting a respectable 74, while Nicklaus was stumbling through a round of 81, to finish well back?

Remember the isolation of Peete, when the cameras were so bent on ignoring him that they were zoomed not on Calvin putting but on Jack watching Calvin putt—Calvin out of the frame?

Well, this time at the U.S. Open in San Francisco, ABC did it again . . . And this time the director of the telecast was not Barbara Donaghue as in 1985 . . . In fact, this time no credit trail was run at the end of the telecast, so the person responsible for the obliteration of Thorpe remains anonymous.

Peete, the second black to qualify for entry, failed to make the 36-hole cut, laboring to a 148, one stroke over the survival point of 147 . . . Eventual winner was Scott Simpson by one stroke over Tom Watson.

Now, it is easy to understand why the cameras do not focus on players whose scores have skyrocketed to the point where only their relatives can be interested . . . But when the pictures follow virtually every stroke of one player through the entire round and totally—yes, totally—ignore his playing partner, it invites suspicion.

This was when ABC came up with an exact replica of its earlier treatment of Peete, simply replacing Calvin with Jim, and Nicklaus with Bernhardt Langer.

The white guy, Langer, finished at 4-over-par, the black guy, Thorpe, at 3-over, a mere one-stroke difference.

If that smacks of AFRO polarization, then let it. There is no guilt feeling, since the identification is made only because there may have been some viewers who are not familiar with Thorpe, and ABC didn't let them see for themselves.

In all probability, ABC is spoiled by the fact it can get away with doing the whole picture on its *Monday Night Football* and *Monday Night Baseball* and even its *Wide World of Sports* because there's little need to concentrate on individuals such as in the one-on-one situation in golf.

Golf, like tennis, is generally looked upon as a game for middle and upper class whites . . . And while NBC has tennis (and does an acceptable job with it), ABC picks up the golf telecast and treats it with arrogance . . . Evidence suggests that in the mind of ABC, attention should be confined to the society of Perrier and manicured lawns . . . not to people like Thorpe whose family cuts those lawns.

As a consequence, twice in the last five years, ABC displayed a blatant lack of sensitivity, and clear evidence that despite its hiring of people like O. J. Simpson, Reggie Jackson and Lynn Swann, some of its pronouncements on race relations are pure lip-service.

There are tens of thousands of blacks who play and love golf . . . There was only one black player in contention in the final round of Sunday's telecast.

Thorpe was in the fifth twosome to tee off in that closing round, which meant that he was among the ten top men in the standings.

His 9th place finish qualified Thorpe for both the 1988 U.S. Open and for the Masters next April . . . So, ABC won't have the opportunity in April to do its milky-way performance, but it will get another shot to encore in June . . . CBS has the Masters TV rights.

While Thorpe, with a final score of 284, received no attention whatever on the final day, the ABC cameras kept visible Mac O'Grady (284), Larry Mize (283), Lennie Clements (284), Ben Crenshaw (283), Seve Ballesteros (282), and even Keith Clearwater with his 288.

Is that polarization? . . . With or without purpose?

And finally, there could be an unmistakable grating sound coming from the audio when black viewers were assaulted with constant Jim McKay reminders: "We're going to take a break here, but you won't miss a thing."

Except Jim Thorpe.

As a former pitcher in organized baseball, I understood the "brushback" pitch, but time after time, would speak out against the "beanball," no matter the target. Too often the knockdown balls seemed aimed at the heads of black players.

Scum!

There is no other name suitable for a family newspaper that best describes pitchers who throw beanballs at major league batsmen . . . They are nothing more nor less than unsportsmanly scum.

In mind, of course, are the two episodes of last week, in which Andre Dawson of the Chicago Cubs and Willie Wilson of the Kansas City Royals were made the targets of opposing pitchers Eric Show and Ken Schrom, respectively . . . In Dawson's case, the ball which struck him in the face caused an injury that required nine stitches and had him bleeding from the mouth. As one player said, "It looked like something from a war movie."

You've heard all the platitudes and disclaimers the perpetrators employ in the wake of such incidents . . . It wasn't intended; the victim leaned into the pitch . . . It was simply a case of establishing the pitcher's right to the plate . . . all that manure.

Even National League president Bart Giamatti and umpire John Kibler whose crew worked the Cubs-Padres game in which Dawson was struck, used the cop-out: "You can't read the mind of the pitcher. Besides, pitchers are trying to win games. They feel they have a right to brush back hitters; winning is their livelihood."

It is an old argument, one that begs an equally old rebuttal: "brushbacks" and "beanballs" are completely different . . . The well-intentioned "brushback" is thrown tight to the body—shoulders to ankles . . . The infamous "beanball" is aimed at or behind the opponent's head (aware that the normal reaction of a batter is to move backward to escape an errant pitch).

Tapes of the Show-Dawson incident clearly indicate that the delivery from the moment it left the pitcher's hand headed directly for the batter's helmet.

And about that other worn-out claim: "the ball got away" . . . There were 16 fights resulting from pitches that "got away" (nine in the AL and seven in the NL) between mid-June and the All-Star break . . . And the pitchers who, intentionally or not, triggered the brawls were schooled in control from three to five years in the minor leagues . . . and in some cases as with Show (7) and Schrom (6) in the majors.

Let us wonder whether it is fair to inject a hint of racism in this look at the Dawson and Wilson incidents . . . Because, if that is attempted, the indictment would be weakened by the realization that these fellows are but two players among an estimated 600 in major league baseball.

And neither has suffered the fate—yet—of men like Tony Conigliaro, Don Zimmer and Ron Hunt, all white . . . and all of whose careers were suddenly blunted by "beaning."

However, here is a statement of fact that may make one think: over the 40-year span between Jackie Robinson's appearance on the major league scene and Dawson-Wilson, the players most often zonked by pitched balls wore names like Sam Jethroe, Minnie Minoso, Jack Roosevelt Robinson, Frank Robinson, Willie Mays, Orlando Cepeda, Tommy Davis, Joe Foy, Al Oliver, Joe Morgan, George Bell . . . and Paul Blair and Don Baylor.

The reasons for isolating the last two: Blair was never the same player after suffering a fractured jaw in the seventies, and Baylor two weeks ago set an all-time record for being hit by a pitcher.

Is it worth noting that such names as Mickey Mantle, Duke Snider, Stan Musial, Joe DiMaggio, Ted Williams, Pete Rose, Dave Kingman and Carl Yastrzemski do not appear in this revelation?

Why do guys hurl life-threatening objects from a distance of 55 feet (allowing for a 5-foot stride) at the heads of other guys at speeds up to 92-miles-an-hour?

Because they're scum!

It will be a cheerful day in this chair when the ideal solution comes . . . That will occur when a pitcher who is known even to his teammates as a "headhunter," knocks down an opposing batter . . . Then when the guy sees his intended victim headed for the mound with evil in his eyes, he looks around his infield, then to his dugout.

And sees no one coming to help him.

This December 1987 column on Bobby Knight, basketball coach at the University of Indiana, wasn't the first time this subject was visited. In 1985, it was suggested that the university president was overly tolerant of Knight's behavior in a piece called "Blessed Boor."

Bobby Boor

Admittedly, commenting on an incident that is a week old is not always worth the time it takes for the comment . . . But, inasmuch as boors always will be around in one shape or another, it should never be too late to respond to their boorishness.

If one like Bobby Knight ever gives up center stage, another is certain to come from behind the curtain to take over . . . One can be equally certain, though, that the University of Indiana basketball coach will be an almost impossible act to follow.

Judging by the attitude he displays, Bobby Knight long since has passed the stage of basketball knighthood . . . He is in AFRO estimation a Jesus whose thorns are not on his brow but in his mouth.

The week-old incident is the one in which Bobby Boor pulled his team off the floor during an exhibition game against the touring Soviet National team . . . The act was Bobby Boor's way of retaliating against a referee's whistle . . . Bobby Boor never has liked game rules . . . He sees no need for them since he has his own . . . He never has liked referees since he feels the game should be played his way, so referees are a hindrance . . . And Bobby Boor doesn't like whistles because they are blown by referees trying to enforce rules.

Actually, the Indiana coach is not alone in this practice of protesting official calls . . . Many others do it in various forms.

There was the pit-bull brutishness of the late Woody Hayes at Ohio State . . . the angelic rowdiness of Al McGuire at Marquette . . . the play-for-pity braying of Lefty Driesell at Maryland . . . and yes the subtle harassment by Nat Frazier at Morgan.

But all of them must [stand] back and doff dubious hats to a guy who has taken the part of an international clod.

Add this insult of a Russian guest to the Pan Am Games smashing of a cop's nose in Puerto Rico, and the aforementioned reference is understandable.

During his career as the Hoosier coach, Bobby Boor once tossed a sportswriter out of his locker room because he didn't like a piece he had authored . . . He once physically bounced one of his players into his sideline seat in clear view of a packed house and television audience (the kid was a sophomore).

In addition to the Puerto Rican incident, Bobby Boor once playfully fired a blank shot at a reporter, explaining that he did it to keep from going crazy . . . He once took the microphone and chided a hometown crowd for failing to cheer for him and his players.

He has since been accused of calling an opposing coach a "chicken SOB" and of cursing the Big Ten commissioner, banging a scorer's table, blasting the cheerleaders of an opponent and tossing a chair across the floor of a crowded arena.

Last week, after leaving the visiting Soviet athletes standing on the floor aghast, Bobby Boor said: "I'm sorry."

About time?

Yet, while all this misconduct is reprehensible it is not regarded here as Bobby Boor's most serious offense.

As this desk has said repeatedly: coaches and athletic directors are teachers first . . . Winning or losing a basketball game is not nearly so important as setting examples for his young disciples . . . Throwing chairs, smashing noses, cursing authority, exhibiting utter disdain for rules, insulting guests and wearing a constant scowl, certainly cannot be categorized as acceptable examples.

College brochures invariably try to sell the idea that athletics in their system is the instrument for building character and teaching values.

At Indiana's basketball office, they need an asterisk.

John Thompson, the basketball coach at Georgetown University, also appeared in the column more than once but in a more favorable light. The June 1990 effort here came a few years after CBS-TV sports anchor Brent Musburger had been accused of taking to the air to parrot before a national audience the words of Curry Kirkpatrick. The columnist wrote that Kirkpatrick had authored a scurrilous attack on Georgetown's style of play under Thompson in Sports Illustrated, *a magazine described as usually an objective publication.*

John Thompson: A Lesson in Loyalty, Values

In 1972, as the college basketball season was in its beginning stages, banners were hanging over the windows blotting out the Washington sunlight from McDonogh Gymnasium.

Slogans which ran the gamut of racist sleaze were inscribed on each: "Go back where you belong, n----r" read one. "Get lost, blackbird," said another.

"If you know what's good for you, you'll forget this job," read still another. Then came the coup de grace: "Go, nobody likes dead crow."

Now, McDonogh Gymnasium, 18 years ago was the site of Georgetown University's basketball games which had been a disgrace to the institution for nearly two decades.

The malicious messages symbolized the attitude, and underwrote the welcome being extended the incoming coach.

He was John Thompson.

The horde of predominately white neighborhood fans, a majority of the white faculty and student body and, perhaps, Washington in general were hard-pressed to accept the incursion of a black high school coach into the athletic life of prestigious Georgetown University.

But the school's Jesuit fathers stuck by John Thompson and their decision to hire him.

Tensions eased somewhat when the Georgetown Hoyas began turning around what had been a perennial losing situation and were beginning to become a viable contender in college basketball.

Within 10 years from his arrival under extremely stressful conditions, John Thompson built Georgetown into a national power in basketball.

The Jesuit fathers were still with him, quietly—not adamantly—proud of him and his achievements.

Other colleges dropped subtle lures before his eyes. Then came the pros who wanted him—Boston, San Antonio, Houston and now Denver.

Only in the last instance did John Thompson hesitate before quietly rejecting the kind of money that would guarantee lifelong security for his family and himself.

Perceiving John Thompson as a man of intense loyalty, one might easily understand why he refuses to leave what he considers to be unfinished business with the Jesuits who trusted him when he was caught in the fire of racism.

His action last Friday proved that no amount of money could cause him to betray that trust. It also delivered a message to the Jesuits and to all the young men who have played under him: that his sense of values are exactly the same as are those he has tried for 18 years to instill in them.

John Thompson's statement at the time he announced his decision to remain at Georgetown: "I am a teacher."

In the pro job he was offered, he would have no one to educate.

He would have no young people to guide and protect.

He'd have no hopeless kids to whom he could provide the help and inspiration needed to complete their education—kids who believed in him when he recruited them as marginal students and with no certain way of entering college.

He infuriated thousands of television viewers and basketball folk when he walked out early last year to begin a 2-game boycott, many regarding the move as "showboating."

Those who railed at him, however, failed to comprehend that this was a characteristic John Thompson statement on behalf of young athletes, black and white.

That this was his way of telling the world that certain academic guidelines imposed by the NCAA were victimizing the very kids who needed adult help in avoiding the pitfalls of an uneducated society.

John Thompson's loyalty and values make him a man loved by a few, liked by many and hated by others.

But respected by all.

Here's a fun one and the butt of the joke is no other than the column writer.

Confession: This Time I Truly Was No Star

If you're a regular customer at this desk, you may have read the piece at another time . . . It has been written before, so I am hopeful that you will be tolerant.

You see, this is last-time (seasonal) golf weekend . . . It also is the weekend for our little "choir rehearsal" (poker party) and as sometimes happens, the concentration at the moment is on things not so mundane as a job.

Anyway, this happened a long time ago, so there just may be enough new readers that I can get away with it.

A group of Hollywood stars had formed a team of movie and stage actors to tour the country on a campaign to pick up some money to fund a variety of charities nationwide . . . It was a baseball entourage that booked games in cities where there were major league ball parks, and the idea was to compete against home teams made up of media personalities, the receipts going to a legitimate local charity.

The visiting actors' roster included Nick Adams of the TV series, *The Rebel,* Harvey Lembeck of *McHale's Navy,* Chuck Connors of *The Rifleman,* Steve McQueen of *Wanted, Dead or Alive,* John Drury of *The Virginian,* and a relative unknown (at the time), Vince Edwards who later starred as *Ben Casey* in the television series.

The late Bob Addie of the *Washington Times-Herald,* accepted the assignment of organizing the local (D.C.–Baltimore area) media team.

Aware that I had played on several outstanding black teams earlier in life, Addie called and invited me to join his group.

Although it had been 10 years since I quit playing—and I was well past my prime even then—I compounded Bob's mistake (of inviting me) with another mistake (my own) in accepting.

Incidentally, any hesitance I may have felt was quickly dissipated by (my late wife) Barbara's insistence that it would "be fun . . . I'm with you on it, so go ahead."

Fortified by her support, I showed up at the stadium at the appointed time . . . Of course, I had neither glove nor spikes, those which I used long years earlier having been dispatched—especially the shoes, since well-worn athletic shoes don't fill the house with an aroma of cooking greens or fresh strawberries.

So, I took the field with a brand-new borrowed glove and a pair of spikes that fit like miniature canoes, graciously loaned by a willing compatriot . . . Infield practice went well, if a boot or two here or there could be overlooked.

The game began with Bob Addie "getting out of the way of the regulars" a one-inning lineup, me being held out to take over in the second inning with the "star group" to play the rest of the way.

In the stands, Barbara and several of our friends throughout the first inning were screaming: "We want Sam, we want Sam! Send in Sam!"

Sam went in, at shortstop.

On the first pitch from Burt Hawkins of the *Evening Star,* Harvey Lembeck singled . . . Then Vince Edwards walked . . . With men on first and second, Nick Adams hit a ground ball to me.

Like riding a bike, an old ballplayer never forgets the mechanics of moving in front of the ball, bending to cup it in the glove and then straightening up for the throw.

That was the third mistake of the continuing saga, straightening up . . . When I did so, Father Time took over, playing check and checkmate in my head.

I saw three first basemen where one had been before I stooped . . . Naturally, I picked the wrong one to throw to . . . Kareem Abdul-Jabbar on stilts couldn't have caught my throw, so when order was restored Lembeck was in the dugout, Vince Edwards was picking up the bat discarded by Nick Adams, and Nick was perched on third base . . . I'm sure it was the only time ever that a player hit a 2-run triple to shortstop.

From the stands, well above the sound of the boos, I could hear Barbara's screeching voice:

"Take Sam out, the bum!!"

A number of the players who made the rosters of two of the "greatest teams,"
as selected by a national magazine, never would have been in their positions
had it not been for the barriers that kept black players from competing, as I
judged the talent firsthand. This 1963 column looks at two of those great
teams and the players.

"Greatest Teams" Need Asterisks

Well now you young folks, go find yourselves chairs and turn on television
... this may be a little above your heads, or before 'em or something. We of
the thinning pates and disappearing molars are about to take off on a series
being carried by a nationally read monthly magazine.

The publishers are calling it "Greatest Sports Teams" and the two most
recent baseball aggregations are those of the 1927 New York Yankees and
the 1942 St. Louis Cardinals. We've heard so much about those "wonderful" Yankees of the Babe Ruth–Lou Gehrig era and the spectacular Cardinals beloved as the "Gashouse Gang," that "A to Z" has begun to wonder
whether these clubs would have shown the same personnel had it not been
for the racial bars which since have been erased. In other words, how many
of the fellows on these two clubs would be basking in the limelight of baseball history if they had not been protected by the self-imposed astigmatism
of the game?

For example, suppose major league baseball had been accessible to all
baseball players during the reign of the Yankees in the mid-twenties and
while the Cardinals were riding over the rest of the crop in the early forties.
How would they have lined up?

Gehrig may have been at first base because he was a tremendous player.
But along about that time the door was closed to a couple of other tremendous ballplayers—Jim Beck with the Lincoln Giants and Ben Taylor of the
Indianapolis ABCs. A lot of people would have found it difficult to choose
among the three. Then at second base, the Yankees had a man described as

"the perfect ballplayer" in Tony Lazzeri. Maybe he was. But Will "Ouija" Monroe of the Chicago American Giants and Frank Warfield of the Baltimore Black Sox were doing everything Tony could do, except where he was doing it.

The Yankee shortstop at the time was one Mark Koenig, a good, journeyman athlete who couldn't have carried either the glove or the bat of John Henry Lloyd of the Atlantic City Bacharach Giants, nor for that matter, of Dobie Moore of the Kansas City Monarchs. You've heard many wondrous tales about "Jumping Joe" Dugan, who guarded third base for those "greatest" Yankees. But Joe might not have been in the lineup if manager Miller Huggins had been able (and willing) to use Oliver Marcell of the American Giants or Henry Blackmon of the ABCs.

Pete Torrienti of the American Giants could run, hit and throw with the Yanks left fielder Bob Meusel. Oscar Charleston of the Lincoln Giants (called by ex-major leaguers Bullet Joe Bush and irascible Rogers Hornsby "the best player who ever lived") would have chased Jack Combs out of the ballpark. And in right, where Ruth domiciled, there was a country-fair performer named Pete Hill of the American Giants.

New York fans probably would never have heard of Benny Bengough, the first-string catcher in 1927, were it not for the barriers that held the Hilldales Lou Santop, the Black Sox's Joe Lewis and the American Giants Bruce Petway at bay. And the Cubans (then operated by Alex Pompez, the same guy who's turning up most of San Francisco Giants phenoms of today) had a hard-bitten little backstopper named "Blue" Perez. He's the fellow who had to throw out Ty Cobb three times in four tries during a postseason barnstorming series before the Detroit Tigers base-stealing ace could be convinced he was for real.

The pitchers of the Yankees of 1927? Waite Hoyt, Herb Pennock, Bob Shawkey, George Pipgras and some other pretty good throwers . . . But aw gee fellows, what a difference it would have made had you been forced to win your jobs in a pool that included Cyclone Joe Williams of the Lincolns, Bullet Rogan of the Hillsdales, Frank Wickware of the Americans and Rube Foster, who once served as coach of New York Giants pitchers in the John McGraw era.

Now, for the 1942 Cardinals, the "Gashousers" or whatever you've been inclined to call them. They had Johnny Hopp at first base. Buck Leonard of the Homestead Grays or Showboat Thomas of the Black Yankees, would have sat him on the bench (this is a positive statement, no ifs, ands or buts). At second, the Cards alternated Frank Crespi and Jimmy Brown. But they wouldn't have done so if manager Billy Southworth had had the likes of Marvin Williams of the Philadelphia Stars or Sammy Hughes of the Baltimore Elites in tow.

Shortstop was manned by "Mr. Baseball," as they called Marty Marion. There was no such accolade for Sam Bankhead of the Grays, Devil Wells of the American Giants, Dick Lundy of the Newark Eagles or Pee Wee Butts of the Elites, but an awful lot of baseball minds would have gladly sacrificed the titled former for any one of the latter four.

Whitey Kurowski was the Redbird third baseman in 1942. He should thank his stars there was no competition for his job from any one of a half-dozen tan third sackers . . . Ray Dandridge of the Eagles, Jud Wilson and Howard Easterling of the Grays, are just off the top. Dandridge played in the high minors (when they got around to letting him in, as late as his 47th year of life). Easterling had hands as light and fast as a magician's. And all three could swing the bat in such manner as to dwarf the efforts of the St. Louis hero.

Now the outfield of the Cardinals was comprised of Terry Moore in center, Enos Slaughter in right and Stan Musial in left. Take any one of several—Jerry Benjamin of the Grays, Larry Doby of the Eagles, Sam Jethroe of the Cleveland Buckeyes or Henry Kimbro of the Elites—and Moore would have been no more. Slaughter was something much of a ballplayer, but Chicago's Ted Steele might have made him exceed his own reputation as a terrific hustler. Musial, well, I guess you're supposed to quit when you're ahead, so we'll leave him be.

Catchers? Walker Cooper was all right for the Cardinals, but would he have been if Josh Gibson, Bizz Mackey or Roy Campanella had been battling him for the job? And pitchers like Mort Cooper, Lon Warneke and Max Lanier had good names. They didn't have to match their talents with those of Satchel Paige, Laymon Yokely, Stringbean Williams, Terry McDuffie, Jonas Gaines and Bill Byrd, though . . . and that helped.

"Sports Greatest Teams" revive the memories of some fine ballplayers. The 1927 Yankees had Babe Ruth and the 1942 Cards had Stan Musial, but the remainder are no more than asterisks, BC (before colored).

Every June for years, I kept my calendar clear in order to be able to try bowling from a wheelchair with the "Perky Hornets," a group of multiple sclerosis victims. Often the late AFRO photographer I. Henry Phillips or son Tim Lacy came along. This column was in 1991, but in 1995, the Perky Hornets presented me their handwritten P.H.B.F. Award, which speaks for itself:

"Fifteen years ago you came to us not as a celebrity but as a friend, bringing love, compassion and understanding. Through your sports column you made us newsworthy. Many awards and honors have been bestowed upon you. We are adding another.

"To: Dr. Sam Lacy, P.H.B.F., Perky Hornets Best Friend Award.

"A friend is a gift whose worth cannot be measured except by the heart. — Perky Hornets, M.S. Bowlers, 6/5/95."

Time for the Annual "Perky Hornets" Love-in

This one is easy.

No need to be searching for words . . . Nor to be fretting over whether, why, when or how: whether feelings will be hurt is of no concern since the subjects here have endured misfortune and disappointments with stoicism through most of their lives . . . and the why is answered with the simple explanation that writing it gives me a better look at myself . . . when to write it poses no problem because any time is appropriate to pay tribute to courage and divine-like tolerance.

Now comes the how.

How to write this is the easiest to conjure, because when I reach the time of year to describe my annual love-in with the "Perky Hornets Bowling League," the words flow like those of the passionate lawyer or the inspired preacher.

You see, if you have not met the Perky Hornets previously, these are men and women of all ages and ethnic and religious backgrounds who find themselves victims of multiple sclerosis.

Under the aegis of Red Cross and the MS Society of Maryland, they ease their discomfiture with therapy in the form of various competitive activities, the most widely acclaimed, perhaps, being bowling in a league comprised of teams that are classified according to the nature of affliction.

Some competitors bowl from wheelchairs, others stand and roll the balls holding to chairs anchored by volunteers. Still others must use slides for releasing their shots.

In each case and with each participant, a volunteer is present to assist . . . These volunteers, incidentally, are of a noble breed whose patience and compassion can come only from the source of a loving heart.

And so it arrives every first Monday in June, and with it comes my (11th) time to display my personal triumph over a wheelchair and a bowling ball . . . But not over Vince Bagli of WBAL-TV, who had to be a show-off, beating me, 61-46, in our one-on-one bowl, to the delight of the Perky Hornets.

Yet, later, when it was announced that cuts in funding would mean discontinuance of several of their more popular activities, the reaction of our hosts was spontaneous but brief . . . A quick sigh of disbelief was followed by resumption of the camaraderie which invariably marks these yearly get-togethers.

This is the sort of lesson I receive when I visit these outings . . . the kind of thing that compels me to recall my own dark moods in the wake of mistreatments I imagined in the year since I was last here.

The broken fingernail, the bout with indigestion, the arthritis seizure that they would happily accept in trade.

And I pray for them, and I hang my head in shame.

I was traveling with the Brooklyn Dodgers and other teams with black players when Roy Campanella came up. Larry Doby had nicknamed him "wheels" because when Doby, Jackie Robinson, Don Newcombe, Joe Black and others traveled, they preferred his astute handling of cars to that of anyone else. It was ironic that Campy was driving a rented vehicle when he had the accident that left him paralyzed. I talked to Campy from time to time and when he died in 1993, called him one of the two most courageous athletes I ever knew, the other being tennis star Arthur Ashe.

Despite expenses that ran $20,000 or more some months and hospitalization for weeks at a time, Campanella tried to be upbeat whenever he spoke to me. He once described how the accident occurred on an icy night:

"The car wouldn't behave. I tried to steer it away from the side of the road. I fought the wheel. The brakes were useless.

"I made a desperate effort to swerve and felt a chill in my spine when I saw I couldn't. I saw this telephone pole right where I was heading. If this had been my own station wagon which is 300 pounds heavier, and had snow tires, I might have gotten it out of the skid.

"How could a man know when he was taking the last steps of his life?"

In a November 1992 column, I found it difficult emotionally to get through a talk with Campy as he approached his seventy-first birthday.

34 Years Later: Voice from a Wheelchair

The voice came back over the phone, weak and interspersed with gravel . . . Roy Campanella was struggling to communicate with one of the few friends wife Roxie will agree to pass through to him.

Once robust, full of life and a hell of a baseball player, Campy today is physically broken, having spent the last 34 years battling an assortment of nature's most devastating ailments.

Roy Campanella marks his 71st birthday on Thursday (19th), but by necessity it will be devoted to acknowledging how grateful he is for having been given the will to survive heart disease, diabetes, cancer and pneumonia—along with their respective side effects.

As his croaky words squeezed through the artificial voicebox in three to five-second intervals, my mind took a cruel backspin to the image of a happy little round man who bashed out 20 and more home runs a year for the high-riding Dodgers, and captured three National League MVP awards in five years (1951, 1953, and 1955).

A peppy little screamer who handled the fire of pitchers like Don Newcombe, Rex Barney, Ralph Branca and Joe Hatton with the same ease that he adapted to the crazy stuff of Preacher Roe, Joe Black and Russ Meyer, Campy was a superstar in a galaxy of stars.

Then came the raging snowstorm and ice-packed roads of a January night in 1958.

Driving home after closing his off-season liquor store in Harlem, Roy Campanella lost control of his car and slid into a telephone pole 10 minutes from his Glen Cove, Long Island, home.

Paralyzed from the waist down, the hero of many Ebbets Field nights was sentenced by fate to a wheelchair that has held him captive for the past 34 years.

But, while his body has deserted him, Roy Campanella's indomitable spirit has not been lost.

"I'm fine," he says, not once referring to the fact that his most recent April-to-October hospital stay was the latest of a series of lengthy bouts with internal disorder, surgeries and reported schedules with an assortment of therapists.

What he did mention, though, was a healthy appreciation he has over the progress of his children.

When I spoke of not wanting to make him labor any longer through the unexpected interview, he pleaded, "Wait, Sam, I want to tell you what it is that enables me to forget the pains and all.

"Roy (Jr.) is an independent television and film producer in L.A. Tony has his own public relations firm in Atlantic City, and Princess is a broker in the Wall Street stock market.

"They'll all be here next Thursday."

"Happy birthday, old fellah," I mutter, wishing I could say more.

There were some interesting remarks, criticisms, and predictions made at the time, and after, Branch Rickey tapped Jackie Robinson as a player for the Brooklyn Dodgers, making him the first black in the majors in modern time.

Some of these were recalled when Robinson was tapped to become a member of baseball's Hall of Fame.

Jackie Proves this Irony of Destiny

Election of Jackie Robinson to the Hall of Fame is crammed with irony . . . Several then-prominent baseball figures predicted when he was chosen to break the game's color line, that Jackie wouldn't even "make" the majors— now he enters the Hall of Fame.

Fifteen years ago, pitcher Bob Feller of the Cleveland Indians was one of the more outspoken individuals willing to be quoted on Robinson's chances of success as the first tan player in organized baseball.

Five months hence, Feller and Robinson walk into the ivy-covered shrine at Cooperstown, New York, hand in hand.

Said Feller at the time: "As far as his (Robinson's) playing ability is concerned, he belongs to the 'good field, no hit' category . . . they're a dime a dozen . . . Jackie's a sucker for an inside pitch . . . he'll be in a tough spot . . . I'm not prejudiced against him, either . . . I hope he makes good, but, frankly, I don't think he will."

Sixteen years ago, outfielder Dixie Walker, one of the most popular players in Brooklyn history, gave reassurance to the southern brotherhood with the prediction that Jackie would never make the grade . . . "He isn't with the Dodgers yet," he asserted . . . "I don't think there's anything to be worried about."

Walker not only became an expendable and was subsequently traded by the Dodgers, he hasn't "made" it to the Hall of Fame, and in the balloting that last month shot Jackie into the shrine, Dixie wound up with the total of one vote.

Seventeen years ago, Jackie was one of three colored prospects who went to Fenway Park for an alleged tryout with the Boston Red Sox. He and Sam Jethroe (who also played big league ball later) and infielder Marvin Williams were given the cold shoulder. Fenway Park is located in Boston, the same city that houses the executive offices of the Baseball Writers Association from which the announcement of Robinson's election was announced.

Manager of the disinterested Red Sox at the time was Joe Cronin, now president of the American League. Cronin is one of two ex-players voted into the Hall of Fame just ahead of Jackie.

The late W. G. Bramham appeared extremely hurt when Branch Rickey broke the baseball color line with the signing of Jackie on October 23, 1945. Bramham at the time was commissioner of the minor leagues, a sort of miniature Ford Frick. As head of the minors, his jurisdiction covered the International League and the Montreal Royals, with whom Robinson was to break in.

Quipped Bramham: "Father Divine will have to look to his laurels, for we can expect Rickey Temple to be in the course of construction in Harlem soon. It is those of the carpetbagger stripe of the white race, under the guise of helping, but in truth using the (colored people) for their own selfish ends, who retard the race."

Needless to say, W. G. never distinguished himself as officer or diplomat and it wasn't long before another minor league czar was functioning.

As everyone reading this must know, the incidents which cropped up during the 10 hectic years of Robinson are countless. Aside from the spoken predictions, there were many that remained unspoken . . . There was animosity on the part of teammates and opponents alike . . . there was hostility among club officials and in the stands and press boxes. But it invariably boiled down to one inescapable conclusion: Many people of all levels despised Jackie Robinson but all of them respected him.

To explain why, "A to Z" can think of no better way than to relate something that occurred in 1956. That was the year the State of Louisiana passed legislation (since rescinded) barring interracial athletics and even went so far as to force the withdrawal of Shreveport from the thriving Texas League. Bill Keefe of the *New Orleans Times-Picayune* and one of the Deep South's most widely read sports columnists, supported passage of the bill with a scathing denunciation of the use of colored players in general, and of Jackie Robinson, the man who started it all, in particular.

Upon reading the column, Robinson sat down in his room at the Netherlands Plaza Hotel (where the Dodgers stayed in Cincinnati) and wrote to Keefe . . . "I am writing," he said, "not as Jackie Robinson, but as one human being to another. I cannot help, nor possibly alter what you think of me. I speak to you only as an American who happens to be an American Negro and one who is proud of that heritage. We (colored people) ask for nothing special. We ask only, in sports, that we be permitted to compete on an even basis and, if we are not worthy, then the competition shall, per se, eliminate us. Certainly you, and the people of Louisiana, should be capable of facing such competition.

"Myself, and other colored players in the majors," Robinson wrote further, "stop in hotels with the rest of the club in towns like St. Louis and Cincinnati. These hotels have not gone out of business. No investment has been destroyed. The hotels are, I believe, prospering. And there has been no unpleasantness.

"I wish you could see this as I do, but I hold little hope. I wish you could comprehend how unfair and un-American it is for the accident of birth to make such a difference to you. I assume you are of Irish extraction. I have been told that, as recently as 50 years ago, want ads in newspapers carried the biased line 'Irish and Italians need not apply' in certain sections of our country. This has been forgotten, or at least overcome.

"You call me 'insolent.' I will admit I have not been subservient, but would you use the same adjective to describe a white ballplayer—say Ted Williams, who is, more often than I, involved in controversy. Am I insolent, or am I merely insolent for a Negro (who has courage enough to speak out against injustices such as yours and people like you)?

"I am happy for you, that you were born white. It would have been extremely difficult for you had it been otherwise."

Two weeks before the results of the Baseball Writers Association Hall of Fame voting were announced, Bill Keefe wrote in his column: "I have cast my vote for Jackie Robinson . . . he deserves to be elected."

At Christmas time in 1994, I shared with AFRO readers a spiritual experience that took place in a church service outside my own denomination that strengthened my faith. There was such a positive reaction it was thought others following this example might also reap dividends.

Try on a New Church for Christmas

A merry Christmas to you fans in this holiday break from sports, whatever your religious affiliation may be.

For what it may be worth to you, I was born and raised in a Catholic family. However, my siblings and I were fortunate to be reared by a mother who might have been accused of maverick tendencies by some.

In that day of Catholicism the church was considered even more provincial than it is presently. It was not until recently, say within the last 10-15 years, that the Vatican issued its first decree accepting other beliefs as comparable in the eyes of God.

That is why I have come as close as I dare to suggesting that my mother (bless her soul) was a maverick of her era. She taught the four kids in our house that any form of religion, so long as there was some type of worship, was legitimate and to be respected.

Christmas, she would preach in her quiet way of deploring the commercial aspect of the holiday, represented celebration of the Divine Birth, whether the celebration be by Baptists, Episcopalians, Presbyterians, Buddhists or Moslems . . . and the questioning of these or other faiths was the equivalent of sacrilege in the eyes of Rose.

My father was a deacon in the Baptist church . . . and she married him.

All of which is to say that at this time every year my thoughts go back to a spur-of-the moment decision I made not too long ago.

I accompanied a friend to a Baptist service at a small church in the Baltimore area. He was a coworker who spent the Sabbath as a lay preacher, and I have to admit that my visit was engendered by curiosity more than by anything else.

But, as it turned out, the timing could not have been better. I cannot remember a moment in my life that I was made more aware of what Christian worship could mean to some of us—and should mean to all of us.

As a product of Catholicism, there had been little previous exposure to the kind of fervor that gripped the entire congregation. The singing ranged from mournful hymn to lively spiritual. The hand clapping was contagious, as was the swaying of bodies to the beat of the song.

The minister's sermon was at the same time a plea, a cajole, a challenge and a defy. The testimonials, mostly by women who rose from their seats as the spirit moved, were inspirational messages that would have done credit to any man of the cloth.

To say that I was moved by this new experience is to put it mildly. When the collection basket was taken, it marked the first time in memory that I didn't feel my pocket was being picked.

As I stated earlier, a number of years have passed since that visit, but flashbacks of the experience occur frequently. And when they do, quite often my mind paints a picture of what it must have been like in the early plantation scenes, scenes from which stem most of our so-called "soul" lifestyle—the song of adversity, the joy of fellowship, the rejection of fear and, most of all, the undying faith in eternal salvation.

And that picture brings into clear focus the reason that all the forms of oppression contrived by mankind, will never be able to keep people of such spirit shackled. Here in that small church on the outskirts of Baltimore, was for me a fresh, lively awareness.

So, in this next week while fitting yourself for a hat, or suit or shoes, why not try on a new church for Christmas?

Your own faith may be strengthened.

On the verge of observing my ninety-first birthday in 1994, I penned this senior citizen piece that hopefully has some significance for all of us.

If You Can Avoid the Alternative, Don't Get Old

But if you insist, bear some things in mind:

First off, be assured that, unless you are into your 9th decade, you will not have experienced some of the good things, bad things, ordinary things and extra-ordinary things that have touched my life.

For which I shall be eternally grateful.

Most of you, I'm sure, missed the days of the unlocked house doors, the boilers on the stoves for the family laundry . . . the daily ritual of meals together (after the Old Man comes home from work) along with blessing of the food.

The pot-bellied stove in the parlor, the gas lights ignited with matches . . . the knickerbockers for the boys and cotton stockings for girls . . . marriage (sometimes) before sex . . . and kids able to go to college without need for parents to mortgage their lives.

The lamplighter, fine autos for $300 . . . gas for cars at nineteen cents a gallon, bread at five cents a loaf and sugar at five cents a pound out of a barrel.

But those are all memories now . . . Things have changed as the years have rolled by, and the warning clouds gather for those of you who may envy a real old geezer.

You lay out the half-dozen or so pills that have been prescribed for you to take during and after meals . . . Two thirds through the meal, the pills are missing and you're not sure whether you've taken them or they've just disappeared.

You will chuckle about that, and recall that yesterday when you put the first forkful in your mouth, the food itself just sat there until you got up and went into the bathroom to get your teeth out of their overnight cup of water.

Comes the day, too, that when preparing for work, when every second counts, you may find yourself searching frantically for the glasses you are using to look for them.

Your thoughts will take in the sometimes anxious, sometimes humorous incidents of young adulthood.

In my case, it was the flight that couldn't land in Washington because of storminess and that had me sitting there with a sleeping Tim at my side, and wondering whether the fuel will last long enough for me to put those little legs on solid ground again.

On the other hand, was my penchant for wearing white in the heat of summer . . . And the little white kid seeing me about to leave the train in Lewiston, Maine, turning to his mother and shouting "Mommie, here's the porter!"

Arriving at the training camp of Archie Moore, I told the story, and throughout my four-day stay there, I was "Sam the Porter."

The sleeping hours will transform dreams into nightmares . . . Nightmares which shock you into awakening in a room that has the windows going around in circles and the ceiling closing down or you . . . Suddenly your skin starts crawling and you hasten to throw on the lights to search for phantom bugs.

Of course, all these are personal experiences and may or may not have comparisons in your life . . . But I'm offering them in case there are some you can relate to, especially if the years are on the upgrade.

Your doctor may tell you to drink milk to ease your ulcer, and on the next visit you will be told that too much milk has produced the kidney stones which keep you doubled over with pain.

Gradually, I come to realize that the world is becoming dimmer by the year and that a strange quiet is entering my life.

The light bulbs need increasing wattage and every little brown spot on the kitchen floor appears to have legs . . . The radio requires more volume and conversations between TV actors become more guttural.

On the golf course (if you have become engrossed in that consumptive activity) the ball is visible in flight, but once it descends below the horizon its whereabouts becomes a mystery.

At the office, a coworker tells me that I have become increasingly crotchety . . . On the other hand, my son reads my column and complains that I've mellowed . . . So, what the heck, when you reach my age you should be entitled to some inconsistency.

But, as Sunday with its 91 label nears, there is one assurance that feeds my ego . . . Despite all my inconsistencies and lapses of memory, I don't have to rehearse my prayers.

You can bet on that.

SAMUEL H. LACY SR.

Professional Experience

1944–present	Sports editor, *Afro-American* newspapers, Baltimore, Maryland; writer of weekly sports column, "A to Z"
1968–1976	Sports commentator, WBAL-TV, Baltimore
1940–1943	Assistant national editor, *Chicago Defender*
1937–1939	Sports editor, *Washington Afro-American*
1934–1937	Sports editor/managing editor, *Washington Tribune*
1930s	Sports commentator, radio stations WOL and WINX

Other Experience

1960–present	Covered Olympic games in Los Angeles (1984), Montreal (1976), Munich (1972), Mexico (1968), Tokyo (1964), Rome (1960). Accredited for 1980 Olympics in Moscow.
1937–1944	Coached Alpha Phi Alpha basketball team; coached Washington Young Women's Christian Association and national champion women's basketball teams

Honors and Awards

Induction into the writers wing of the National Baseball Hall of Fame, 1998
Journalism Legends Award from the United Negro College Fund, 1998
Frederick Douglass Award from the University System of Maryland
    Board of Regents, 1998

Red Smith Award (Walter Wellesley Smith), from the Associated Press
  Sports Editors, 1998
Honored at the 23rd All Sports Hall of Fame dinner in New York
  City, 1998
Winner of the 1998 Excellence in Sports Journalism award from
  Northeastern University's Center for the Study of Sport in Society
  and NU's School of Journalism
Honorary Doctor of Humane Letters, Loyola College, Baltimore, 1997
Honorary Doctor of Laws Degree, Morgan State University, May 1995
A.J. Liebling Award from Boxing Writers Association of America,
  New York, New York, 1995
Inducted Society of Professional Journalists Hall of Fame, 1994
Inducted Maryland–Delaware–D.C. Press Association Hall of Fame,
  1994
Lifetime Achievement Award, Orioles Advocates, 1992
First place, sports column category, Maryland–Delaware–D.C. Press
  Association editorial contest, 1992
National Association of Black Journalists, Lifetime Achievement Award,
  Kansas City, Missouri, 1991
D.C. Kiwanis Man-of-the-Year, Bolling AFB, 1991
Old Hilltop Award, Preakness Alibi breakfast, 1991
"Contributions to the Veracity of Baseball" at 37th annual Tops in Sports
  dinner, 1990
"Lifetime Achievement Award in Journalism" by *Sports Illustrated*
  magazine, 1989
Elected to Black Press Hall of Fame, 1988
Named one of top black journalists by "Miller Brewing Company
  Gallery of Greats," 1987
CIAA Officials Hall of Fame, Richmond, Virginia, 1986
"Man of Year," Pigskin Club, Washington, D.C., 1985
Inducted into Maryland Media Hall of Fame, first black enshrined and
  one of only nine journalists elected in its fifty-two–year history, 1984
"Sam Lacy Day" organized by the City of Baltimore and the Mayor's
  Office of Special Projects, August 7, 1980
Honoree at "An Evening With Sam Lacy" where 1,500 patrons
  contributed $28,000 to Project Survival Youth Program, 1979

Inducted into the Maryland chapter of the International Boxing Hall of
Fame, 1978
Inducted into Black Athletes Hall of Fame, Las Vegas, Nevada, 1975
National Newspaper Publishers Association writing awards, 1964, 1968,
1970, 1972
Commendation from Branch Rickey and Bill Veeck in recognition of
excellence in baseball writing, 1948

Civic/Professional Organizations

Member, Baseball Hall of Fame Committee of Negro Baseball,
1970–1974
Member, Boxing Writers Association of America, 1960
Member, President's National Committee on Physical Fitness,
1952–1954
Member, Football Writers Association, 1953
Member, Baseball Writers Association of America (first black), 1948
Member, Eastern Board of Officials. Officiated in high school, college,
and professional basketball games, starting in 1936

Volunteer Activities

Participant in sports-related fundraising events with the following:
  Johns Hopkins Children's Clinic
  Maryland State Heart Fund
  Maryland State Cancer Fund
  Multiple Sclerosis Society
  Project Survival
  Save-a-Heart

INDEX

A

Aaron, Henry (Hank), 86, 91, 92, 93, 94, 95, 120, 123, 125, 146, 147, 191, 192, 217
Aaron, Tommie, 123
Abbott, Robert S., 44
Ackerman, Val, 200
Adams, Ace, 62
Adams, Nick, 229, 230
Adams, Willie, 137
Addie, Bob, 229, 230
Addison, Vivian, 108
Afro-American newspapers, 5, 56, 60, 61, 65, 72, 78, 81, 89, 97, 100, 107, 111, 114, 116, 118, 137, 140, 158, 161, 164, 168, 170, 173, 183, 208, 216, 222, 225, 234
Akinwande, Henry, 206
Alexander, Kermit, 133
Alexander, Lamar, 144
Alexis, Lucien Jr., 41
Ali, Muhammad, 12, 159, 160, 161, 196, 203
Allen, Andrew, 25
Allen, Dick, 121, 122
Allen, Richie, 157
Alou, Felipe, 155, 188
Alston, Walt, 122
Alter, Adrian, 142
Altrock, Nick, 25
American Athletic Union, 170, 171
American Basketball Association, 120, 123
American Basketball League (ABL), 118, 199
American Football League (AFL), 103
American Giants, 232
Amoros, Sandy, 86, 89
Anaheim Angels, 217
Anderson, Dave, 3, 4
Anderson, Jack, 6
Angelos, Peter, 217
Angels, Anaheim, 217
Angels, California, 122, 157
Antwine, Houston, 104
Arkansas Razorbacks, 188
Armas, Tony, 220
Aronoff, E. Joseph, 39

Arum, Bob, 179
Ashburn, Richie, 159
Ashe, Arthur, 7, 18, 140, 146, 172, 173, 177, 178, 197, 235
Ashford, Emmett, 122
Athletics, Kansas City, 93
Athletics, Oakland, 89
Athletics, Philadelphia, 62
Atlanta Braves, 120, 125, 191
Atlanta Daily World, 78
Atlanta Glory, 199
Atlanta Hawks, 188
Atlantic City Bacharach Giants, 232
Attles, Al, 123
Auerbach, Red, 119, 120, 188

B

Bagli, Vince, 13, 101, 161, 235
Baker, Art, 103
Baker, Dusty, 188
Baker, Gene, 119, 124
Ball, Celeste, 108
Ballard, Lula, 29
Ballesteros, Seve, 143, 222
Baltimore Black Sox, 232
Baltimore Bullets, 164
Baltimore Colts, 111, 112, 113, 114, 115, 119, 127, 129
Baltimore Elites, 63, 233
Baltimore News American, 101, 114
Baltimore Orioles, 84, 85, 88, 91, 94, 95, 97, 102, 115, 116, 117, 217, 218
Baltimore Sun, 101, 114
Bankhead, Dan, 10, 62, 65, 66, 70, 76
Bankhead, John, 10
Bankhead, Sam, 62, 64, 76, 233
Banks, Ernie, 82, 95, 112, 122, 124, 191, 192
Barber, "Toots," 19
Barksdale, Don, 119
Barney, Rex, 66, 236
Baseball Writers Association of America, 3, 5, 99, 100, 238, 240
Bassett, "Pepper," 53

Bassey, Hogan "Kid," 169
Bauer, Hank, 157
Baylor, Don, 188, 220, 224
Baylor, Elgin, 22, 96
Baylor, "Mutt," 19
Bears, Chicago. *See* Chicago Bears
Beason, Mrs., 21
Beck, Jim, 231
Beckwith, John, 98
Bell, Bobby, 210
Bell, Cool Papa, 165, 166
Bellamy, Walt, 145
Belle, Albert, 191, 193
Bengough, Benny, 232
Benjamin, Guy, 130
Benjamin, Jerry, 233
Bennett, W.M., 170
Berbick, Trevor, 179
Berra, Yogi, 81, 83
Bethea, Elvin, 134
Bethea, Rainey, 34
Betz, Pauline, 168
Bey, David, 179
Bickerstaff, Bernie, 123, 188
Bill, Bobby, 103
Bills, Buffalo. *See* Buffalo Bills
Bing, Dave, 22
Bingham, William J., 41
Birmingham Stallions, 132
Black, Jim, 195
Black, Joe, 8, 89, 90, 122 , 235, 236
Black, Julian, 32
Blackburn, Jack, 32
Black Coaches Association, 189
Blackmon, Henry, 232
Black Sox, Baltimore, 232
Black Yankees, 233
Blaik, Earl, 104
Blair, Paul, 13, 117, 158, 224
Blanks, Larvell, 124
Blanks, Sid, 104
Blefary, Curt, 116
Blue, Vida, 153, 154
Blues, Vera Cruz, 62, 63
Blue Stockings, Toledo, 60
Blyleven, Bert, 158
Bolt, Tommy, 138
Bolton-Holifield, Ruthie, 200
Bonds, Barry, 123, 193
Bostic, Joe, 30, 55

Boston Braves, 56, 65
Boston Celtics, 96, 97, 102, 119, 123, 126
Boston Globe, 3
Boston Patriots, 128
Boston, Ralph, 174
Boston Red Sox, 4, 56, 86, 158, 189, 220, 238
Boudreau, Lou, 66
Bowe, Riddick, 206
Bowens, Sam, 116
Bowser, Andrea, 108
Boyd, Bob, 93
Bracken, Charley, 127
Braddock, Joe, 51
Bradley, Phil, 132
Bradshaw, Terry, 129
Bragan, Bobby, 67
Brailford, Barbara, 108
Branca, Ralph, 236
Branham, W.G., 238
Brannick, Eddie, 79
Braucher, John, 118
Braves, Atlanta. *See* Atlanta Braves
Braves, Boston, 56, 65
Braves, Milwaukee. *See* Milwaukee Braves
Breadon, Sam, 66
Briscoe, Marlin "The Magician," 128
Brock, Lou, 156, 157
Brock, Mrs. David, 60
Broncos, Denver. *See* Denver Broncos
Brooklyn Dodgers, 55, 56, 60, 61, 62, 64, 65,
    66, 68, 69, 71, 76, 78, 79, 80, 86, 88, 89,
    90, 92, 98, 99, 113, 121, 122, 183, 235,
    238
Brooks, Mark, 194
Brooks, Zip, 82
Brookshire, Tom, 130
Broun, Heywood C., 4
Brown, Charles, 108
Brown, Dady, 119
Brown, Edgar, 139
Brown, Jim, 95, 96, 110, 111, 112, 146
Brown, Jimmy, 233
Brown, John, 103
Brown, Larry, 114
Brown, Paul, 96
Brown, Pete, 138
Brown, Walter, 97
Brown, Willie, 103, 120
Browns, Cleveland. *See* Cleveland Browns
Browns, St. Louis, 79

Bruton, Billy, 92, 93, 94, 96
Bryant, Ron, 123
Buccaneers, Tampa Bay. *See* Tampa Bay
    Buccaneers
Buchanan, Junious, 103
Buckeyes, Cleveland. *See* Cleveland Buckeyes
Budig, Gene, 5, 189
Buffalo Bills, 128, 129, 152
Buford, Don, 13, 117, 146
Bullets, Baltimore, 164
Bunche, Dr. Ralph, 77, 135
Buncom, Frank, 103
Burns, Ben, 44
Burns, Charlie, 113
Burrell, Otis, 174
Bush, Bullet Joe, 232
Butler, Phil, 23
Butts, Pee Wee, 233
Byars, Keith, 216
Byrd, Bill, 232
Byrd, Butch, 103
Byrd, Curly, 41

C

California Angels, 122, 157
Calloway, Cab, 77
Camacho, Hector, 203, 206
Campanella, Princess, 237
Campanella, Roxie (Mrs. Roy), 236
Campanella, Roy, 7, 54, 64, 66, 67, 71, 72, 73,
    76, 77, 78, 80, 82, 89, 90, 158, 192, 233,
    235, 236–37
Campanella, Roy Jr., 237
Campanella, Ruthe (Mrs. Roy), 68
Campbell, Chris, 203
Campbell, E. Simms, 6
Campbell, Marion, 132
Campbell, Soup, 42
Cantor, Eddie, 33
Cardinals, St. Louis. *See* St. Louis Cardinals
Carew, Rod, 86
Carlos, John, 175, 178
Carlton, Steve, 219
Carnera, Primo, 32
Carpin, Frank, 156
Carter, Arthur M., 28, 29, 34, 43, 46, 58, 165
Carter, Lee Jr., 142
Carty, Rico, 76, 125
Casale, Martin, 94
Cavaliers, Cleveland, 126, 188

Cavalli, Gary, 200
Cayton, Al, 59
Celtics, Boston. *See* Boston Celtics
Cepeda, Orlando, 155, 224
Chamberlain, Wilt, 123, 146, 196
Chambers, Delores, 108
Chambers, Ted, 170
Chandler, Senator A.B. "Happy," 47, 48, 65
Chapman, Ben, 66
Chargers, San Diego. *See* San Diego Chargers
Charleston, Oscar, 163, 164, 166, 232
Charlotte Sting, 200
Chavez, Julio Cesar, 204, 205
Chavis, Gordon, 137
Chenier, Phil, 147
Chicago American, 5, 98
Chicago American Giants, 63, 232
Chicago Bears, 102, 127, 132
Chicago Bulls, 193
Chicago Cubs, 119, 122, 124, 223
Chicago White Sox, 5, 70, 81, 82, 84, 89, 91,
    93, 97, 121, 156, 189, 191, 192, 193
Christopher, Frank, 23
Christopher, Mrs., 23
Cincinnati Post, 71
Cincinnati Reds, 88, 93, 156
Cincinnati Royals, 133
Clark, John L., 35
Clark, Perry, 127
Clayton, Zach, 214
Clearwater, Keith, 143, 222
Clemente, Roberto, 86
Clements, Lenny, 143, 222
Clemons, Ricky, 4, 187
Cleveland Browns, 95, 110, 111, 112, 128, 141
Cleveland Buckeyes, 56, 63, 233
Cleveland Cavaliers, 126, 188
Cleveland Indians, 5, 66, 69, 70, 75, 76, 78, 82,
    91, 113, 116, 124, 156, 217
Cleveland Nets, 199
Cleveland Pipers, 118, 119
Cleveland Plain Dealer, 4, 100
Cleveland Press, 100
Cleveland Rockers, 200
Clifton, Nat "Sweetwater," 119
Clinton, President Bill, 74, 208
Coachman, Alice, 77, 168
Coates, Jim, 157, 158
Cobb, Ty, 24, 232
Cobb, W. Montague, 91

Cobbledick, Gordon, 100
Cochran, Johnnie Jr., 193
Cocoa, Louis "Kid," 39
Coetzee, Gerrie, 179
Cohen, Marvin, 111
Colas, Carlos, 63
Coleman, Don, 120
Coleman, Jerry, 87, 88, 89
Coleman, Joe, 158
Coleman, Leonard, 4, 56, 187, 189
Coleman, Nick, 86
Collier, Reggie, 132
Collins, Marva, 105
Colorado Xplosion, 199
Colts, Baltimore. *See* Baltimore Colts
Columbus Quest, 199
Colvin, Ernest, 109
Combs, Jack, 232
Conigliaro, Tony, 158, 224
Conley, Jess, 59
Conlon, Jock, 77
Connolly, Maureen, 168
Connors, Chuck, 67, 229
Considine, Bob, 99
Cooper, Chuck, 119, 120
Cooper, Cynthia, 200
Cooper, Mort, 233
Cooper, Tarzan, 42
Cooper, Walker, 233
Cosell, Howard, 102, 161
Covington, "Pee Wee," 19
Covington, Wes, 86, 93
Cowboys, Dallas. *See* Dallas Cowboys
Crabbers, Santurce, 56
Crawfords, Pittsburgh, 63
Crawley, Sylvia, 199
Crenshaw, Ben, 143, 222
Crespi, Frank, 233
Cromwell, John, 23
Cronin, Joe, 122, 164, 238
Crosetti, Frank, 82
Crosley Field, 71
Crowe, George, 92, 122
Crump, Diane, 176
Crutchfield, Jim, 62
Cubans, New York, 63
Cubs, Chicago. *See* Chicago Cubs
Cunningham, Randall, 132
Curtis, Hymie, 19
Curtis, Joey, 215

Custis, Bernie, 127
Cuyler, Kiki, 32
Cy Young Award, 77, 153

D

Dallas Cowboys, 96, 130, 132
Dalton, John, 127
D'Amato, Cus, 160
Dandridge, Ray, 63, 163, 165, 233
Daniels, Clemon, 104
Danny, Claro, 63
Dark, Alvin, 155
Darnon, Pierre, 173
Davenport, Lindsay, 198
Davidson, Don, 97
Davis, Al, 127
Davis, Allison, 16
Davis, Commander, 41
Davis, Ernie, 103, 111
Davis, Hilda, 16
Davis, Mike, 134, 147
Davis, Tommy, 224
Dawes, Dominique, 203
Dawson, Andre, 223, 224
Dawson, Jack, 161
Dawson, Long William, 77
Day, Doris, 154
Day, Laraine, 57, 68
Day, Leon, 53, 165
Dean, Walter, 109
DeFrancis, Frank, 109
DeFrantz, Anita, 202
Dejoie, C.C., 104
DeMoss, Bingo, 164–5
Dempsey, Jack, 159
Denny, Cleveland, 214
Dent, Jim, 195
Denver Broncos, 128, 133
Denver Rockets, 120
Derby, Kentucky, 58, 59
Despino, Sam, 188
Despino, Sam Jr., 181, 182
Detroit Pistons, 119, 120, 123
Detroit Tigers, 96, 232
Devers, Gail, 203
Dickey, Bill, 81
Dickey, Eldridge, 128
Dihigo, Martin, 164, 166
DiMaestri, Joe, 89
DiMaggio, Joe, 44, 224

Dixon, Bill, 134
Dixon, Dave, 103, 211, 212
Doby, Larry, 5, 66, 67, 69, 70, 71, 74, 82, 116, 122, 126, 156, 189, 233, 235
Dodgers, Brooklyn. *See* Brooklyn Dodgers
Dodgers, Los Angeles. *See* Los Angeles Dodgers
Dokes, Michael, 179
Dollar, Jimmy, 108
Donaldson, Ray, 114
Donoghue, Barbara, 143, 221
Dooley, Vince, 106
Dowds, Roger, 173
Downing, Al, 97, 145
Drake, Solly, 86
Drew, Charles, 16
Driesell, Lefty, 184, 225
Drury, John, 229
Drysdale, Cliff, 173
Dubenion, Elbert, 103, 210
Dugan, "Jumping Joe," 232
Duncan, Todd, 37
Dungy, Tony, 188
Dunn, Mike, 114
Duran, Roberto, 214
Durocher, Leo, 47, 65, 75, 84
Dykes, Jimmy, 175

E
Eagles, Newark. *See* Newark Eagles
Early, Penny Ann, 175
Easterling, Howard, 233
Ebbets Field, 56, 65, 176, 236
Eckert, William D., 122
Eckstine, Billy, 136
Edmonton Eskimos, 130
Edwards, Bruce, 67
Edwards, Vince, 229, 230
Eisenhower, President Dwight D., 91
Elder, Lee, 141, 142, 143, 172, 195, 196, 197
Elites, Baltimore, 63
Ellington, Edward Kennedy "Duke," 16, 18
Ellis, Alex, 96
Ellis, Cornelius "Neagie," 19
Els, Ernie, 194
Elway, John, 133
Embree, Mel, 13, 113
Embry, Wayne, 123, 126, 188
Epiphany Roses, 99
Erskine, Carl, 89

Estalella, Bobby, 62
Evans, Lee, 174, 175
Evans, Rob, 127
Evans, Vince, 129, 132
Evening Star, 230
Expos, Montreal. *See* Montreal Expos
Eynon, E.B., 23

F
Faison, Earl, 210
Fauntroy, "Bill," 19
Feeney, Charles S. "Chub," 79
Feldman, Harry, 62
Feller, Bob, 166, 237, 238
Fels, Ben, 26
Fergerson, Duke, 152
Ferris, Dan, 171
Fichter, Ross, 141
Field, Marshall, 44
Fielder, Cecil, 193
Fields, Pam, 164
Flaherty, Francis X., 99
Fleischer, Nat, 160
Flood, Curt, 88, 93, 133, 134, 159
Florida Marlins, 191
Florio, Clem, 161
Flournoy, Robert, 109
Floyd, Ray, 138
Football News, 106
Ford, Dan, 86
Foreman, George, 203
Fortune, Porter, 105
Foss, Joe, 103
Foster, Andrew "Rube," 164, 166, 232
Foundation, Jackie Robinson, 74
Foy, Joe, 224
Francis, Norman, 104
Frazier, Joe, 203
Frazier, Nat, 225
Frick, Ford, 66, 238
Fucher, Bill, 129
Furr, Phil, 39

G
Gaines, Jonas, 233
Gainford, George, 100
Gaither, Jake, 128
Gant, Anita, 29
Gardella, Danny, 62
Garrison-Jackson, Zina, 197, 199

Garron, Larry, 104, 210
Gaston, Cito, 188
Gault, Prentice, 96
Gehrig, Lou, 163, 231
George, William, 16
Georgetown Hoyas, 227
Georgetown University, 227–8
Giamatti, Bart, 223
Giants, Chicago American, 63
Giants, Newark, 60
Giants, New York. *See* New York Giants
Giants, San Francisco. *See* San Francisco
    Giants
Gibbs, Joe, 132
Gibson, Althea, 139, 140, 141, 146, 197, 198,
    199
Gibson, Bob, 88, 121, 189
Gibson, Josh, 26, 40, 53, 76, 164, 165, 166, 233
Gifford, Frank, 130
Gilchrist, Cookie, 103
Gilliam, Jim, 122
Gilliam, Joe, 8, 129
Gilliam, Junior, 89
Gimelstob, Justin, 198, 199
Glascoe, Raymond, 16
Glory, Atlanta, 199
Gloster, Cecil, 16
Golden State Warriors, 123
Golota, Andrew, 206
Gomez, Chilie, 62
Gomez, Reuben, 78, 89, 90
Gomez, Wilfredo, 214, 215
Goode, Mal, 6
Goodloe, Dr. W.A., 33
Graham, Donald, 108
Graham, Otto, 112
Granger, Lester B., 29
Grant, Jim "Mudcat," 147, 175
Grays, Homestead. *See* Homestead Grays
Grayson, Dave, 103
Green, Dennis, 188
Green, Elijah "Pumpsie," 86
Green, Samuel (KKK Grand Dragon), 68
Green Bay Packers, 127
Greenberg, Hank, 75, 78
Greer, Sonny, 18
Grier, Marvin, 104
Griffey, Ken Jr., 147, 193
Griffin, Marty, 207
Griffin, Governor Marvin, 104

Griffin, Pete, 170
Griffith, Calvin, 86
Griffith, Clark, 24, 38, 70, 74, 86
Gross, Milton, 100
Grove, Lefty, 32
Guerra, Fermin, 76
Gulsyas, Estvan, 172
Gumbel, Bryant, 148
Gunts, Brent, 13

H
Hackney, Gainor, 208
Haden, Pat, 129
Hall, Grover C., 105
Hall, Pete, 128
Ham, Bus, 77, 110
Hammond, John, 135
Hardaway, Anfernee "Penny," 193
Hardwick, Otto, 16, 18
Harlem Globetrotters, 177, 187
Harper, Lucius, 44
Harraway, Charlie, 114
Harris, Bucky, 86
Harris, James, 128, 129, 130, 131
Harris, Oren D., 159
Hart, Tom, 169
Haskins, Clem, 190
Haskins, Don, 190
Hastie, William, 16, 77
Hatcher, Ron, 112
Hatton, Joe, 236
Hauser, Joe, 32
Hawkins, Burton, 10, 230
Hawkins, Tom, 96
Hawks, Atlanta, 188
Hayes, Bob, 174
Hayes, Elvin, 175
Hayes, Woody, 225
Haynes, Abner, 103, 211, 212
Haywood, "Red," 19
Henderson, Erskine, 59
Hendricks, Elrod, 13, 117
Heningburg, Gus, 102
Herald Tribune, 100
Heredia, Ramon, 63
Hernandez, Joe, 112
Hicks, Fred L., 180
Hill, Grant, 147
Hill, Mack Lee, 103
Hill, Pete, 232

Hill, Winston, 103
Hilton, Roy, 114
Hingis, Martina, 197, 198
Hodges, Gil, 66, 67
Hoffman, Pam, 141
Holland, Skeets, 117
Holman, Bud, 67
Holman, Joe, 50
Holmes, Derrick, 214, 215
Holmes, Justin, 183
Holmes, Larry, 179, 203
Holmes, Talley, 139
Holtz, Lou, 149
Holyfield, Evander, 204, 205, 206
Homestead Grays, 57, 60, 62, 164, 233
Honesty, Francis, 19
Hope, Willie, 19
Hopkins, Mrs. E.L., 107
Hopp, Johnny, 232
Hopper, Clay, 61
Horne, Lena, 77
Hornsby, Rogers, 232
Houston Astros, 116, 188
Houston Comets, 200
Houston Post, 106
Houston, G. David, 19
Houston, Wade, 127, 144
Howard, Elston, 80, 83, 85, 87, 88, 97, 122, 145
Howard University, 91
Hoyt, Waite, 232
Hudspeth, Highpockets, 163
Huggins, Miller, 232
Hughes, Sammy, 233
Humphrey, Hal, 145
Hundley, James "Blip," 19
Hunt, Roy, 224
Hunter, Eddie, 33
Hunter, Jim, 23
Hunton, Ben, 16
Hurd, Babe, 58
Hurt, Eddie, 169, 170, 172

I
Idelson, Jeff, 4
Indiana, University of, 225–6
Indiana Pacers, 126
Indianapolis ABCs, 231
Indianapolis Clowns, 177
Indians, Cleveland. *See* Cleveland Indians

Innis, Del, 159
Irsay, Robert, 113, 115
Irvin, Monte, 69, 79, 89, 90, 122, 139, 164, 165
Irvin, Win (Mrs. Monte), 78, 164, 166

J
Jabbar, Kareem Abdul, 174, 196, 230
Jackie Robinson Foundation, 74
Jackson, Bo, 216
Jackson, C.C., 174
Jackson, Eric, 200
Jackson, Hal, 28
Jackson, Mannie, 187
Jackson, Onree, 128
Jackson, Reggie, 143, 219, 222
Jackson, Reverend Jessie, 187
Jackson, Sonny Man, 39
Jacksonville Jaguars, 133
Jaworski, Ron, 129
Jeffrey, Burton, 68
Jeffries, Leroy, 20
Jethroe, Sam, 56, 79, 156, 158, 224, 233, 238
Jockeys Hall of Fame, 107
Johnson, Abby "Tiny," 29
Johnson, Brooks, 177
Johnson, "Cocky," 109
Johnson, Connie, 84, 85
Johnson, Dr. Mordecai W., 37
Johnson, Earvin "Magic," 196
Johnson, Gus, 146
Johnson, Jack, 32
Johnson, "Jinx," 19
Johnson, John, 44
Johnson, Judy, 163, 165, 166
Johnson, Mamie, 177
Johnson, Maurice, 16
Johnson, Michael, 195, 202
Johnson, President Lyndon Baines, 92
Johnson, Walter, 25
Jolson, Al, 33
Jones, Jimmy, 129
Jones, K.C., 119, 123
Jones, Sam "Toothpick", 119, 157, 158, 159, 191
Jones, William "Dofey," 27
Jones, Willie, 159
Jordan, Michael, 28, 147, 193, 195
Joss, Addie, 163
Joyner-Kersee, Jackie, 203

K

Kaline, Al, 157
Kansas City Athletics, 93
Kansas City Monarchs, 5, 56, 60, 124, 177,
    232
Kansas City Royals, 223
Karris, Alex, 130
Keefe, Bill, 239, 240
Kellett, Don, 112, 113
Kemp, Jan, 106
Kennedy, President John F., 111
Kenner, Burrell, 19
Kentucky Derby, 58, 59
Kerr, Paul, 162
Kibler, John, 223
Kilgallen, Dorothy, 154
Kimbro, Henry, 233
King, Billie Jean, 176, 198
King, Carolyn, 182
King, Clyde, 123
King, Don, 204, 205, 206
King, Dr. Martin Luther Jr., 91
King, Joe, 5, 99
King, Mr. and Mrs. Gerald, 182
Kingman, Dave, 224
Kirkpatrick, Curry, 227
Klein, Lou, 62
Knight, Bobby, 225–6
Knight, Phil, 195
Knoetze, Kallie, 179
Koenig, Mark, 232
Koger, Ann, 176
Korby, Karl, 23
Kournikova, Anna, 198
Kuhn, Bowie, 162, 166
Kupchak, Mitch, 147
Kurowski, Whitey, 233
Kusner, Kathy, 176

L

Lacy, Alberta Robinson, 27
Lacy, Barbara Robinson, 11, 13, 27, 229, 230
Lacy, Erskine Henry, 14
Lacy, Evelyn (Mrs. Benjamin Hunton), 14, 15,
    16
Lacy, Henry Erskine, 15
Lacy, Raymond, 14
Lacy, Rose, 14, 241
Lacy, Rosina (Mrs. Lawrence Howe), 14, 15
Lacy, Samuel Erskine, 14, 25, 241

Lacy, Samuel Howe (Tim), 4, 17, 27, 38, 70,
    184, 234
Lacy, Vernice (Mrs. Tim), 17
Ladd, Ernie, 103, 210, 211, 212
Lakers, Los Angeles, 96
Lamb, Chris, 98
Landis, Judge Kenesaw, 45, 46
Lane, Frank, 81, 84
Laney, Al, 100
Lang, Chick, 107, 108
Langer, Bernhardt, 143, 221
Lanier, Max, 62, 233
Lapchick, Richard, 187
Lautier, Louis, 24
Lawrence, Brooks, 88, 122
Lazzeri, Tony, 232
Lee, Jimmy, 58
Lee, Scrip, 26
Leibovitz, Hal, 4, 100
Lembeck, Harvey, 229, 230
Leonard, Buck, 38, 164, 165, 166, 232
Leonard, Sugar Ray, 161, 203, 206, 214
Leslie, Lisa, 200, 207
Lewin, Edith, 6
Lewis, Carl, 203
Lewis, George, 58
Lewis, Ike, 59
Lewis, Joe, 232
Lewis, Johnny, 122
Lewis, Lennox, 204, 205, 206
Lewis, Oscar, 58
Lewis, Walter, 132
Lincoln, Keith, 210
Lincoln Giants, 231
Lipscomb, Big Daddy, 13
Liston, Sonny, 160, 196
Little, Sally, 195
Little League World Series, 181–3
Lloyd, Earl, 119, 120
Lloyd, John Henry "Pop," 26, 165, 166, 232
Lloyd, Pat, 26
Lobo, Rebecca, 200
Lofton, James, 134
Logan, Bonnie, 176
Lollar, Sherm, 89
"Long Shot Red," 108
Look Magazine, 102, 121
Lopez, Hector, 86, 97
Los Angeles Angels, 192
Los Angeles Dodgers, 74, 154, 192, 217

Los Angeles Examiner, 99
Los Angeles Lakers, 96, 196
Los Angeles Raiders, 127, 132
Los Angeles Rams, 113, 129, 130
Los Angeles Sparks, 200
Louis, Joe, 7, 25, 32, 33, 34, 51, 77, 138, 185
Louisiana Weekly, 104
Lucas, Bill, 125
Lundy, Dick, 26, 164, 165, 233
Lynch, Jair, 203

M
Mack, Connie, 74
Mack, Darrell, 116
Mackey, Bizz, 165, 233
Mackey, John, 133, 146
MacPhail, Larry, 47, 57, 58, 61
MacPhail, Lee, 95
Maddux, Greg, 191
Maglie, Sal, 75
Mahoney, Ann, 177
Maisel, Bob, 101
Malone, Mary, 184
Malone, Moses, 184
Mamakos, Steve, 39
Manley, Abe, 165
Manley, Effa, (Mrs. Abe), 165
Mann, Carol, 176
Mantle, Mickey, 157, 224
Marcelle, Oliver, 165
Marciano, Rocky, 160
Marichal, Juan, 123
Marion, Marty, 233
Maris, Roger, 157
Marquard, Rube, 163
Martin, Christy, 206
Martin, Glenn L., 43
Martin, Jack, 21
Martindale, Billy, 142
Maryland, University of, 82, 99
Maryland Jockey Club, 107
Mason, John, 33
Mathews, Eddie, 123
Matlock, Roy, 64
Matthews, Ralph Sr., 29, 41, 42
Matthews, Robert III, 12
May, Don, 175
Mays, Gary, 22
Mays, Willie, 82, 84, 86, 90, 101, 102, 123,
     155, 156, 157, 191, 192, 217, 224

McAlpin, Harry, 28
McAshan, Eddie, 129
McCall, Oliver, 204, 205
McCarver, Tim, 156, 157
McClaren, Jack, 139
McCovey, Willie, 123, 155
McCullum, Sam, 134
McDaniels, Jimmy, 59
McDonald, Arch, 32
McDuffie, Clyde, 23
McDuffie, Terris (Terry) "The Great," 55, 233
McGlone, Bill, 111
McGovern, Peter J., 180
McGowan, Roscoe, 8, 100
McGraw, John, 232
McGuire, Al, 225
McGuire, Mickey, 95
McHale, John, 94
McKay, Jim, 148, 194
McKay, John, 129, 131
McKenley, Herb, 169
McKenzie, Stan, 164
McLendon, Donn, 156
McLendon, Johnny, 118, 119, 120
McNeil, Lori, 197, 199
McQueen, Clifford, 180
McQueen, Steve, 229
Memphis Red Sox, 66
Memphis Showboats, 132
Metcalfe, Ralph, 52
Metrevelli, Alexander, 172
Mets, New York, 74
Meusel, Bob, 232
Meyer, Russ, 236
Mexico City Red Devils, 62
Miami Dolphins, 130
Miles, Clarence, 116
Miller, Bill, 169
Miller, John, 154
Miller, Larry, 175
Milwaukee Braves, 92, 93, 94, 97
Milwaukee Brewers, 158
Milwaukee Bucks, 123, 126
Minneapolis Star-Tribune, 4, 86
Minnesota Twins, 158
Minor, Davage, 119
Minoso, Minnie, 82, 91, 95, 156, 158, 191, 224
Minoso, Orestes, 69, 70, 71
Mirnyi, Max, 199
Mitchell, Arthur W., 44

Mitchell, Bob, 96
Mitchell, Clarence, 109
Mitchell, Clifford C., 31
Mitchell, Lydell, 114
Mix, Ron, 211, 212, 213
Mize, Larry, 143, 222
Modell, Art, 141
Molina, Rafael Leonidas Trujillo, 64
Monarchs, Kansas City. *See* Kansas City
    Monarchs
Monroe, Will "Ouija," 165, 232
Monroe, Earl, 146, 164
Monterey Monties, 63
Montgomery, Lou, 37
Montgomery Advertiser, 104
Montreal Expos, 122, 188, 191
Montreal Royals, 58, 60, 61, 62, 65, 238
Moon, Warren, 130, 131, 132
Moone, Dobie, 232
Moore, Archie, 243
Moore, Lenny, 13, 113
Moore, Terry, 233
Moorer, Michael, 204, 206
Morgan, Connie, 177
Morgan, Joe, 224
Morgan, Walter, 195
Moss, Elizabeth (Bettye Murphy Phillips), 43
Motley, Marion, 77
Motton, Curt, 13
Muchnick, Isadore, 56
Murphy, Colonel Raymond, 119
Murphy, D. Arnett, 137
Murphy, Dr. Carl, 42, 43, 45, 46, 57, 164
Murphy, Isaac, 58, 107
Murphy, John H. III, 45
Murphy, William H. "Billy," 205
Murray, Eddie, 217–20
Murray, Morris, 28
Murray, Mrs. Carrie, 219
Murray, Norman, 28
Murray, Raymond, 28
Musburger, Brent, 148, 227
Musial, Stan, 155, 224, 233
Myers, Calvin, 108, 109

                    N
NAACP, 93, 102, 145
Namath, Joe, 129
National Baseball Hall of Fame and Museum,
    3, 4, 5, 74, 100, 162, 163, 164

National Baseball League, 4, 56
National Basketball Association (NBA), 202
National Football League (NFL), 96, 110, 114,
    126
National League MVP Award, 77, 78
Naulls, Willie, 119
NCAA, 202, 228
Neal, Charley, 86
Negro National League, 56, 59, 126, 162, 163
Nelson, Larry, 221
New England Blizzard, 199
New England League, Nashua, N.H., 64
New Orleans Breakers, 132
New York Cubans, 63
New York Daily News, 99, 100, 163
New York Giants, 60, 62, 68, 85, 119, 121, 123,
    128, 164, 232
New York Herald Tribune, 98
New York Knicks, 126, 196
New York Liberty, 200
New York Mets, 74
New York Mirror, 5, 99
New York Post, 100
New York Times, 3, 100
New York World Telegram, 5, 99
New York Yankees, 70, 80, 81, 82, 83, 84, 85,
    87, 93, 97, 122, 188, 193, 220, 231, 232,
    233
Newark Eagles, 5, 56, 63, 126, 164, 165, 233
Newark Giants, 60
Newcombe, Don, 64, 72, 75, 76, 77, 78, 89, 235
Newhouse, Robert, 134
New Orleans Times-Picayune, 239
Nicklaus, Jack, 143, 221
Nixon, Mike, 111
Noble, Ray, 79
Nock, George, 114
Norris, Mike, 148
North, Andy, 221

                    O
Oakland Athletics, 89, 153
O'Connell, Stephen, 105
O'Connor, Leslie, 47
O'Doul, Lefty, 163
Offert, Gertrude, 29
O'Grady, Mac, 143, 222
Oklahoma Outlaws, 132
Olesker, Michael, 101
Oliver, Al, 224

Oliver, John J. Jr., 183
Olmo, Luis, 62
Olympic Games, 167, 169, 201, 203
O'Malley, Walter, 121
O'Neal, Shaquille, 147
O'Neil, John "Buck," 119
Orioles, Baltimore. *See* Baltimore Orioles
Orlando Magic, 193
Orr, Dr. Daniel, 214
O'Sullivan, Chester, 161
Overton, Monk, 58
Owen, Mickey, 62
Owens, Jesse, 33, 52, 122, 174

P

Pace, Orlando, 193
Page, Greg, 179
Paige, C.D., 170
Paige, Satchel, 53, 59, 62, 64, 69, 70, 71, 76, 79, 80, 164, 165, 166, 233
Paparella, Joe, 76, 77
Parker, Dan, 100
Parker, Jim, 111, 113
Parks, Rosa, 91
Parrott, Harold, 47, 71, 99
Partlow, Roy, 65
Pasquel, Jorge, 62
Patterson, Floyd, 160
Paula, Carlos, 10, 82, 86
Payne, Ethel, 6
Payne, Mrs., 21
Payne, Tom, 18, 19, 26
Peete, Calvin, 143, 144, 195, 221
Pena, Tony, 137
Pennington, Art, 63
Pennock, Herb, 232
People's Voice (New York), 55
Perez, "Blue," 232
Perkins, James, 59
Perky Hornets, 234–5
Perry, Doc, 18
Perry, Gaylord, 123, 124
Perry, Joe, 113
Perry, Lowell, 139
Peters, Hank, 217, 218
Petway, Bruce, 232
PGA, 144
Philadelphia Athletics, 62, 76
Philadelphia Eagles, 127, 132
Philadelphia Phillies, 62, 66, 80, 159, 219

Philadelphia Stars, 63, 233
Philadelphia Warriors, 196
Phillies, Philadelphia. *See* Philadelphia Phillies
Phillips, I. Henry, 234
Phillips, Wendell, 20
Phoebus, Tom, 158
Phoenix Mercury, 200
Piggott, Bert, 170
Pinson, Vada, 93
Pipers, Cleveland, 118, 119
Pipgras, George, 232
Pirates, Pittsburgh. *See* Pittsburgh Pirates
Pistons, Detroit. *See* Detroit Pistons
Pitino, Rick, 190
Pittsburgh Courier, 5, 56, 97
Pittsburgh Crawfords, 63
Pittsburgh Pirates, 119, 121, 122, 191
Pittsburgh Steelers, 113, 129
Player, Gary, 142
Plunkett, Sherman, 104
Polo Grounds, 68, 75
Pompez, Alex, 232
Pope, Dave, 82, 116
Portland Power, 199
Portland Trail Blazers, 123
Posey, Cum, 40, 57
Poston, Carl, 193
Poston, Kevin, 193
Povich, Shirley, 100
Powell, Art, 103
Powell, Congressman Adam Clayton, 77
Powell, Dick, 165
Powell, Marvin, 134
Powell, Renee, 176
Power, Vic, 80, 81, 86
Powers, Jimmy, 100
Preakness Stakes, 107
Pugh, Johnny, 19

R

Radcliffe, Alex "Doubleduty," 165
Raft, George, 57
Rainey, Joseph H., 47
Rams, Los Angeles. *See* Los Angeles Rams
Randolph, Leo, 214
Raspberry, William, 6
Rayford, Floyd, 218
Razorbacks, Arkansas, 188
Red Devils, Mexico City, 62
Red Sox, Boston. *See* Boston Red Sox

Red Sox, Memphis, 66
Reds, Cincinnati. *See* Cincinnati Reds
Reed, Matt, 114
Reed, Willis, 126, 145
Reeder, Sylvester, 23
Reehorn, Sean, 183
Reese, Beasley, 134
Reese, Pee Wee, 66
Reichler, Joe, 84, 120, 163
Reid, David, 203
Reilly, Patrick, 144
Reinsdorf, Jerry, 189
Rennie, Rud, 98, 100
Reusse, Patrick, 4
Rhames, Ving, 206
Rhodes, Ray, 188
Rhodes, Ted, 135, 136, 137, 195, 196, 197
Rice, Grantland, 4
Rice, Jim, 220
Richards, Paul, 116
Richardson, Nolan, 127, 188, 190
Richman, Milton, 5, 9, 100
Richmond Rage, 199
Richmond Times-Dispatch, 173
Richmond Virginians, 82
Ricketts, Dave, 122
Rickey, Branch, 7, 46, 47, 48, 54, 57, 58, 60, 61,
    64, 66, 67, 68, 73, 76, 86, 94, 95, 113,
    121, 176, 183, 238
Riddles, Raymond, 180
Rigney, Bill, 158, 192
Riley, "Aggie," 19
Ring magazine, 160
Ripken, Cal Jr., 217, 220
Ripken, Cal Sr., 217
Ripken, Kelly (Mrs. Cal Jr.), 217
Ripken, Vi (Mrs. Cal Sr.), 217
Rixey, Eppa, 163
Roberts, Clifford, 142
Robertson, Oscar, 133
Robeson, Paul, 44, 45, 46
Robinson, Bill "Bojangles," 32, 33
Robinson, Brooks, 116, 117, 146, 157
Robinson, Charlie, 113
Robinson, Earl, 94, 95, 120, 192
Robinson, Eddie, 123, 131
Robinson, Floyd, 93, 192
Robinson, Frank, 7, 13, 76, 86, 93, 102, 146,
    156, 157, 158, 189, 191, 192, 224
Robinson, Henry, 16
Robinson, Humberto, 92
Robinson, Jackie, 8, 11, 12, 25, 48, 54, 56, 75,
    77, 78, 79, 81, 82, 86, 89, 90, 92, 95, 97,
    154, 165, 183, 185, 224, 235, 237–40
Robinson, Jackie Jr., 154, 155, 176
Robinson, Michaelyn, 27
Robinson, Mrs. Bill, 33
Robinson, Rachel (Mrs. Jackie), 67, 68, 72, 73,
    74, 154
Robinson, Sugar Ray, 59, 100, 107
Roe, Preacher, 236
Roeder, Bill, 8, 99
Rogan, Joe "Bullet," 5, 165, 232
Rogers, Will, 31
Roof, Phil, 158
Rooney, Art, 113
Roosevelt, President Franklin D., 41, 43
Rose, Pete, 224
Roseboro, John, 122
Rosen, Carl, 135
Rosenbloom, Carroll, 112, 113, 129
Rosenbloom, Georgia (Mrs. Carroll), 113
Roses, Epiphany, 99
Ross, Kevin, 105
Rowan, Hobart, 6
Rowe, Billy, 97
Rowland, Jennifer, 176
Roxborough, John, 32
Royals, Montreal. *See* Montreal Royals
Rozelle, Pete, 111
Rubin, Chanda, 197, 198, 199
Rubin, Barbara Jo, 176
Rudolph, Wilma, 171, 172
Ruffin, Red, 44
Runyon, Damon, 4
Rupp, Adolph, 190
Russell, Bill, 96, 97, 102, 119, 120, 123
Russwurm, John, 6
Ruth, Babe, 24, 98, 146, 231, 233
Ryan, Red, 165

                        S
Saban, Lou, 128
Sacramento Monarchs, 200
Saitch, Eyre, 139
Salazar, Lazaro, 63
Salter, George, 181
Salter, Robert, 181
Sample, Johnny, 112
Sanders, Deion, 147

Sanders, Red, 67
Sanders, Tom, 119, 126
San Diego Chargers, 130, 211, 213
San Diego Conquistadors, 123
San Francisco 49ers, 111
San Francisco Giants, 155, 157, 188, 192, 193, 232
San Jose Lasers, 199
Santiago, Jose, 69
Santop, Lou, 232
Santurce Crabbers, 56
Saperstein, Henry G., 138
Satterlee, Josh, 183
Sayers, Gale, 102, 112
Schaefer, Governor William Donald, 109, 115
Schiro, Mayor Victor, 211, 212
Schmeling, Max, 34
Schroeder, Jay, 132
Schrom, Ken, 223, 224
Schultz, Barney, 156
Scott, Henry O., 24
Scott, Ray, 123
Scott, Walter, 153
Scott, William "Scottie," 45
Scull, Angel, 82, 86
Seattle Mariners, 132, 193
Seattle Pilots, 120
Seattle Reign, 199
Seattle Seahawks, 152, 153
Seattle SuperSonics, 123
Seay, Dick, 26
Segal, Abe, 172, 173
Seghi, Phil, 124
Seidman, Robert B., 41
Seldon, Bruce, 204
Selig, Bud, 74, 189
Selmon, Lee Roy, 134
Senators, Washington. *See* Washington Senators
Sengstacke, John, 44, 45
Shahravan, Nina, 207
Shapiro, John, 109
Sharkey, Jack, 34
Shaugnessy, "Shag," 62
Shaw, Buck, 104
Shawkey, Bob, 232
Shea Stadium, 74
Sheffield, Gary, 191
Sheingold, Peter M., 183
Shell, Art, 126

Shelton, Ron, 197
Short, Bob, 96
Short, Ed, 97
Show, Eric, 223, 224
Sidat-Singh, Samuel, 36, 37
Sidat-Singh, Wilmeth, 35, 36, 41
Sifford, Charlie, 135, 136, 137, 138, 143, 195, 196, 197
Simms, Jesse, 74
Simms, Willie, 59
Simpson, Dennis, 28, 29
Simpson, Harry, 88
Simpson, O.J., 129, 143, 222
Simpson, Scott, 221
Singh, Vijay, 194
Skinner, Bob, 122
Slaughter, Enos, 233
Slowe, Lucy, 139
Smith, Al, 82, 93
Smith, Ed, 164
Smith, Ken (Kenny), 5, 99
Smith, "Lefty," 19
Smith, Milt, 88, 159
Smith, Orlando Henry "Tubby," 190
Smith, Red, 4
Smith, Sylvester, 139
Smith, Theo, 63
Smith, Tommie, 174, 175, 178
Smith, Vashti, 164
Smith, Wendell, 5, 30, 56, 57, 97, 98, 162, 165
Snell, Matt, 145
Snibbe, Robert, 41
Snider, Duke, 224
Snow, Felton, 38
Snyder, Cameron, 114
Sober, Pincus "Pinky," 170, 171
Society of Professional Journalists, 5
Solem, Ossie, 36
South Africa, 167, 170, 171, 172, 173, 177, 178
Southworth, Billy, 233
Spearman, Henry, 53
Spiller, Bill, 135, 136, 195
Spink, J.G. Taylor, award, 3
Spinks, Leon, 214
Spinks, Michael, 214
Sporting News, 100
Sports Illustrated, 171, 227
St. Louis Browns, 79
St. Louis Cardinals, 62, 66, 67, 70, 77, 93, 156, 231, 233

St. Louis Rams, 193
Stanky, Eddie, 66
Stanton, Roger, 106
Starbird, Kate, 200
Stars, Philadelphia, 63
Steadman, John, 101, 114
Stearnes, Turkey, 165
Steele, Ted, 233
Steiger, Gus, 8
Stein, Russell, 128
Steinbrenner, George, 118, 119
Stengel, Casey, 4, 65, 80, 81, 82, 83, 219
Stewart, Elaine W., 188
Stewart, Ollie, 168
Stephens, Sandy, 128
Stern, David, 200
Stone, Ed, 63
Stone, Toni, 177
Stoneham, Horace, 79, 84
Stoudamire, Damon, 188
Stover, George, 60
Stroble, Bobby, 195
Sukeforth, Clyde, 57, 65
Summerall, Pat, 130
Summers, Freddie, 128, 129
Susie, Aunt, 18, 19
Sutton, Alex, 137
Swann, Lynn, 143, 222
Sweeney, Ed, 118
Swoopes, Sheryl, 200
Swope, Tom, 9, 71
Sykes, Doc, 165

T
Taliaferro, George, 113, 127, 139
Talliferro, Ernest, 31
Tampa Bay Buccaneers, 130, 131, 132
Tate, John, 179
Taylor, Ben, 165, 231
Taylor, Charley, 112
Taylor, Johnny, 63
Tebbetts, Birdie, 93
Temple, Ed, 168, 169
Thomas, Dave "Showboat," 55, 233
Thomas, Eugene, 170
Thomas, Frank, 193
Thomas, Isiah, 188
Thomas, Joe, 114
Thomas, John, 111
Thompson, Frank, 52

Thompson, Hall, 144
Thompson, Henry, 76, 78, 79, 89, 90
Thompson, John, 153, 177, 190, 227–8
Thompson, Maria (Mrs. Henry), 78
Thompson, Ted, 18
Thorpe, Jim, 143, 195, 220–3
Thrower, Willie, 127
Tiff, Margo Antoinette, 199
Tigers, Detroit. *See* Detroit Tigers
Tittle, Y.A., 128
Toledo Blue Stockings, 60
Torrence, Gwen, 203
Torrienti, Pete, 232
Townsend, Ron, 196
Traber, Jim, 219, 220
Traynor, Pie, 24, 163
Trevino, Lee, 143
Truman, Harry S., 16
Tullis, Jim, 128
Tunnell, Emlen, 119, 139
Tunney, Gene, 160
Turner, Harry "Soup," 19
Turner, Joe, 39
Turner, Mr., 19
Tymous, Otero, 29
Tyson, Mike, 204, 205
Tyson, Pete, 28, 29

U
Udall, Stewart L., 111
United States Football League (USFL), 132
United States League, 56
University of Maryland, 82, 99
Unseld, Wes, 147, 175
UPI, 100
Upshaw, Gene, 133
Utah Starzz, 200

V
Vargo, Ed, 156
Veeck, Bill, 5, 69, 81, 113, 126
Vera Cruz Blues, 62, 63
Vernon, Mickey, 70
Vincent, Lee, 108
Vinson, Charlie, 144

W
Wagner, Honus, 35
Wagner, Leon, 192
Waitkus, Eddie, 159

Walk, Neal, 175
Walker, Billy, 58
Walker, Daryl, 188
Walker, Dixie, 67, 238
Walker, LeRoy, 169, 170, 177, 201
Walker, Moses Fleetwood, 60
Walker, Welday, 60
Walker, Wesley, 134
Walker, William O., 24
Wall Street Journal, 195
Walton, John, 132
Warfield, Frank, 232
Warfield, William, 16
Warlick, Ernie, 103, 211, 212
Warneke, Lon, 79, 80, 233
Warner, Ted, 72
Warren, Mike, 174
Washington, Elinor Parker, 22
Washington, MaliVai, 18, 197
Washington, Ora, 29, 139
Washington, Rudy, 189
Washington Bullets, 123
Washington Post, 77, 100, 110
Washington Redskins, 110, 111, 114, 132
Washington Senators, 70, 82, 86, 89, 158
Washington Times-Herald, 229
Watson, Bob, 188
Watson, Tom, 221
Watts, J.C., 131
Watts, Ray, 79
WBAL-TV, 99, 164, 235
Weaver, Earl, 158
Weaver, Mike, 179
Weaver, Monte, 32
Webb, Bryan, 176
Webb, Elias, 36
Webb, Pauline, 36
Webb, Waldo, 37
Webster, Marvin, 22
Weiss, George, 81, 83, 88
Wells, Devil, 164, 233
Wells, Willie, 62
Welsh, George, 216
West, Charley, 128
West, Jim, 26
Westmoreland, Dick, 103, 211, 212
Whetsel, Arthur "Sheif," 18
White, Bill, 79, 93, 102, 120, 147, 187
White, Cheryl, 176
White, Jackie, 177

White, "Runt," 19
White, Walter, 30
Whiteside, Larry, 3, 4
White Sox, Chicago. *See* Chicago White Sox
Whitford, Mal, 169
Wickware, Frank, 232
Wilkens, Lenny, 120, 123, 188
Wilkerson, Doug, 134
Wilkes, Ernie, 88
Wilkins, J., 83
Wilkinson, John, 23
Wilks, Ted, 175
Williams, A.D., 96
Williams, Alex, 79
Williams, Cyclone Joe, 232
Williams, Doug, 130, 131, 132, 133
Williams, Edward Bennett, 115, 218, 220
Williams, "Geechie," 19
Williams, Marvin, 56, 233, 238
Williams, Richard, 198
Williams, Serena, 197, 198, 199
Williams, Stringbean, 26, 165, 233
Williams, Sydney, 127
Williams, Ted, 41, 155, 157, 158, 224
Williams, Venus, 197, 198, 199
Wills, Gertrude (Mrs. Maury), 154
Wills, Maury, 102, 126, 154
Willson, Admiral, 41
Wilson, Artie, 69
Wilson, Don, 116
Wilson, Earl, 86
Wilson, Hack, 32
Wilson, John, 62
Wilson, Jud, 38
Wilson, Kenneth, 12
Wilson, Ralph, 119
Wilson, Willie, 223, 224
Wimbish, Robert, 93
Winchell, Walter, 154
Windrell, Walter, 107
Winfield, Dave, 220
Wininger, Bob, 138
Winkfield, Jimmy, 59
Winkler, Jimmy, 58
Winters, Nip, 26
Wismer, Harry, 110
Wittemore, Jim, 99
Wolters, Kara, 200
Women's National Basketball Assn. (WNBA),
    200, 201, 207

Wood, Harry "Freak," 28, 29
Wood, James "Biddy," 107
Wood, Willie, 129
Woodard, Lynette, 177
Wooden, John, 188
Woods, Earl, 196
Woods, Kultida (Mrs. Earl), 197
Woods, Tiger, 147, 194, 195, 197
Wooten, John, 99, 141
Word, Barry, 215, 216
World Boxing Council (WBC), 179
World Telegram, 99
Wright, Bill, 63
Wright, John, 8, 60, 61
Wrigley, Phil, 124

Y
Yancey, Bill, 164, 165

Yancey, Joe, 169, 170
Yankees, New York. *See* New York Yankees
Yankee Stadium, 80
Yastrzemski, Carl, 224
Yokely, Laymon, 233
Yost, Eddie, 89
Young, Buddy, 13, 113, 119, 139
Young, Dick, 5, 8, 99, 163
Young, Frank A. "Fay," 30
Young, M. Wharton, 91

Z
Zimbelman, Jodi, 152, 153
Zimmer, Don, 224
Zoeller, Fuzzy, 197